Rogue Revolutionaries

EARLY AMERICAN STUDIES

Series Editors
Daniel K. Richter, Kathleen M. Brown,
Max Cavitch, and David Waldstreicher

Exploring neglected aspects of our colonial,
revolutionary, and early national history and culture,
Early American Studies reinterprets familiar themes
and events in fresh ways. Interdisciplinary in character,
and with a special emphasis on the period from about
1600 to 1850, the series is published in partnership with
the McNeil Center for Early American Studies.

A complete list of books in the series
is available from the publisher.

Rogue Revolutionaries

The Fight for Legitimacy
in the Greater Caribbean

Vanessa Mongey

PENN

UNIVERSITY OF PENNSYLVANIA PRESS

PHILADELPHIA

Published by
University of Pennsylvania Press
Philadelphia, Pennsylvania 19104-4112
www.upenn.edu/pennpress

Printed in the United States of America
on acid-free paper
10 9 8 7 6 5 4 3 2 1

Library of Congress Cataloging-in-Publication Control Number: 2020004167
ISBN 978-0-8122-5255-2

CONTENTS

KEY FIGURES

LOUIS-MICHEL AURY. Born near Paris, France; joined the navy during the revolution as a sailor; deserted his post in the West Indies; became an independent corsair; appointed commandant general of the naval forces of the Republic of Cartagena; clashed with Simón Bolívar; embarked on a more independent career, setting up headquarters on the islands of Galveston (1816–1817), Amelia (1817), and Providencia (1819–1821).

BENJAMIN AND PHILIPPE, ALIAS TITUS, BIGARD. Brothers born in Guadeloupe, France; served in the revolutionary corsair fleet; moved to the Swedish colony of St. Barthélemy; set up a mercantile house; lobbied for voting rights and political representation of free men of color; funded an expedition against Puerto Rico in 1822.

AGUSTÍN CODAZZI. Born in Lugo, northern Italy; enlisted in the Napoleonic army; crossed the Atlantic Ocean in 1817 to join the Spanish American independent movements on Amelia and Providencia; returned to Italy and bought a farm; became a cartographer and geographer in Venezuela and New Grenada; recruited German migrants for Venezuela; died in Colombia.

MANUEL CORTÉS CAMPOMANES. Born in Madrid, Spain; began his career as a professor; instigated the antiroyalist San Blas conspiracy; deported to Venezuela, where he plotted an anticolonial coup; worked with Spanish American insurgent exiles in London; joined the first republic of Venezuela in 1811; moved to the Republic of Cartagena; participated in an expedition against Mexico from Galveston, Texas, in 1817; became an editor and bookseller in Belgium.

SÉVÈRE COURTOIS. Born in Ouanaminthe, northern St. Domingue, France; left colony first for Cuba and then for Louisiana; enlisted in a battalion of free men of color in the Battle of New Orleans of the Anglo-American War of 1812; joined the Republic of Cartagena; served in Simón Bolívar's army; became an independent privateer; moved to Providencia, western Caribbean; oversaw the unification of Providencia to the Republic of Gran Colombia; participated in the revolutionary conspiracy against Cuba in 1823.

HENRI LOUIS LA FAYETTE VILLAUME DUCOUDRAY-HOLSTEIN. Born in Schwedt, northeastern Germany; volunteered in the French army; captured in Spain; escaped to the United States; enlisted in the Republic of Texas in 1813; joined the Republic of Cartagena; became Simón Bolívar's chief of staff; plotted a revolutionary expedition against Puerto Rico in 1822; settled as a language teacher and a writer in Albany, New York.

COSTANTE FERRARI. Born in Reggio, northern Italy; joined the Napoleonic army; volunteered for South American independence movements at Amelia and Providencia; returned to Italy and bought a farm with Codazzi; fought in the Greek war of independence; fought in a liberal rebellion in Italy in 1831; traveled to Venezuela in 1834–1835; led a battalion of volunteers in the Italian revolutions of 1848; died in Reggio.

MARCELIN GUILLOT. Born in St. Domingue, France; evacuated during the revolution probably to Cuba and then to Louisiana; enlisted in the battalion of free people of color in New Orleans during the Anglo-American War of 1812; moved to Galveston, Amelia, and Providencia; fought in the Battle of Lake Maracaibo with the republican forces in 1823; became an army officer in Gran Colombia.

BAPTIS IRVINE. Born in Baltimore, eastern United States; journalist; fought with the Maryland militia during the Anglo-American War of 1812; promoted the cause of Spanish American independence as the newspaper editor of the *New-York Columbian*; served as a U.S. special agent in Venezuela in 1818; participated in a revolutionary plot against Puerto Rico in 1822.

GEORGES NICHOLAS JEANNET-OUDIN. Born in Arcis-sur-Aube, northcentral France; his brother was an army general and his uncle, George Danton, was a political leader during the revolution; posted in Guyana (April 1793 to November 1794 and April 1796 to November 1798) and in Guadeloupe (1800); recalled to the metropole; fled to North America and founded the Champ d'Asile colony in Texas in 1818; led a revolutionary expedition against Puerto Rico in 1822; died in France.

JUAN BAUTISTA MARIANO PICORNELL. Born in Palma de Mallorca, Spain; joined scientific and literary societies; taught in Madrid; wrote treatises on education and pedagogy; involved in the 1796 antiroyalist San Blas conspiracy; transported to Venezuela, where he participated in the anticolonial La Guaira conspiracy; took refuge in the United States; joined the first Republic of Venezuela in 1811; returned to the United States; joined an expedition against Texas; became president of the "provisional government of the free men of the Interior Provinces of Mexico" in 1813; rallied the Spanish royalist cause in New Orleans; died in Cuba.

JOSEPH SAVARY. Born in Saint-Marc, western St. Domingue; went to Cuba and Louisiana; joined Spanish American insurgent movements on the Louisiana/Texas border; participated in the republic of Texas from 1812 to 1813; led a battalion of free men of color during the Battle of New Orleans in 1815; moved to Galveston Island; settled in New Orleans with his wife Eugenie, also a native of St. Domingue.

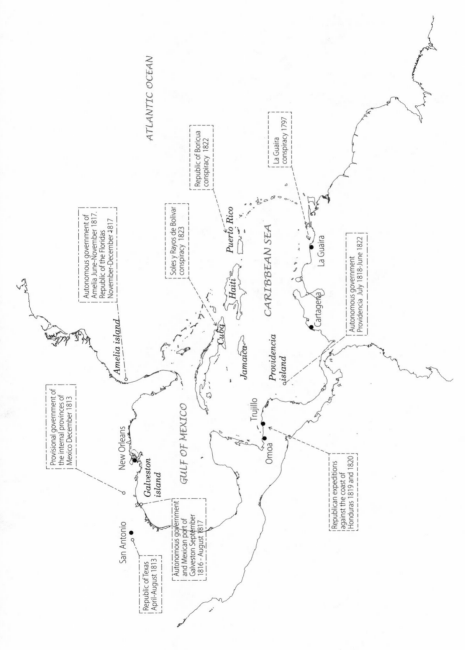

Map 1. Revolutionary projects in the Greater Caribbean.

ATLANTIC OCEAN

Republic of Boricua
conspiracy 1822

La Guaira
conspiracy 1797

Autonomous government of
Amelia June-November 1817.
Republic of the Floridas
November-December 1817

Soles y Rayos de Bolívar
conspiracy 1823

Puerto Rico

Autonomous government
Providencia July 1818-June 1822

Amelia island

Cuba

Haiti

CARIBBEAN SEA

La Guaira

Provisional government of
the internal provinces of
Mexico December 1813

Jamaica

Cartagena

New Orleans

Providencia
island

GULF OF MEXICO

Trujillo

Galveston
island

Omoa

Republican expeditions
against the coast of
Honduras 1819 and 1820

San Antonio

Autonomous government
and Mexican port of
Galveston September
1816 - August 1817

Republic of Texas
April-August 1813

Foreigners of Desperate Fortune

To talk revolutions, to imagine revolutions, to place oneself
mentally in the midst of a revolution, is in some small degree
to become master of the world.
—Alejo Carpentier, *Explosion in the Cathedral* (1962)

In September 1822, *The Mary* departed Philadelphia in the direction of
Puerto Rico, one of the last Spanish colonies in the New World. Many vessels sailed the Caribbean region at this time of the year, transporting sugar,
molasses, and rum from the West Indies; wines from Spain and France;
textiles from India; silk and porcelain from China; and mahogany, indigo,
and cochineal from Honduras and Brazil. Unlike other ships, *The Mary* was
engaged in a different kind of commerce: it was exporting revolution. The
ship carried rifles, pistols, and gunpowder. In the hull lay a box filled with
proclamations announcing the creation of a new republic. When the expedition ran into a fateful storm, a U.S. admiral celebrated the downfall of these
"foreigners of desperate fortune, who, in their imaginations," he sneered,
"fancied any project lawful that should put them in possession of . . . a portion of the Spanish colonies, under the pretense of establishing Independent Governments."[1] The admiral mocked these men's revolutionary dreams
whose sole purpose, as he saw it, was to take advantage of a volatile situation
to conduct contraband trade.

A closer look at the documents stowed in the hull of *The Mary* tells a
slightly different story about these "foreigners of desperate fortune." They not
only sought personal fortune but also wished to create a haven of liberty and
equality. Although they had never stepped foot in Puerto Rico, they had carefully drafted the blueprints of their new country: "A free, independent, and
wise Government [that] will give us happiness, strength, and consistency [in]
the new republic of   ." The line ended with a blank as if this imagined
republic could be transported and implanted anywhere.

This book is a study of the empty space in this sentence: it traces a history of geopolitics to little-known individuals who belonged to the same multinational and multiethnic networks and who repeatedly launched revolutions and claimed territories. This empty space signaled a revolutionary ideology bent on altering the world order fractured by the disintegration of empires. Historians tended to dismiss the republic imagined on *The Mary* and a host of related polities floating on the blue Caribbean waters in much the same way contemporary authorities did, as quixotic and failed schemes, or, in the words of U.S. officials, "chimeras of the wildest nature." But the floating dream in the hull of *The Mary* was at the heart of broader transatlantic changes, among them a fierce battle over the right of revolution and sovereignty. It was a contest over legitimacy.

Legitimacy is never self-evident or inevitable; it tentatively coalesces, as sociologist Pierre Bourdieu wrote, "only as the result of dogged confrontations."[2] Prime among these "confrontations" are revolutions, which create voids and represent transitional and transformative moments. Revolutions are unlawful by definition: they involve a violation of the law in existence when the uprisings take place. They become lawful only in hindsight as revolutionaries replace the legitimacy of existing regimes with a new legitimacy of their own making. Success depends heavily not just upon the mobilization of resources and supporters but also upon the ability to monopolize, or at least secure, the language of legitimacy. Tracking the instances when revolutionaries sought recognition but failed demonstrates that legitimacy was a process produced by a history of discourse and practice rather than an ahistorical attribute. New countries could no longer turn to tradition or even divine rule to justify their existence, and legitimacy became the sine qua non for state sovereignty.[3] These men were state-entrepreneurs who never turned into statesmen.[4] They lost the battle for legitimacy, paving the way for the reordering of the international system to the detriment of projects labeled "piratical" and to the advantage of a select number of nation-states.

The age of revolutions was a nearly century-long "world crisis" triggered by intensified warfare, expanding trading routes, new technologies, and debates about rights. This was a moment in which new social contracts were forged between people and states, in which the great winner was the modern state.[5] Yet, as the men on the decks of *The Mary* remind us, this quintessential moment that witnessed the rise of modern nation-states also saw the rise of failed revolutions and ephemeral states. The desire for change ricocheted back and forth across the Atlantic world. Political legitimacy was up for grabs, and a wide range of groups and individuals claimed it: wealthy slaveowners in North America, bourgeois merchants in France, enslaved laborers in the Caribbean, and Creole priests and intellectuals in South America.

Upheavals tumbled into the nineteenth century and prompted intense debates on the right of revolution (the right not just to overthrow governments that no longer met the needs of the people but also to establish new regimes). The absence of clearly codified precedents made it difficult to decide under which circumstances overthrowing a government was acceptable and who had the right to do so.[6] In the Anglo-American world, the debate over the legitimacy of the 1688–1689 Glorious Revolution created the fear that a right of revolution would lead to continual turmoil. In *Two Treatises of Government*, revised in 1689, English philosopher John Locke argued that people could instigate a revolution against the government when it acted against their interests. In some cases, Locke deemed revolution an obligation to safeguard against tyranny, and the 1776 Declaration of Independence of the United States cited this idea of people's collective right to cast off an arbitrary king. The right of revolution was included in article 35 of the French Constitution in June 1793: "When the government violates the rights of the people, insurrection is for the people, and for every portion thereof, the most sacred of rights and the most indispensable of duties," but this constitution was never officially enacted. The revolution led by enslaved Africans in 1791 on the French Caribbean colony of Saint-Domingue proved a crucible for testing the right of revolution, and governments around the world promptly shunned the new black-led independent country of Haiti. The right of revolution became emblematic of the possibilities and limitations of popular sovereignty: it legitimized insurrections—and the birth of new countries and new governments—retrospectively but also had the potential to unleash a torrent of revolutions and revolutionaries.

The demises of older systems and competing power structures brought contingency to the fore.[7] The actors of this book and the states they attempted to create might have been outliers, but they were not anomalies. In the first half of the nineteenth century, many polities throughout the Americas were evanescent and their existence contested. The list is too short to be exhaustive: Madawaska on the border between the United States and Canada, Tucumán and Entre Ríos in Argentina, Riograndense in Brazil, and Franklin, Muskogee, West Florida, and Texas in the United States, among others. Gran Colombia survived for about ten years before being replaced by the independent states of Venezuela, Ecuador, and New Granada. Even the United States was a weak and tentative state whose survival was by no means certain. All countries in the postcolonial America, often with weak foundations, inherited the same challenges to their authority as their predecessors and faced a challenging path toward consolidation.[8] Even if some colonies did secede, European imperialism remained a strong presence in the Caribbean while other regions in the Americas experienced a resurgence of royalism.[9]

We need a more expansive definition of revolution that includes various attempts to forcibly overthrow regimes and generate alternative social, economic, and political orders. Exploring the multiple forms that revolutions take and the actions and ideologies of those who conduct them shows that even so-called failed revolutions that did not create lasting states initiated significant changes on local and regional societies and on the wider international system.

*   *   *

The best way to understand how a system came to exist is often to listen to voices from the outside, from the perspective of failure: here, a cast of a dozen individuals with interconnected stories. By recovering these individuals' ambitions and their evanescent polities, *Rogue Revolutionaries* makes four overarching points. First, these men created a space of political experimentation and innovation in the Greater Caribbean. One of the earliest and most completely globalized regions in the world, the region was a fertile ground for the cross-pollination of goods, ideas, and peoples; it was a revolutionary rendezvous. In the absence of internationally recognized and enforceable norms and laws, these men created entities that held an ambiguous position between states with a legitimate chance of recognition and pirate nests conducting contraband trade.

Second, whether these revolutionaries intended to turn these experiments into durable states is difficult to determine with any degree of confidence. In their own time, these men did not necessarily see the ephemerality of their efforts as failure. Sometimes revolutions founded independent nation-states that endured. Most often, however, revolutions created transient polities that remind us not to naturalize the transition from empires to nations as inevitable. The attempts at revolution planning and state making were not staging grounds for the eventual rise of sovereign nation-states. Looking at contending political futures peels back the calcification of entrenched states to reveal the chaos of the coalescing international order.

Third, by stigmatizing alternative projects as piratical, anarchical, and conducive to racial conflicts, the states that survived the revolutionary era were those that successfully constructed an endogenous and exclusionary system, notably through the principle of diplomatic recognition. Recognition was not just about how states accepted one another; it was also about how they invented and defined the new international system. A few European and American powers recognized each other as belonging to the same group, separating themselves from their illegitimate rivals. Legitimacy became produced and reproduced by the practice of states themselves.[10]

Fourth, this group biography is an intellectual prosopography that reveals the political dimensions of mobility and dislocation. One of the benefits in following individuals across borders is that they shatter the walls of insular histories. Their stories were fragments of a mosaic formed by people who shaped their ideas on the move. Situating these revolutionaries in their regional, global, and intellectual contexts also supports the idea that the emergence of nation-states was a contingent and hazardous development. The processes of legitimation at the individual and national levels did not simply mirror each other: they were dynamically linked and mutually constitutive. Shifting attention to personal trajectories offers the possibility of writing a history of the revolutionary era in which individuals were as much the products of a larger canvass of global forces as they were the instruments in producing global forces.[11]

To construct a veneer of legitimacy for their political projects, revolutionaries drew on a repertoire of legal principles and historical precedents and adapted it into an eclectic blend that reflected their reality and served their political and economic interests.[12] One of the strongest influences on these revolutionaries was their experiences in the maritime world. Life at sea was a space of solidarity and cooperation but also of hierarchy and violence. Ships created mobile international communities that amounted to polities in their own right.[13] Starting in the late eighteenth century, revolutions revived the practice of privateering, a form of naval warfare conducted by privately owned ships authorized by a government, through commissions or letters of marque to attack and capture enemy vessels. North American leaders commissioned privateers to fight Britain during the war of independence and the War of 1812. The French revolutionary government did the same. After the breakdown of the Iberian Empire following Napoléon's invasion of the Iberian Peninsula in 1808, Latin American insurgents turned to privateering in their war with Spain.[14] Thousands of foreigners joined the Latin American independence movements.[15]

Certain of these foreigners sought privateering commissions from Latin American agents and reinterpreted them as licenses to export revolution.

They used them not only to avoid prosecution for maritime predation but also to justify territorial seizure over Spanish colonies. Mobilizing privateering commissions as tools of revolutionary politics, they scripted their revolutions as part of a hemispheric fight against European imperial tyranny and displayed an often-strategic attachment to Spanish American independent movements. This autonomy gave them a greater degree of freedom and a greater latitude for action.

Another influence on these revolutionaries originated in the French revolutionary and the Napoleonic wars.[16] Many of the actors in this book fought in militaries on land and at sea, in Europe and in the Caribbean. They drew from the brief but powerful moment (1792–1799) when France's revolution metamorphosed into an expansionist mission through the forcible annexation of foreign territories.[17] They claimed the right, or rather the duty, to liberate people from the yoke of despotic Spain. Sailing the tempestuous tide of revolutions, these men believed that the cause of liberty was the cause of humankind.

These revolutionaries articulated a philosophy I call "cosmopolitan patriotism." It was "patriotism" to the extent that the authors of this revolutionary propaganda intended to create independent republics out of New World colonies. When most people lacked an identifiable national consciousness and keenly felt local ties, revolutionaries redefined the concept of patriotism, turning it into a capacious concept.[18] This patriotism was "cosmopolitan" in that it consistently claimed to advocate for the welfare of humanity rather than a particular national or ethnic group. These men fused a moral cosmopolitanism—the view that all human beings belong to a single community—with a political cosmopolitanism, the attempt to establish a new, worldwide order.[19] Yet the cosmopolitanism these men practiced and conceptualized was not emancipatory for all. They often sponsored their exciting quest for liberty, equality, and fortune from slave trading or from products produced by slave labor.

*   *   *

Although I work among several fields of historical research about the revolutionary Atlantic—the crisis of the Iberian Atlantic, the role of nonelite groups, and the rise of new sources of political legitimacy—I position my study specifically at the intersection of two literatures. The first centers on the interconnectedness of multiple revolutions.[20] This book not only brings new voices to this narrative but also uses these voices to flip our perspective and place the margins at the center. A few scholars have moved beyond the revolutions that founded enduring independent nation-states to examine imagined possibilities.[21] What this book emphasizes is the contested production of legitimacy in these liminal sites and how European and American powers depicted them as deficient and illegitimate. The transformation of these imagined possibilities into anomalous ventures is part of an enduring stigmatization of large parts of the world and their populations.

This book not only adds depth to accounts of the revolutionary Atlantic but also analyzes these revolutionaries through insights drawn from international relations. Spurred by the end of the Soviet Union and the rise of radical Islam in the 1990s, a vast literature now exists on so-called failed and unrecognized states.[22] Failed or weak states, in particular, are defined as enjoying external sovereignty without or with only limited internal sovereignty, while unrecognized or contested states survive without external sovereignty and claim to have achieved internal sovereignty.[23] What such labels have in common is that they designate deviations from the ideal type—sovereign nation-states—and are almost entirely located outside the Global North.

Recent postcolonial scholarship has shown that Western-centric norms of state development have uncritically framed the failed state narrative.[24] "Failed state" is not simply a label but a powerful ideology that often justifies military interventions based on a Western ideal of what a state should look like. Rather than adhere to a successful/failed and ideal/defective state binary, scholars have adopted a more flexible, divisible, and multifaceted continuum of legitimacy. The fact that recognized and sovereign states are perceived as the norm in the international system reflects this Western-centric global imaginary.[25] This book shows that the narrative construction of certain political projects as deviations from the norm, as failures, and as illegitimate dates back to the age of revolutions.[26]

Eschewing a purely chronological approach, each chapter weaves the stories of two or more revolutionaries into an analysis of larger historical processes. This approach emphasizes themes and topics that crossed the revolutionary Atlantic. It also stresses the role of human agency in geopolitical transformations and reminds us that "revolutions are fundamentally about people."[27] Chapter 1 examines what made a government legitimate. It looks at such blueprints of ephemeral states as privateering commissions, declarations of independence, and constitutions to show that the road to sovereignty did not run smooth. Looking at legal, political, and practical issues of state creation, this chapter traced the efforts of revolutionaries to gain both local and global acceptance. Tackling the question of what made information legitimate in a world where rumors were rampant, Chapter 2 traces the circuits of communication created by a mobile and multilingual print culture. It explores the materiality of intellectual production. Printing presses followed or even blazed trails of revolution around the Atlantic world, enabling revolutionaries to disseminate their radical cosmopolitan beliefs. Chapter 3 asks what made equality legitimate when circumscribed by structures of racial disenfranchisement. Revolutionaries structured their revolutions around equal political and civil rights, yet they often preserved slavery and profited from slave trading. The pursuit of self-determination and anticolonial solidarity grew out of an exploitative soil. Chapter 4 examines what made a revolution legitimate, particularly in legally and jurisdictionally contested spaces such as the Caribbean. This chapter traces what happened when revolutionaries failed to secure support internationally and received instead the labels of pirates, outlaws, and instigators of race wars. It shows how this stigmatization paved the way for international cooperation to stifle this type of political and social subversion. Finally, Chapter 5 raises the question of what made a historical memory legitimate. It studies vehicles of historical self-presentation—memoirs, maps, petitions—as meeting points between the personal and the structural. These vehicles show that affiliations and political identities were repeatedly performed, reproduced, and challenged. Entangled in a relation among history, memory, and political power, revolutionaries wrote their own stories within a context of narrowing alternatives and triumphing nation-states.

The globe is covered today with a multitude of countries branded as failed or fragile states that achieved de facto independence but failed to gain widespread international recognition.[28] Some exist for decades while others disappear after a few years. Like the "chimeras of the wildest nature" denounced by U.S. officials, these places never established themselves in the international system. They rarely, if ever, appear on official maps or in schoolbooks. Yet they beg the question of whether our understanding of *successful* revolutions and states is not deeply flawed. Is a revolution only successful if it creates an enduring state? Is a state successful because it is long lasting? Is it because it is recognized by others? Who is the source of this legitimacy? The answers to these questions have shaped our understanding of political fragility and stability to this day.[29]

CHAPTER 1

Ghostly Governments

Statehood and Sovereignty

Every step of Louis-Michel Aury's career had led to this moment. In July 1818, a mere week after landing on the island of Providencia in the western Caribbean, Aury announced the creation of his new headquarters to the rest of the world. In an address republished in newspapers across the Americas, he invited "gallant foreigners" and other "friends wandering without a country" to join his crusade to bring liberty and independence to the world. "Come amongst us as brothers," he promised, "to enjoy that political and religious liberty, of which the ferocity of the despots and fanaticism wanted to deprive you."[1] As he wrote these words, a hurricane had struck the island, supplies ran low, and his "gallant legions" were dying of hunger and disease.

Aury "always dreamed of republic," wrote one of his collaborators.[2] Providencia was Aury's third attempt at revolution launching and state making: he had previously carried the banner of liberty to the islands of Galveston in Texas and Amelia in Florida. At his side stood Sévère Courtois, a free man of color from Saint-Domingue who took over the Providencia government after Aury passed away. Lasting four years, the establishment in Providencia was Aury and Courtois's longest accomplishment and the crowning achievement of their state-entrepreneurial careers. It ended in June 1822, when the town council adopted the Cúcuta Constitution, turning Providencia into a territory of Gran Colombia.

What existed in Providencia during these four years is a riddle waiting to be solved: a contested state-like entity that achieved de facto control over its claimed territory and was self-governing with a republican at the head of a military government. Both Aury and Courtois used the name "government" for the polities they set up across the Greater Caribbean.[3] Contemporaries called them "criminal" and "fraudulent."[4] The concept of a popularly

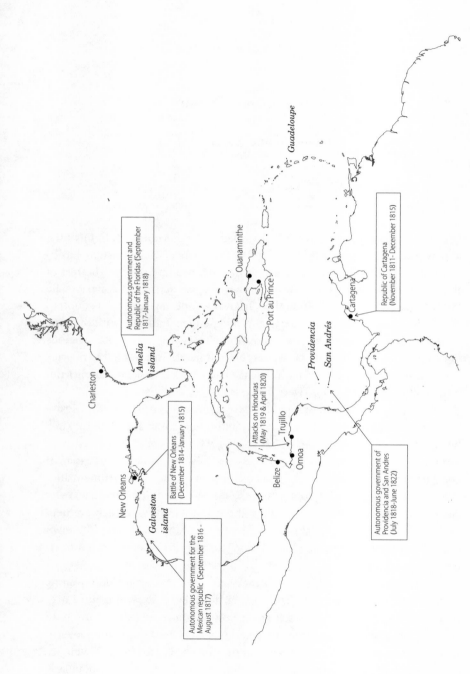

Charleston

Amelia
island

Autonomous government and
Republic of the Floridas (September
1817–January 1818)

New Orleans

Galveston
island

Battle of New Orleans
(December 1814–January 1815)

Autonomous government for the
Mexican republic (September 1816 –
August 1817)

Ouanaminthe

Port au Prince

Guadeloupe

Attacks on Honduras
(May 1819 & April 1820)

Trujillo

Belize

Omoa

Providencia
San Andrés

Cartagena

Republic of Cartagena
(November 1811–December 1815)

Autonomous government of
Providencia and San Andres
(July 1818–June 1822)

Map 2. The political projects in which Louis-Michel Aury and Sévère Courtois participated, 1810–1822.

legitimated sovereignty slowly replacing a dynastically legitimated sovereignty was the beginning of modernity, scholars argue, but Aury and Courtois's ghostly governments reveal the tensions deeply embedded in this transition.[5] If people had a right to create a state (the famous opening phrase of the U.S. Constitution "We the People"), then *anybody* could initiate their own government. As numerous new political entities sprang into existence in the Atlantic world, no consensus existed on what entities qualified as sovereign, independent states.

Aury and Courtois's floating governments were mere blips on the historical radar, standing on a spectrum between exotic lures or piratical nests. Even the best biographies of Louis-Michel Aury brush over his political ambitions, choosing to focus instead on his tribulations and adventures.[6] Most historians focus on other countries' reactions to Aury's actions, explaining how the U.S. government invaded Amelia, paving the way for the treaty with Spain that ceded Florida to the United States, or they focus on how Providencia became part of Gran Colombia.[7] However, connecting Aury and Courtois's governments solely to "recognized" countries such as the United States and Colombia reproduces a preordained narrative that alternative entities were bound to fail, framing them as preludes to U.S. or Colombian national expansion. This chapter instead places these ghostly governments at the center of its analysis, focusing on the ways their leaders engaged with the wider world in their quest for legitimacy. It does not consider these governments anarchical anomalies or "forgotten islands of international disorder" but argues that Aury and Courtois deftly scripted governments that could and did pose as legitimate—even for just a few months or years.[8]

Aury and Courtois's ghostly governments give us insight on the debate around the importance of foreign recognition in the creation of states. A traditional and constitutive approach to sovereignty holds that recognition has "provided the *imprimatur* of statehood to seceding entities for over two hundred years" and legitimized certain states as members of the wider international community.[9] Although the revolutionaries of Providencia failed to gain formal diplomatic recognition, they actively traded and negotiated with other countries and colonies. By focusing on the factors that enabled these state-like entities to exist and how these entities enabled their creators to pursue their political and pecuniary ambitions, this chapter demonstrates that sovereignty and statehood were not indivisible, one-size-fits-all concepts. People claimed, asserted, and acknowledged them in pieces or in fragments but rarely as a whole. The concepts of sovereignty and statehood were extremely elastic and malleable.

The Quest for Fortune

"Since chance brought me to this country, fortune, which had before been against me, has started to be favorable." Louis-Michel Aury wrote these words in Cartagena in 1814, anxious to share some good news with his relatives in Paris, including his beloved younger sister. The following year, chance brought him to befriend a fellow restless soul, Sévère Courtois, born in Ouanaminthe, in northeastern Saint-Domingue. One of the most important ports in the Spanish Caribbean, Cartagena seceded from Spain and became an independent republic in 1811. Aury's expertise and enthusiasm helped him rise through the ranks. As he explained to his family, "I have had different engagements with the corsairs that I have commanded, which have won me marks of distinction from the government I serve."[10] Then twenty-six years old, Aury had been searching for these "marks of distinction" for the past ten years.

Aury lived most of his life at sea, and this experience shaped his vision of the world. He entered the French navy at the age of thirteen after his father passed away. Life as a sailor was not for the faint-hearted. Wages were low, working conditions were harsh, and diseases were frequent. The letters he wrote his family conveyed his loneliness. An adolescent in a world of adults, Aury earnestly reported every growth spurt ("I am now five feet three inches," he happily wrote in January 1804).[11] Money was a constant problem; he did not have enough to buy proper clothing, and he clung to any book on which he could get his hands. A novice sailor, he had to perform the most unpleasant tasks. Aury remained silent about the other sailors—except one who promised to teach him mathematics. When he learned of the death of his mother, he became concerned about the future of his sister. He effusively thanked his relatives for providing for her—"until I am able to help her myself," he promised.[12] Providing for his only sister would become Aury's life goal.

Rivalries between Britain, France, and Spain gave Aury the opportunity to make a name for himself. A corsair took him prisoner in 1803 in Guadeloupe; he stayed onboard eleven months before jumping ship and swimming back to liberty.[13] He never rejoined the French navy. One of Aury's collaborators, Agustín Codazzi, described Napoléon's coronation in 1804 as a turning point: "Educated in the principles of the revolution, he had been suckled in such feelings of liberty that he abandoned the service of his *patrie* when Napoléon crowned himself emperor. . . . He preferred to live among free people than among his compatriots, who had so quickly forgotten the bloodshed for liberty."[14] Despite this public repudiation of Napoléon, Aury was happy to take advantage of the opportunities offered by the Napoleonic wars and received privateer commissions to attack Spanish and British ships from Guadeloupe until the British invaded the French colony in 1810.[15]

Privateering was the prerogative of sovereign monarchs, princes, and states according to the treatise *Droit des Gens* or *Laws of Nations* (1758) by the Swiss jurist Emer de Vattel—the dominant theoretical framework for understanding international law and for implementing it into diplomatic practice. Sovereigns issued privateer commissions, or letters of marque, a piece of paper that extended the sovereign state's jurisdiction, laws, and protection into the ocean.[16] Privateers acted under the authority of a sovereign and, in return, received that sovereign's protection against criminal proceedings. Aury associated privateering and patriotism: "Corsairs," he reassured his relatives, "wage war as loyally as the ships of his imperial majesty."[17]

Privateering shaped U.S., British, and Spanish war efforts, but in Aury's case, privateering shaped his ambitions. A shy sailor no more, Aury grew into a leader of men. He became a ship captain. He learned to tap into and exploit other people's longing for adventure. He persuaded investors to finance his expeditions and talked men of sundry backgrounds into joining his ranks. Aury equipped his first vessel around 1805, attacked British and Spanish ships, and brought seized goods to Charleston, Baltimore, and New Orleans. The British navy captured the ship into which he had invested 2,500 gourds. When fortune eluded him, he moved to Louisiana. There, he bought and repaired a small boat.[18] Aury targeted Spanish slave ships and sold enslaved Africans in Louisiana, contravening the 1808 U.S. slave trade ban.[19] Aury's list of enemies continued to grow when U.S. authorities apprehended his new ship in 1810, killing and wounding twelve of his sailors. With a tinge of melancholy, he wrote his sister that he hoped that "[Fortune] will not always persecute me."[20]

Fortune appeared in the shape of hundreds of men, most of them free people of African descent, pressuring the junta of Cartagena to sign a declaration of independence in November 1811.[21] The following year, a constitution secured suffrage for male heads of households and property owners, regardless of color or birth. The government soon turned to privateering, and President Manuel Torices invited foreigners to come to Cartagena, filling the city streets with foreign sailors and soldiers.[22] Torices also sent a copy of the constitution to U.S. president James Madison, asking that vessels flying the Cartagena flag be allowed to enter U.S. ports.[23] This news reached Aury, and he embarked with Juan Antonio Hernandez, a Haitian sailor, to Cartagena in December 1812.[24] Aury's embrace of Spanish American independence allowed him to reconcile the ideals of the French Revolution and his hatred of monarchies with his naval expertise.

In Louisiana, Sévère Courtois certainly heard about what was happening on the Colombian coast but decided to place his bets with the U.S. republic. Courtois was born into a prominent land-owning family in Saint-Domingue. The military career was a family tradition; his grandfather was a recipient of the royal and military order of Saint Louis and his older brother, Joseph, was an officer in the Napoleonic army.[25] As one brother faced the British Empire in Europe, the other fought the same enemy in the Americas. In December 1814, Sévère joined a battalion of free men of color from Saint-Domingue led by Major Joseph Savary and fought in the Battle of New Orleans against the British. Listed a sergeant major, Courtois probably had previous military experience. He later claimed that he had been working for the "just cause of America" since 1812; it is therefore very likely that he participated in the failed Republic of Texas with Joseph Savary.[26] Dissatisfied with their treatment by the U.S. army, many volunteers deserted. Courtois and other officers petitioned Andrew Jackson in March 1815 to demand protection against the "vexations" and "humiliations" free men of color experienced in the state of Louisiana.[27]

When no remedy in Louisiana was forthcoming, Courtois crossed the Gulf of Mexico and joined the Republic of Cartagena. As in Louisiana, Courtois rubbed shoulders with other transplants: a fifty-man garrison was exclusively manned by Haitians.[28] Cartagena was the place where Aury and Courtois's fortunes converged. When Courtois arrived, Aury had become commodore of the naval forces. He had grown into "a fine looking, well-made man, about six feet high," the newspapers observed, "with a countenance possessing strong traits of intelligence."[29] The two men became friends.

Aury and Courtois's time in the cosmopolitan port city fueled their political ambitions. The Republic of Cartagena represented an era of considerable social and political transformation in which men of African descent played a central role in the construction of republican politics and revolutionary egalitarianism. However, starting in August 1815, the social and racial experiment of Cartagena turned into a death trap. The Bourbons were back in power in Spain and launched a reconquest of the Americas. Royalist forces organized a grueling five-month siege, and the independence leaders left a city ravaged by hunger and disease. A third of the population perished. In December 1815, Aury led a flotilla of thirteen vessels of refugees to Les Cayes on the southwestern coast of Haiti. Forty-five passengers died on the way.[30] It was in these tragic circumstances that Courtois returned to his native land.

Hundreds of refugees from the continent sought refuge in the republic in the south of Haiti, including Simón Bolívar, H. L. V. Ducoudray-Holstein, and Manuel Cortés Campomanes. Haitian president Alexandre Pétion's hospitality did little to dampen the rivalries and divisions among the refugees. No leader of the independence movement had yet emerged.[31] At a meeting in early 1816, Aury adamantly refused to vote for full and unlimited powers for Bolívar and advocated a joint command.[32] Despite Aury's resistance, Bolívar became the leader of the insurgent movement.

Discords about the future of the independence movement may have been raging around Aury, but his mind was 45,000 miles away. His sister was twenty-six, single, and alone in Paris. Victoire Aury remained the only fixed emotional center for her itinerant brother. He sat down in Port-au-Prince and instructed his sister about matters of the heart. A virtuous and honorable man should be her choice, Aury wrote, and she ought to develop these qualities herself. He promised to send her money and even suggested she might join him wherever he found fortune in the Americas. After all, he wrote her, "It is happiness that I desire for you."[33] To provide for his sister, Aury had to establish himself. The fall of the Republic of Cartagena dashed his hopes of securing a position. Things were tense in Haiti. As most other leaders rallied behind Bolívar, Aury found a way out in the person of Joseph Savary, Courtois's former commanding officer in the Battle of New Orleans, who was in Haiti as an agent of the Mexican independence cause.[34] As Aury philosophized to his family, "One must have traveled the world for ten or thirteen years to know the value of what you love."[35] Aury felt that fortune was waiting for him somewhere in this world.

Aury and Courtois's sojourns in Cartagena and Haiti shaped how the two revolutionaries understood sovereignty and statehood. Both Cartagena and Haiti were unrecognized and contested states. Even if foreign powers refused to recognize their independence and sovereignty formally, they functioned as autonomous states as evidenced by Cartagena commissioning its own privateers. Various actors such as merchants, ship captains, colonial officials, and admiralty judges recognized the de facto sovereignty of Cartagena and Haiti. In turn, this lack of formal recognition shaped state building. Autonomous but fragile, the Haitian state protected itself by becoming heavily militarized.[36] Cartagena could not resist Spanish military forces. Drawing from their experiences in both locations, Aury and Courtois would incorporate three lessons into their next enterprises—privateering as a prerogative of sovereignty, the importance of de facto recognition of statehood through trade (especially maritime trade), and the importance of strong military leaders.

This Is the Age of Revolution

The Republic of Cartagena was just one of many ephemeral attempts at state creation in the Greater Caribbean. Others included two republics of Venezuela on the southern rim of the Caribbean basin; Muskogee, West Florida, and the Maroons of Prospect Bluff on the northern rim; and, further east, the secession of André Rigaud's State of the South from the Haitian republic.[37] After all, as London's *Morning Chronicle* noted in a report on Aury, "This is the age of Revolution."[38]

The year 1816 was grim for independence movements in the Greater Caribbean. The movement in Mexico was not faring much better than the one in Colombia and Venezuela, including a series of setbacks and the execution of one of the main leaders, José María Morelos. The viceroy of New Spain introduced a policy of reconciliation, and many insurgent leaders accepted his amnesty. Others went into exile in Haiti or in the United States, including José Manuel de Herrera, who appointed Aury governor of the province of Texas and general in the Mexican republican army.[39]

Courtois did not join Aury and the Mexican cause. Courtois instead volunteered in Bolívar's expedition against the continent as a ship captain. In May 1816, the expedition left Haiti and disembarked on the island of Margarita before moving to Carúpano. For mysterious reasons, Bolívar sent Courtois back and treated him, one observer noted, "harshly and in a haughty manner."[40] Royal forces repelled the expedition, which returned to Haiti. Bolívar organized a more successful expedition a few months later, but Courtois was not involved.

Meanwhile, across the Caribbean Sea, Aury left Haiti with 400 soldiers, fifty officers, and seven ships and took control of Galveston Island in the last days of spring 1816. He declared it independent in the name of the Mexican republic. Galveston was a narrow barrier island, half sand, half marsh. A few months after settling on the island, in early September, a group of Haitians broke into Aury's cabin in the middle of the night and demanded he became their prisoner. When Aury refused, the men shot him. Severely injured, Aury was unable to stop the seditious crew as they stole 600 pesos, arms, munitions, and three of his ships. Aury had promised the Haitian volunteers that they would become privateers and sell their prizes in New Orleans. When they realized that Matagorda was a "desert," they returned to the comfort of their native island. Most Haitian volunteers nevertheless remained on the island, trusting Aury to deliver on his promises. A Spanish observer noted that 200 "negroes" remained in Galveston.[41]

While Aury acted in the name of the Mexican republic, he was at the helm of his own small government. Aury was no longer a simple privateer. He set up a government that extended its sovereignty over a piece of land. As civil and military governor of Galveston, he appointed a marshal, a customs collector, a notary public, judges, and civil and military officers, as well as set up war councils and admiralty courts.[42] In an address to the U.S. Congress, Aury assured them that "the establishment of Galveston was legally formed, and that was done by the existing authorities there, was . . . for the welfare and aiding by every possible means the patriot cause."[43] He oversaw the construction of a village on the east end of the island, using sailcloth and scrap timber to build around one hundred houses. Deer and wild fowl populated the island, fish swam in the bay, and oysters thrived in the marshes. Foodstuffs came from the mainland or from seized Spanish ships.[44]

One of the prerogatives of sovereignty was the ability to practice privateering against an enemy power. The Mexican Congress, one of Aury's followers argued, had entrusted him with forming a government in Galveston, "with all the necessary authorities, by arranging the several branches of public administration."[45] Aury no longer received letters of marque; he issued them. Written in Spanish and with Aury's name and title displayed on top, the privateer commissions listed the names of the vessel, the owner, the captain, the size of the crew, and the number of arms aboard. A seal emblazoned the documents.[46] A Spanish captain saw nearly twenty captured ships come into Galveston in the nine months he was in prison there.[47] Aury commissioned eighteen to twenty privateers, brought prizes before the admiralty court, and arranged for the judged goods and enslaved people to be sold in New Orleans.[48]

Aury's headquarters were some 600 miles from New Orleans: local authorities such as the collector of customs and the judges of the district court were on the front lines to monitor activities between Louisiana and Galveston. They also had to ascertain the legitimacy of Aury's government. The New Orleans collector scoffed that Galveston's government was "illegal and piratical" and of an "ambulatory nature."[49] Squelching trade proved difficult, however. The financial interests of Louisiana merchants undermined the efforts of the customs collector who repeatedly complained about violations of the slave trade act. He calculated that Aury smuggled around 650 enslaved

Africans from Galveston into Louisiana, keeping some of them as sailors on his ships.[50]

Spanish authorities viewed Aury's establishment as a hotbed of revolutionary contagion. The arrival of Spanish republican general Xavier Mina in November 1816 confirmed their fears. Forces in Galveston were rumored to be planning an attack against Mexico, and "under the assertion of giving liberty to the inhabitants, the true objective was to pillage and put the province of Texas under the harsh yoke of a foreigner."[51] Spanish authorities wove a web of informants and spies who infiltrated revolutionary networks. The brothers Jean and Pierre Lafitte entered the service of Spain. In April 1816, Jean arrived in Galveston and staged a coup while Aury escorted Mina to the Mexican port of Soto de la Marina. When Aury returned, he declared that "he had no desire to surrender his authority and rights" and briefly moved his headquarters to nearby Matagorda Bay.[52] Most of those who remained with him were Haitians or Afro-Caribbeans: a passenger aboard a Cuban vessel angrily noted that men of African descent wearing military uniforms inspected the ship's papers and acted on Aury's behalf.[53] Aury formally disavowed connections with the establishment in Galveston, informing both Mexican minister Herrera and the collector of New Orleans that the judge of the admiralty, the collector, and other authorities had left with him.[54]

Aury's experience in Galveston only fueled his hunger for recognition. He was a man with "a burning imagination and a formidable ambition," one of his collaborators noted, "[who] was looking for glory everywhere."[55] Aury set his eyes on the Spanish colony of Florida, which stood in a highly coveted location. Control of the Gulf Coast east of New Orleans was critical for transporting cotton and other products to the United States. An 1812 attempt by U.S. agents to seize Amelia Island failed, and the island remained in Spanish hands until the arrival of Gregor MacGregor, a Scottish adventurer.[56] While in Philadelphia, MacGregor received a Pan-American commission signed by three Spanish American agents: Pedro Gual for New Granada, Lino de Clemente for Venezuela, and Martin Thomson for Rio de la Plata. In June 1817, MacGregor traipsed south, recruiting U.S. Americans to Amelia Island. Although the port was fortified, the local garrison surrendered without a shot. MacGregor set up a provisional government but felt isolated. In early September, he gathered his officers and left the island. On his way out, he met Aury and his ships.[57]

Aury's source of revenue was maritime trade. Amelia was a perfect location for this purpose. Through networks of trails, inland rivers, and ocean routes, the island linked to plantations in neighboring Georgia and other markets in the United States. Amelia was also near the sea routes of many Spanish ships transporting their cargos from the main ports of Veracruz and Havana to the peninsula. When Aury replaced MacGregor, he initiated several changes. Politically, Aury's connections with the United States were more tenuous than MacGregor's. While MacGregor had recruited U.S. American soldiers and sailors and sold shares of Florida land, Aury did not trust the U.S. government. His misadventures along the Gulf Coast in the 1810s were still fresh in his mind. Aury was nominally an officer of the Mexican army, and he initially hoisted the Mexican flag.[58]

Aury brought new faces to the island. Several observers commented on the number of officers and soldiers of African descent, with some reports claiming there were 300 black soldiers living in Amelia.[59] These men's belief in racial equality increasingly clashed with white U.S. Americans' belief in racial hierarchy. A U.S. newspaper reported that Aury's men "insist[ed] upon equal rights and privileges with the whites," and his collaborators were "otherwise very insolent; indeed even as to assume equal command." Worst of all, newspapers noted, they "aspired to a perfect equality, if not mastership."[60]

Autumn 1817 was brutal for the republicans, and yellow fever took its toll. Yet Aury endeavored to make a state. Amelia was a marshy and sparsely populated island with 200 permanent inhabitants. The main town, Fernandina, consisted of about forty houses, along with a church, warehouses, and a few stores. To provide public services, Aury arranged for a hospital and designated a refugee from Saint-Domingue as doctor.[61] As enmities and tempers flared, Aury forcefully asserted his authority over the island. He formed three battalions around loose national, ethnic, and linguistic lines: the first with U.S. Americans and Englishmen, the second with soldiers and officers of African descent (mainly Haitian or Afro-Caribbean) who declared themselves "ready to give their lives for the Republic," and the third, a melting pot of other nationalities—French, Polish, Prussian, Italian, and a few Spaniards.[62]

The legal landscape of Amelia demonstrates Aury's strategy to legitimize his political project. Aury claimed full authority on the territory and its population. Washington instructed a U.S. ship to station near the island, officially to prevent the movement of enslaved people and weapons out of Amelia and into U.S. territory. The captain of the U.S. brig received a request from a U.S. citizen imprisoned on Amelia. Aury refused to forfeit his prisoner, explaining that the man's "disturbance of social order" landed him in jail. Dispelling the image of Amelia as a place of lawlessness, Aury explained that "this rising republic" had adopted both the laws of the United States and the Law of Nations. The message to the U.S. captain was succinct but conveyed two forceful messages: the first was that Amelia was a sovereign territory; the second was that it was a place where law and order prevailed, with tribunals and admiralty courts ready to act against any contravention.[63]

Aury proclaimed de facto independence for Amelia Island when he adopted martial law in early November. The proclamation encapsulated Aury's cosmopolitan brand of republicanism. National divisions were a danger to the "most glorious cause" of republicanism. Aury strove to unite all inhabitants, declaring, "Men of all nations, we are freemen, let us forever be united by the love of liberty and hatred to tyranny."[64] Behind these lofty ideals, Aury alleged that a public emergency justified an unusual extension of power, or "state of exception."[65] By suspending existing laws, Aury consolidated his power as independent head of state.

Aury lifted martial law when a ship brought 200 additional men to the island, including the experienced Pedro Gual and Vicente Pazos.[66] Gual was a native of Caracas exiled in the United States after the fall of the first republic of Venezuela; he was a representative of New Granada. Pazos was a former newspaper editor from Buenos Aires who launched a Spanish-language newspaper after touching ground in Fernandina: *El Telégrafo de las Floridas*. The arrival of Gual and Pazos solidified Aury's political project. The revolutionary leaders believed that formal independence would protect them from the U.S. ships surrounding the island. After all, as Aury explained to the captain of the squadron, the citizens of the republic had nothing but "respect and interest [for] our neighbors and brethren of the United States."[67]

Aury organized elections to form a provisional government and draft a constitution. "Free inhabitants" who had resided in Amelia for fifteen days could vote, provided they swore an oath to renounce allegiance to "any State not actually struggling for the emancipation of Spanish America," a not-so-thin reference to U.S. neutrality policy. On November 19, a few polling places, hastily set up, opened for the afternoon. The next day, the polls opened from sunrise to sunset. A week later, Aury announced the election of nine representatives: a mix of Spanish Americans, Saint-Dominguan exiles, and U.S. Americans. Aury remained military commander.[68]

The "infant Republic" flourished. The provisional government adopted a constitution in December 1817. The provisional government was "Democratic-Republican" and divided into executive, legislative, and judicial branches—with "the military subordinate and obedient in all cases to the civil authority." The authors cited Alexander Hamilton's *Federalist* No. 70 to justify a single executive. One of the articles hinted at the republicans' expansionist

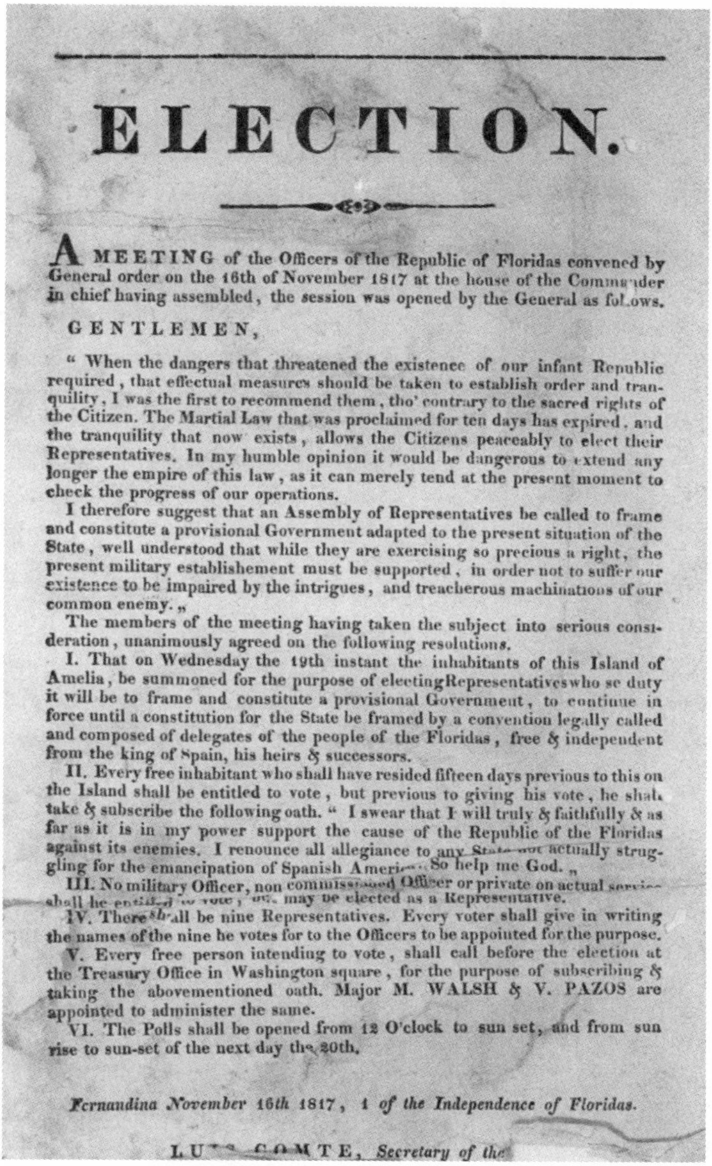

ELECTION.

A MEETING of the Officers of the Republic of Floridas convened by General order on the 16th of November 1817 at the house of the Commander in chief having assembled, the session was opened by the General as follows.

GENTLEMEN,

" When the dangers that threatened the existence of our infant Republic required, that effectual measures should be taken to establish order and tranquility, I was the first to recommend them, tho' contrary to the sacred rights of the Citizen. The Martial Law that was proclaimed for ten days has expired, and the tranquility that now exists, allows the Citizens peaceably to elect their Representatives. In my humble opinion it would be dangerous to extend any longer the empire of this law, as it can merely tend at the present moment to check the progress of our operations.

I therefore suggest that an Assembly of Representatives be called to frame and constitute a provisional Government adapted to the present situation of the State, well understood that while they are exercising so precious a right, the present military establishement must be supported, in order not to suffer our existence to be impaired by the intrigues, and treacherous machinations of our common enemy. „

The members of the meeting having taken the subject into serious consideration, unanimously agreed on the following resolutions.

I. That on Wednesday the 19th instant the inhabitants of this Island of Amelia, be summoned for the purpose of electing Representatives who se duty it will be to frame and constitute a provisional Government, to continue in force until a constitution for the State be framed by a convention legally called and composed of delegates of the people of the Floridas, free & independent from the king of Spain, his heirs & successors.

II. Every free inhabitant who shall have resided fifteen days previous to this on the Island shall be entitled to vote, but previous to giving his vote, he shall take & subscribe the following oath. " I swear that I will truly & faithfully & as far as it is in my power support the cause of the Republic of the Floridas against its enemies. I renounce all allegiance to any State not actually struggling for the emancipation of Spanish America. So help me God. „

III. No military Officer, non commissioned Officer or private on actual service shall be entitled to vote, nor may be elected as a Representative.

IV. There shall be nine Representatives. Every voter shall give in writing the names of the nine he votes for to the Officers to be appointed for the purpose.

V. Every free person intending to vote, shall call before the election at the Treasury Office in Washington square, for the purpose of subscribing & taking the abovementioned oath. Major M. WALSH & V. PAZOS are appointed to administer the same.

VI. The Polls shall be opened from 12 O'clock to sun set, and from sun rise to sun-set of the next day the 20th.

Fernandina November 16th 1817, 1 of the Independence of Floridas.

LUIS COMTE, *Secretary of the*

Figure 1. Call for election, Republic of the Floridas, Amelia Island, November 1817. Wikimedia Commons.

intentions. Every district in Florida desiring to join the republic would be
entitled to send two representatives to the general assembly. Two additional
articles guaranteed freedom of the press and freedom of conscience "as one
of the natural rights of the people of Floridas."[69]

Aury's strategy was to publicize his actions as widely as possible to uphold
the image of a legitimate sovereign state. He forwarded the constitution for
the República de las Floridas, along with invitations to join the republic, to
various newspapers across the Americas: the *Aurora* in Philadelphia, the
Niles' Weekly Register in Baltimore, and the *Correo del Orinoco* in Angostura, among others. These documents quickly reached Europe.[70] The editor
of otherwise pro–Spanish American independence *Niles' Weekly Register*
reproduced Aury's proclamations and decrees while discrediting his political
project. "Amelia seems to have degenerated into a mere asylum of privateers,"
the editor added as an introduction to the texts.[71]

Commerce was good. Aury sent an announcement to U.S. papers that
the port at Amelia did not collect duties on "arms, munitions of war, and
provisions of every kind." Word on the streets of Charleston was that Aury's
followers had seized prizes worth $250,000.[72] A lot of these profits came from
slave trading. The Amelia government sold between 600 and 1,000 enslaved
people into the United States. In November 1817, a U.S. brig captured a prize
vessel with 118 enslaved Africans going into Amelia. The Africans were distributed among planters for "safe-keeping" in neighboring Georgia.[73] An
Amelia privateer took drastic measures to protect his merchandise when he
saw U.S. naval ships: he made 250 enslaved prisoners seized from a Spanish
ship jump overboard in the night. Those who knew how to swim made it
to the shore. The others did not. The survivors were sold to U.S. citizens.[74]
Knocking at the door of the family of nations, Aury shifted enslaved Africans
from one ship to another, from one legal space to another, without any recognition of their humanity.

The Good Neighbor Policy

Reactions to the Amelia republic shows how the U.S. administration gradually
drew a line between entities it recognized as sovereign and those it declared
nonsovereign. The discourse around the Republic of the Floridas revealed a
preoccupation with mobility. President James Monroe argued that Amelia
was a "piratical" establishment, as evidenced by its "itinerant nature."[75] The
itinerant republicanism of Aury and other revolutionaries clashed with the

settler republicanism of the U.S. republic. When the United States expanded westward, it imagined Native territories as unsettled wilderness. The United States set out to settle this space through white homesteads and the establishment of civil society and legal order.[76] They began to apply the same language to Amelia Island: since its founders were marauders who leapfrogged from one place to the next, Amelia was not a legitimate sovereign state. Secretary of State John Quincy Adams concluded, "The marauding parties at Amelia Island and Galveston ought to be broken immediately."[77] The expression "marauding parties" shows how mobility and piracy were racialized in the early nineteenth-century United States, where pirates were mostly associated with uncivilized racial "others" from the North African coast (the so-called Barbary pirates of the 1790s and 1800s).[78]

In the eyes of the United States, Aury's republic was guilty of four crimes: the first was contravening the slave trade ban. The second was breaching the "No Transfer Resolution" passed by Congress in 1811. At the time, a significant number of U.S. citizens had moved to West Florida, and an armed force attacked the Spanish fort at Baton Rouge, Louisiana, and declared its independence from Spain. Shortly after, President James Madison issued a proclamation claiming West Florida for the United States. To legitimize the land grab, the No Transfer Resolution authorized the president to take possession of Florida and any territory adjoining the U.S. southern boundary if it was transferred to a foreign power and threatened U.S. "security, tranquility, and commerce." While the Louisiana Purchase enabled U.S. territorial extension through treaties and international negotiations, the No Transfer Resolution added unilateral military intervention as a new tactic of U.S. foreign policy.[79]

A third accusation was that Amelia threatened the foundations of U.S. racial hierarchy by arming men of African descent and giving them equal rights. This fear ran through a series of letters sent by citizens of Georgia and Louisiana to the House of Representatives. Witnesses claimed that Aury relied on "about one hundred and thirty brigand negroes—a set of desperate bloody dogs." Another wrote that Aury "thinks proper to grant to his party-colored associates the blessings," he sneered, "of a *free government*." Another account explained that the republicans "have declared that if they are in danger of being overpowered, they will call to their aid every negro within their reach. Indeed I am told that the language of the slaves in Florida is already such as is extremely alarming."[80] Accused of encouraging a race war, Aury responded by publicizing the laws of his government that prescribed penalties for assisting or hosting enslaved runaways from the United States.[81]

The last argument against Amelia was that Aury's government made a political farce of the U.S. revolution. Aury expressed his wish that the United States sympathize "with their southern brethren in the struggle for liberty and independence in which they are engaged, as were the United States forty years ago."[82] Located at the southern borders of the United States, Amelia confronted this country with the legacy of its own revolutionary origins. U.S. observers saw the events at Amelia as echoes not of the glorious U.S. Revolution but of the much-feared French Revolution. In their view, Amelia planted the seeds of radicalism dangerously close to U.S. soil. A resident of Saint Mary wrote the *Charleston Courier* that the Republic of the Floridas was going to be "similar to that in the early days of the French Revolution. . . . We expect daily to see a guillotine."[83]

On December 22, 1817, Aury received the message that a U.S. squadron was taking possession of the island. He protested that the United States had no authority over Florida: "the only law you can adduce in your favor, is that of force, which is always repugnant to republican governments, and to the principles of a just and impartial nation." Aury's republic was outnumbered and peacefully surrendered. Either as a sign of goodwill or as a measure to protect his troops from U.S. forces, Aury ordered all his officers and soldiers of African descent to take shelter on a ship anchored offshore.[84]

The concepts of "pirates" and "outlaws" began to sustain a distinction between legitimate and illegitimate political actors. In January 1818, the Congressional Committee on Foreign Relations recommended that the government recognize the Amelia revolutionaries as "reprobated by laws of nations, which recognize them only under the denomination of pirates."[85] The concept of piracy allowed the U.S. government to defend the legality of its military intervention: the Amelia republic was outside the civilized community of states. As historian Deborah Rosen argued, the pirate analogy defined Florida as similar to the high seas: a space that belonged to no nation yet allowed nations to exercise jurisdiction there under certain conditions. Spain was too weak to control the territory.[86] The United States extended its extraterritorial sovereignty over Amelia by asserting the right to punish "pirates" and "marauders." The U.S. government used the same justification during the Seminole War in Florida in 1816–1818.

Important distinctions existed, however, between the Amelia "pirates" and the circumstances of the Seminole War. The U.S. government justified not just military intervention but also military violence by refusing to recognize Seminole Indians and Afro-descendants' claims to rights of territorial sovereignty. They punished them with deportation, execution, and enslavement. The lack of physical violence toward the republicans at Amelia shows that both the veneer of legitimacy Aury had created and the ethnic-national identity he represented (a white Frenchman) provided protection. The U.S. administration considered him a pirate but did not treat him like Seminole Indians or other nonwhite people. He firmly belonged on the right side of the race-based line between civilization and savagery in the eyes of the U.S. government.[87] His foreignness was another layer of protection. Members of Aury's Amelia government came from all around the world, and the United States had no desire to risk the ire of consuls and diplomats by committing acts of violence against them.[88]

The U.S. government characterized the Amelia republicans as pirates to shape legal perspectives on military intervention by questioning the definition of popular sovereignty. President James Monroe decried Amelia as a distortion of the right of self-determination, "where the venerable forms, by which a free people constitute a frame of government for themselves," he objected, "are prostituted by a horde of foreign freebooters for purposes of plunder."[89] Yet Aury articulated his claims to legitimacy so forcefully that the Monroe administration contradicted itself in its frenzy to justify its intervention: MacGregor and Aury had ended Spanish rule in Amelia, they asserted, thus violating the No Transfer Resolution. Yet, with the same breath, they claimed that these leaders had no claims to sovereignty. Amelia had not gone from the hands of Spain to those of a foreign power, they argued; it had fallen into the lap of black-loving, slave-smuggling, itinerant pirates and radical firebrands.[90] This stigmatization enabled the United States to embrace the Law of Nations that guaranteed the right of self-determination while claiming the right to intervene outside of their borders to crush another republic.

Aury attempted to use proper channels to contest U.S. military intervention. In doing so, he launched another skillful, if eventually unsuccessful, entrée into international diplomacy. In the absence of supranational institutions, he commissioned Vicente Pazos to defend his cause and obtain reparations.[91] Pazos spent four months in Washington, sending a protest, *The Exposition, Remonstrance and Protest of Don Vincente Pazos*, to the House of Representatives. Quoting the U.S. Declaration of Independence, Pazos stressed the need for international fraternity. After all, Aury's government was as much a "handful of adventurers" as George Washington had been.[92]

Not only did the United States flout international norms by capturing an island from freedom-seeking insurgents at war with Spain, but they also disregarded their own domestic laws. On the No Transfer Resolution, Pazos pointed out that the United States, as a neutral power, had no right to breach the territorial sovereignty of Amelia. The republic on Amelia was "agreeable to the laws of nations," and therefore, he continued, "no power can assume the authority to interfere with the concerns, nor decide upon the rights of another." Pazos noted that the Amelia constitution protected freedom of press, speech, and trade. He praised Aury as a "worthy officer and distinguished patriot" and was appalled that U.S. opinion and officials had "confounded [him] with pirates and malefactors." Amelia was a "sister republic" alongside the United States against European monarchies. It could be an example to the rest of the world. "The establishment of Amelia was a school," Pazos concluded, and "its inhabitants were republicans."[93]

In the House of Representatives, Henry Clay supported Pazos as part of his broader campaign in favor of South American revolutions. He and a few other representatives argued that Amelia was a legitimate republic, having formed a government, elected a legislature, and appointed officers. Clay presented Pazos's memorial to the House, starting a three-hour debate over whether the House should receive the memorial formally.[94] The secretary of state's response was blunt.[95] Pazos's words had failed to make him see "the proceedings at Amelia Island in a different charter from that in which he had before viewed them."[96] The House eventually refused to accept the memorial of a "self-styled" foreign agent and conceded the U.S. president's right to invade a foreign territory without a declaration of war.[97]

Reactions to Aury show how the contest over legitimacy played a constitutive role not only in the construction of U.S. foreign policy but also of inter-American relationships. Aury's shadow loomed over the relationships between the United States and Latin America. As soon as the news that the insurgent forces had prevailed over Spain reached the U.S. government, the State Department sent Commodore Oliver H. Perry to Angostura to discuss the intervention at Amelia.[98] When Perry met with Vice President Francisco Antonio Zea in July 1819, Zea reassured the U.S. agent that he "was perfectly satisfied with the justice and policy of the United States in expelling from a usurped territory a flag that was never acknowledged by the Venezuelan Republic."[99] The two governments agreed: Aury had abused the right of revolution.[100] Yet Aury had supporters in Venezuela, particularly the editor of the paper *El Correo del Orinoco*, who defended the Republic of the Floridas as legitimate: elections had been organized, a provisional government had been established, and "The Press had already started operating." He insisted that the U.S. government violated the Law of Nations by invading this territory.[101] The *Correo*'s editorial was not enough to sway the government's decision to disavow Aury.

Concerns about Amelia Island crossed the Atlantic. An inquiry by the French minister of foreign affairs prompted the U.S. ambassador in France to justify the military intervention of his government. He answered that Amelia Island was occupied by "a set of unauthorized, outrageous, and dangerous . . . adventurers."[102] The U.S. takeover of Amelia Island finally convinced Spain to ratify the Adams-Onís, or Transcontinental Treaty, in 1819, ceding Florida to the United States.[103] Spain required that, in exchange for Florida, the United States refuse to recognize Latin American independence. The United States remained noncommittal until the treaty was secure in 1821. The following year, it recognized Argentina, Chile, Peru, Colombia, and Mexico.

Even after Aury departed U.S. waters, he still influenced the legal and diplomatic concept of sovereignty in the North Atlantic. The absence of consensus regarding the recognition of new countries, coupled with reluctance on the part of governments to get involved in the conflicts between Spain and its colonies, meant that courts were often the places where international policy was tentatively articulated. Courts adjudicated a number of cases involving Spanish American insurgents and privateers and had to assess the legitimacy of unrecognized states.[104] A significant case reached the U.S. Supreme Court in 1820 against Ralph Klintock, a U.S. citizen sailing under a commission from Aury. The defending party claimed that Aury's commission exempted the prisoner from the charge of piracy. As opposed to previous court decisions, the Supreme Court decided that the U.S. court system could prosecute "outlaws"—U.S. and non-U.S. citizens alike—who operated outside of the interstate system without the authority of a "legitimate" state behind them. In other words, Aury was an unrecognized authority, or rather, the United States did not recognize his authority. The judge concluded that Aury and his crew, including Klintock, belonged to "no nation or State . . . [they] are outcasts from the society of nations."[105]

The Attributes of Sovereignty

"Let's console ourselves that America is large," Aury reassured his followers after they departed Amelia, and "many States are in full revolution: there will be no shortage of land for us." He quietly promised, "I have a project in mind that cannot fail."[106] On a trip to Jamaica, Aury met José Cortés Madariaga, an agent of the Republics of Buenos Aires and Chile, who granted him a commission to promote "Liberty and Independence" in the Caribbean.[107] Two months later, Madariaga wrote his government that Aury had claimed the archipelago of Providencia and San Andrés and adopted a "provisional form of government."[108] Colombia's secretary of foreign affairs, Pedro Gual, who had worked with Aury at Amelia, grudgingly admitted that the government on Providencia had been "issuing letters of marque, granting military titles"; in short, it had been "exercising almost all the attributes of sovereignty."[109] Chile reacted quickly and disavowed Madariaga and Aury publicly. Although Chilean independence leaders briefly authorized privateering in 1817, they were now building a "legitimate" navy and opposed the use of privateers.[110] Aury and the other republicans either never heard of this disavowal or ignored it.

The island of Providencia lies in the far southwestern corner of the Caribbean. A rugged, volcanic mass, five by three miles at its widest point, surrounded by an extensive bank of coral and sand, Providencia possessed a natural harbor in Catalina, a nearby smaller island. England and Spain settled and resettled Providencia many times. Like Galveston and Amelia, Providencia was located at the edge of the Spanish Empire and had experienced various waves of migration, making its attachment to the crown tenuous. In 1803, Spain added the archipelago of Providencia, San Andrés, and a section of the Mosquito Coast to the jurisdiction of the Viceroyalty of New Granada.[111] Providencia's geographic isolation from the colony and its social and economic ties with the Anglophone areas of Jamaica and Honduras enhanced its cosmopolitan nature.[112] When Aury arrived, about 1,200 inhabitants of different national and ethnic backgrounds lived on the island, 800 of whom were enslaved. Free inhabitants tended to be plantation owners who traded cotton and tobacco, supplementing their incomes with turtle shells.[113] After Aury's ships blockaded the port, the governor—a naturalized Englishman— informed him that the inhabitants desired to escape the tyranny of the Spanish Empire.[114] Aury's squadron of 300 men, two small gun brigs, and three privateer schooners took possession of Providencia on July 4, 1818.

At some point during the six months Aury spent at sea between Amelia and Providencia, Sévère Courtois joined him. Two years had passed since they were together in Cartagena and Haiti. Courtois had gained a nefarious reputation; one of Aury's collaborators noted that he was "known in all the sea-bordering countries for his acts of piracy."[115] However, Aury knew an asset when he saw one, and Courtois quickly became a commanding presence on Providencia. Courtois once stated that no cause was more sacred to him than "the holy cause of Liberty and Independence."[116]

Aury had learned his lessons from the U.S. invasion of Amelia. He avoided a formal declaration of independence—possibly a strategy to increase room

for maneuver and greater flexibility. He sent a ship to Jamaica to announce his new republican establishment. Creating links with British authorities was of vital importance since Jamaica was Providencia's main trading partner.[117] He also sent out the word that his troops needed new recruits. News quickly traveled to the United States and Gran Colombia, where notices appeared in newspapers. "The screams of the wounded humanity demand our help," Aury proclaimed, "and require that we do put an end to this age of barbarity."[118] Aury emphasized his allegiance to Chile, Buenos Aires, and Colombia. Providencia was a "department" of Colombia liberated in the name of Buenos Aires and Chile; it was not an independent republic.

In practice, however, Providencia operated as an autonomous government. Aury set up an admiralty court and issued privateer commissions to encourage maritime trade. Reports in Kingston spoke of prize goods "worth a quarter of a million dollars."[119] He set up a system in which privateers paid him a commission of 18 percent on all captures.[120] Reporting on Providencia, the *Bermuda Gazette* snidely remarked, "It seems to be a rule in commencing a patriotic revolution in any part of Spanish America that the establishment of a Court of Admiralty must be among the first acts."[121] Courtois rose through the ranks. He became captain of his own ship, the *Mars*. He, along with what a U.S. traveler described as a "nearly all black crew," seized Spanish vessels traveling around Haiti and Cuba.[122]

The ambiguous status of Providencia could be an asset as well as a problem. Latin American authorities did not recognize Aury's legitimacy but tolerated him. But in 1819, a Venezuelan corsair apprehended and detained one of Aury's corsairs, the *Diana*. Aury wrote the president of the Republic of Venezuela to protest this "manifest violation of the Law of Nations." Aury argued that the *Diana* was flying the "legitimate flags of the republics of Buenos Aires and Chile," and the principles of harmony and friendship united all Spanish American governments. By seizing the *Diana*, Venezuela had committed an act of piracy and even war against a friendly country, he insisted.[123]

To be accepted by the international community, Aury and Courtois offered proofs of territorial control, institution building, and basic services— in brief, proofs that their government was effective. They did some urban planning. Aury and his men found Providencia to abound with thick woodland—perfect for ship and house construction. Gardens supplied such crops as beans, yams, sugar cane, mangoes, plantains, and melons. Aury bragged that in barely two years, his government on Providencia put together "a great neighborhood, with Judges, Markets, stores and shops, and the commerce had been much improved as a result." He had the dock enlarged so that the port could accommodate foreign ships.[124] A hospital was set up from material imported from the United States.[125] Aury and Courtois also systematized social planning. While religion played little role in his personal life, Aury always made it a point of honor to build Catholic churches to enhance the respectability of his governments to the outside world. When a privateer captured a Spanish ship that transported a priest, Aury asked him to be the chaplain of a new church. The priest refused.[126]

Aury's political convictions to export liberty and independence nicely allied with his creative diplomatic strategy. Building on his experiences in Galveston and Amelia, he hoped to tie Providencia to the rest of the Caribbean, not only through trade but also through foreign intervention. "The time, then, has come for the political transformation the New World has been crying for," he announced.[127] One region was of particular interest: the Gulf of Honduras, which had long been the subject of jurisdictional and territorial disputes. Honduras was a province of the captaincy general of Guatemala, but the crown exercised a fragile sovereignty over the region.[128] The Caribbean coast, in particular, the Mosquito Coast—a jagged coastline stretching from Cape Gracias a Dios in the north to the San Juan River in Costa Rica— was also the site of British presence.

The proliferation of geopolitical actors and interests made the Gulf of Honduras an attractive destination for Aury and Courtois's revolutionizing ambitions. The region also produced indigo and cochineal, making it an even more attractive destination for Aury and Courtois's pecuniary ambitions.[129] British and Spanish American insurgent attacks on Spanish shipping at sea made it necessary for exporters to send their indigo overland to Veracruz, depriving Aury and others an opportunity to get their hands on the precious product. Sévère Courtois oversaw the naval forces of two attacks against the coast. On the first attempt in May 1819, Aury and Courtois's squadron stopped at the British port of Belize. Lieutenant Governor George Arthur tried to enforce a strict neutrality policy. As he explained, "General Aury's followers appear to be collected from all Nations, and their ruling profession is, I fear, Plunder, not Patriotism."[130] The revolutionaries left Belize and attacked the Spanish forts of San Felipe and Isabela on the Rio Dulce, where they seized indigo, cochineal, and other goods worth 1,500 pounds.[131]

On their way back to Providencia, they stopped at Belize once again. The lieutenant governor warned the authorities in London that "the utmost caution is necessary to guard against the appearance of our supporting the cause of the Republicans," but he expressed his concern that the revolutionaries could turn against the British settlement. The only course of action, he decided, was to compromise: he allowed the revolutionaries into the port but forbade them from obtaining arms and ammunitions. Local merchants promptly ignored this order, eager to trade gunpowder for indigo.[132] Aury made overtures to George Frederick, recognized by the British as king of the Miskito Coast Indians and educated in Belize and Jamaica. The lieutenant governor of Belize pressured the Miskito king not to back the expedition, causing the alliance to fall apart.[133] A republican settlement in Spanish Honduras meant potential trade disruptions as well as further incentives for enslaved workers to run away. Even without Miskito support, Aury and Courtois led another expedition against the coast of Honduras a year later.

One morning in April 1820, Aury traveled with fourteen ships and 200 men to Trujillo. As he did in Providencia two years earlier, he demanded that the Spanish political and military government join forces with the "Republic." Unlike the governor of Providencia, the Spanish representatives in Trujillo turned down the offer. After two days of fighting, which killed or wounded forty republicans and two royalists, Aury withdrew his troops and redirected them to neighboring Omoa on a small bay along the northwest Caribbean coast of Honduras.[134] There, he attempted to perform the same ceremonies of liberation he had employed on many previous occasions. He first demanded peaceful surrender and promised that should the residents, "Europeans, indigenous or Africans," decline to join the republic, they would be free to leave the region peacefully and take their properties.[135] When the commandant refused, the republicans futilely laid siege to the small town.[136] Forced to withdraw their forces, they returned to Providencia. In just one year, two of the Courtois and Aury's liberating conquests had failed.

Condemned by the Congress of Gran Colombia for attacking Honduras without authorization, Aury drafted a detailed account to defend his reputation. His ambition, he stated, was to establish on Providencia "a lasting establishment from which to launch the thunderbolt aimed at exterminating the enemies of the Independence."[137] Aury's rhetoric had potent millennialist undertones: he claimed that he wished "to shed the beneficial light of Liberty, over a large land, still covered by the darkness of terror, superstition, and despotism."[138] However, Aury realized, the cooperation of "the naturals of the Country" was essential but did not happen in Spanish Honduras. The reason was simple, according to him: "No Liberal idea has yet germinated among this people; no glimmer of Liberty shines in their eyes."[139] Aury and Courtois clearly overestimated the support their republican project would receive. Yet the expeditions were not complete failures. Courtois made more than two thousand pesos from the indigo and cochineal seized in the Gulf of Honduras.[140]

The Colombian government repeatedly rejected Aury's efforts to obtain formal recognition. Bolívar played with the idea of admitting Aury as a ship captain but was reluctant to grant him the commandant-in-chief position he insisted was his due. Luis Brión, the admiral of the Colombian navy, steadily refused to integrate Aury and his fleet into the navy. He refused to have Aury's ships navigate the same seas as Colombian vessels. Aury was "certainly a pirate," Brión insisted.[141] Adding insult to injury, Bolívar wrote Aury in January 1821, "The Republic of Colombia had reached a point when it no longer needs these corsairs who degrade her flag in every sea of the world." The message was loud and clear: "please gather your ships and take them far from Colombian waters."[142] Colombia chose another path to international legitimacy and began to move away from the multiethnic and multinational world of privateering. Vice President Santander created a naval school in Cartagena in 1822 and issued additional decrees for the provision of a navy.[143]

Faced with Gran Colombia's hostile reaction, Aury and Courtois turned to another power in the region for assistance. The two men knew that Haiti supported the Latin American independence movement in the name of hemispheric solidarity. Aury took a trip to Port-au-Prince in 1821 to meet with President Jean-Pierre Boyer to discuss an attack on the Spanish colony of Santo Domingo.[144]

Aury and Courtois saw Providencia as the "asylum of defenders of independence" where sailors and soldiers burned with "patriotism, love of liberty, and devotion for their leader."[145] The life of this leader ended on August 30, 1821, when Aury fell from a horse. He was about thirty-three. He had appointed Courtois as his executor, and the Saint-Dominguan drew up an inventory of his friend's possessions. They included a watch, a sword decorated with gold, a saber, a hat, and some sets of epaulets. Enslaved individuals also formed part of his estate: Coffes, Williamson, Petit, William, Francisco, and young Emilie. Aury stipulated that they be emancipated at the age of twenty-five. The enslaved Francisco and the guns, jewels, clothes, and two hundred gourds went to his nephew. One-third of his estate went to his lover, a woman from San Andrés. His beloved sister Victoire in Paris got the remaining two-thirds.[146] Aury's death prevented the two siblings from being reunited. They did not see each other for twenty years, and Aury missed his sister's wedding to a merchant hosier.[147] Unlike her peripatetic brother, Victoire never left Paris. She died in the city in 1839.[148]

Saint-Domingue-born leaders Courtois and Jean-Baptiste Faiquere suc-
ceeded Aury: Faiquere became governor while Courtois became the commandant of the army and navy, proudly wearing Aury's cockade everywhere
he went.[149] Since Providencia was a military stronghold, this title meant that
Courtois was head of government. He published an invitation to foreign
sailors to join him in Providencia to defend "our asylum."[150] He issued privateer commissions. In a spirit of hemispheric solidarity, he wished to revolutionize Cuba. He reached out to his relatives in Haiti and asked for their
support. He even contacted President Boyer, explaining that his goal was to
give "their liberty to the populations who are now under Spanish yoke."[151]

The power vacuum created by Aury's death pitted his collaborators
against each other. Soon, Courtois's reputation came under fire. He became
the target of a smear campaign led by French general Louis Peru de Lacroix,
another close collaborator of Aury, who felt that Courtois has cheated him of
Aury's estate. Lacroix moved to Cartagena and denounced Courtois as the
leader of a "fraudulent government" and "the head of a political and criminal party of armed individuals . . . devised without any respect for the rules
of civil society and the Law of Nations." Courtois's government, Lacroix
insisted, was "neither dependent [on], nor protected by any government."
While Courtois pretended that his government was "a lawful, beneficial, and
liberal government," it had instead, according to Lacroix, "usurped, illicit,
and overbearing authority."[152]

Lacroix played on fears of a race war with Colombian officials, suggesting
that Courtois, a "despotic sultan," had great influence on the men of African
descent who formed the quasi-totality of the population and the military on
the island.[153] Courtois protested in response that Lacroix's attack campaigns
were calumnious insults and baseless accusations. In a series of letters to the
Gaceta de Cartagena, Courtois foregrounded his service to the republican
cause, his love for "humanity," and his leadership abilities, explaining that he
was "a man able to order, and to preserve the subordination of corsairs."[154]
The volatility of the political and social situation created the need for a strong
leader: Courtois saw himself as the perfect candidate for the role. He accused
one of Lacroix's followers of calling him a "mulâtre capois," or a mulatto from
Le Cap in northern Haiti.[155] Courtois knew what laid behind this seemingly
neutral description: "mulâtre capois" signaled Courtois as a nonwhite foreigner. Fears of race wars had destroyed the careers of other ambitious military leaders of African descent. A few years earlier, after the mestizo general
Manuel Piar demanded better treatment for nonwhite forces in Venezuela, he
was tried for insubordination and sentenced to death.[156] After his experience

during the Battle of New Orleans and having clashed with Bolívar previously, Courtois knew that his status as both a foreigner and an Afro-descendent was precarious.

The internal divisions following Aury's death paved the way for the integration of Providencia into Gran Colombia. These divisions probably forced Courtois's hand in seeking a rapprochement. He knew that his wealth, military expertise, and troops were valuable to the republic. Eager to incorporate both Providencia's territory and forces, the Colombian government blamed Providencia's autonomous government on Aury. With the death of this troublesome leader, Gran Colombia could now annex Providencia peacefully. Aury had ruled with "an absolute and unlimited power" on the island, the Colombians argued, and had silenced the "good patriots" who were now free to join the republic.[157] Courtois and Faiquere held a ceremony June 23 in Providencia and July 21, 1822, in San Andrés to pledge allegiance to the Colombian flag. The islands became the sixth canton of the Province of Cartagena under Faiquere's command. Aury's "private interest" had governed the islands for too long, the Colombian government chided; they were now under proper governance.[158]

Courtois put his fleet to the service of the republic in October 1822 and, in a mutually convenient quid pro quo, was cleared of all accusations of piracy and of racial conspiracy. He could continue to command his corsair ships if he put them in the service of the republic.[159] Courtois sent his service records to the Colombian government, asking for naturalization papers as well as military recognition. He successfully presented himself as "an honorable officer" who had long "served the cause of America" and asked for 800 pesos to repair two of his ships.[160] Courtois carefully manipulated public opinion to deflect fears and critiques. In his confrontation with Lacroix, Courtois was the one with connections, ships, and wealth. He sued Lacroix for defamation of character and won his trial.[161] When the Spanish sent a fleet to the continent in 1823, Courtois and his four ships fought for the republic at the Battle of Lake Maracaibo under the orders of Colonel José Padilla.[162]

The leaders of the Republic of Gran Colombia distanced themselves from itinerant revolutionaries and their inventive use of privateering rights.[163] They wished to expunge Aury's legitimacy completely and commissioned an agent to Chile and Argentina to inquire about their support of Aury's revolutionary pretensions. Colombia encouraged the new American states to end the "abuses" committed by some "pirates flying our own colors."[164] They explained that "the executive took various measures to control these men who had no other motive for their actions than their private interest."[165]

Colombia and Chile were on the same page. Chile's minister of government and foreign affairs had long denied a connection with Aury, insisting that his administration was opposed to the "establishment of those corsairs" who disrupted maritime trade.[166]

Some of Aury's forces remained in Providencia.[167] However, Courtois was not a man who settled. The experience of Providencia had not quenched his political thirst. He might have negotiated with Gran Colombia to integrate its naval forces, but he was steadfast in his efforts to export revolution to the world. Cuba was his next target. In 1823, he participated in the conspiracy called the Suns and Rays of Bolívar (Soles y Rayos de Bolivar) that hoped to establish the Republic of Cubanacán. Courtois collaborated with José Francisco Lemus, a Cuban who had fought in the Colombian army. Lemus infiltrated Masonic groups in Cuba and shared his plans with his network, including free Afro-descendants but also white elites and intellectuals frustrated with Spanish trade restrictions. The captain-general of Cuba informed metropolitan authorities that foreign adventurers sent proclamations and pamphlets to the island. These "false doctrines" and democratic principles, he denounced, seduced "a lot of the youth . . . and some negroes on which [foreign adventurers] rely to spread the word of independence."[168]

The Republic of Cubanacán planned to abolish slavery progressively, with compensation to slaveholders, and to give equal rights to all. "We do not recognize any other distinction than that owned to true merit," one of the proclamations claimed.[169] Just a few days before the planned uprising, Spanish spies uncovered the conspiracy. Authorities made a series of arrests in Havana, including Lemus and 600 other people, and proclaimed martial law. Courtois probably escaped, but the conspiracy of the Suns and Rays of Bolívar marked his disappearance from the archives.

*   *   *

"What makes a government legitimate?" asked Jean-Jacques Rousseau in *The Social Contract*. For him, the answer was a government that served public interest and ruled by laws, or what he called a republic. The only legitimate state was the one in which sovereignty rested with the people.[170] Rousseau was not the only one who struggled with defining and classifying sovereignty and statehood. These debates occurred everywhere: government cabinets, courts, marketplaces, taverns, and ships. A British chief justice acknowledged the difficulties in proving legitimacy in the early nineteenth century: "If a foreign state is recognized by this country, it is not necessary to prove that it

is an existing state; but if it is not recognized, such proof becomes necessary."
He even volunteered his own definition of statehood: "If a body of persons
assemble together to protect themselves, and support their own independence and make laws, and have courts of justice, that is evidence of their
being a state."[171]

Viewed from the outside, Aury and Courtois's small sovereignties gener-
ated a multiplicity of interpretations. U.S. authorities saw them as "government[s] by foreign adventurers . . . distinct from the colonial governments of
Buenos Ayres, Venezuela, or Mexico, pretending to sovereignty."[172] Colombian authorities saw them as the places where Aury "had established a piratical Republic, asylum of pirates and any kind of bandits."[173] British authorities
thought Aury was a "robber . . . at the head of . . . a horde of banditti [and]
renegades."[174] Yet Aury and Courtois unfailingly articulated an ideological
position to validate their claims to territory and sovereignty.

In their correspondences with foreign powers, they steadily presented
themselves as equal diplomatic partners and heads of their own governments.
The ghostly and ephemeral governments engineered by Aury and Courtois
in the Greater Caribbean actively engaged with many actors. Their program,
which blended cosmopolitan republicanism, racial egalitarianism, and economic opportunities (including slave trading), appealed to various groups.
Though they acted in the name of Latin American independence movements, they acquired a degree of autonomy that would have been impossible
from within insurgent navies and armies. They turned the right to revolution
into a contagion on land and at sea. Latin American privateer commissions
turned their ships into floating republics: they seized not only enemy ships
but also enemy territories and secured autonomous governments that issued
their own privateer commissions. Deploying a cosmopolitan rhetoric based
on the idea that republicanism and independence transcended boundaries,
Aury declared that his purpose was to "plant the tree of liberty, to foster free
institutions, and to wage war against the tyrant of Spain, the oppressor of
America, and the enemy to the rights of man."[175]

CHAPTER 2

Traveling Words

Communication Circuits

A few weeks before Christmas 1813, Juan Bautista Mariano Picornell received a letter he had eagerly anticipated. Sitting in a hastily assembled camp on the banks of the Sabine River, the former professor could feel the breeze coming from the Gulf of Mexico nearby. Far from his native Mallorca, Picornell had appointed himself "President of the Provinces of Mexico" over a handful of individuals who hoped to free Mexico from the shackles of Spain. Busy printing proclamations on a small press brought from Philadelphia, Picornell turned his attention to the letter he had just received from his "old friend and colleague," Manuel Cortés Campomanes. Together, they had fought for the cause of freedom for the past twenty years but had not heard from each other for over a year. Cortés Campomanes was in the Republic of Cartagena and asked his old friend to send him not only weapons—promising 25 pesos for each rifle—but also other valuable commodities. He needed books, especially military manuals. "Send me [books] in any language," he asked, "because I haven't got any," a particularly uncomfortable situation as he hoped to train 4,000 soldiers in four years. Even as they stood on opposite coasts of the Gulf of Mexico, the two traveling revolutionaries exchanged news about friends and foes, politics and revolutions.[1]

The age of revolutions was an age of information and misinformation. The late eighteenth century saw tremendous growth in newspapers, gazettes, pamphlets, and books in the Atlantic world.[2] Literacy levels varied, but more people than ever had access to a printing press and were free to broadcast their own stories, making official attempts at censorship futile.[3] An incipient informal market of books began to operate, and information networks among different social groups proliferated. These networks circulated both written and oral materials. This world of print coexisted with a world of

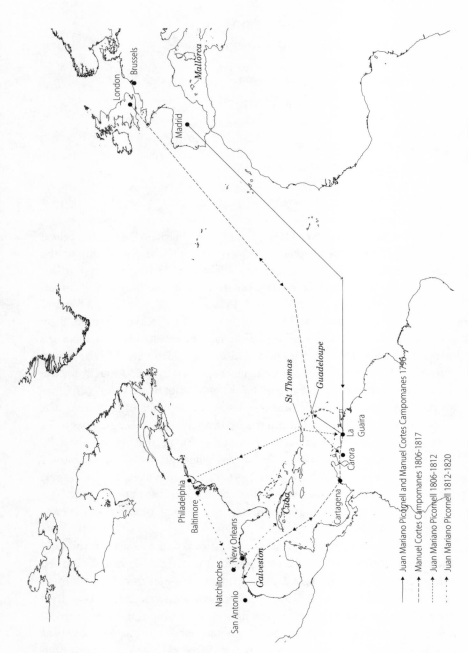

Map 3. The voyages of Juan Mariano Picornell and Manuel Cortés Campomanes, 1796–1820.

whispers. Rumors and verbal exchanges played a crucial role in the spread of information.[4]

Part of this world of stories was the propaganda and advertising campaigns that accompanied these political projects. Propaganda was an act of political theater performed for as wide an audience as possible. Revolutions were fought not only with firearms but also with letterpress printing.[5] When one of their political projects did not come to fruition (like Picornell's provisional government of the internal provinces of Mexico in 1813), they planned another one. They lined their paths with declarations of independence, proclamations, constitutions, and songs. These paper trails achieved three aims. The first was for their authors to have their ideas heard. The second was to recruit and mobilize supporters. The last impulse was to counteract rumors spread by detractors and control the narratives around their projects.

Like the ones that came before them, the revolutions in the Caribbean were revolutions of paper. Ideas circulated through a wide array of printed media during the 1640–1660 English revolution.[6] When printing presses became cheaper and more available, different groups and publicists vied to use print as a weapon to sway public opinion during the U.S. Revolution.[7] As John Adams wrote, "The Revolution was in the minds and hearts of the people. . . . This radical change in the principles, opinions, sentiments, and affections of the people, was the real American Revolution."[8] The disaggregation of European empires on the American continent often created a sense of a common cause among independents. Pamphlets, broadsides, and newspapers articulated proindependence arguments that often turned into nationalism, much as Benedict Anderson argued that national communities were first imagined through print.[9] Revolutionary publicists challenged the legitimacy of colonial regimes in order to proclaim the right to secede from the parent country.

No prior upheaval achieved the multilingual range of the materials produced by these cosmopolitan revolutionaries. The production of these advertising campaigns was a collective process involving a combination of technologies, authors, printers, translators, newspaper editors, and readers on both sides of the Atlantic. They all created an intellectual space that fundamentally reconsidered sources of political legitimacy and the right of every individual to launch—and advertise—a revolution. The multilingualism of this propaganda reflected the existence of an international consciousness during the age of revolutions.[10] The advertising campaigns produced by Picornell and Cortés Campomanes were embedded in the human and material webs of the Greater Caribbean. The portable printing presses that accompanied the expeditions were crucibles in which different traditions mingled and produced new promises for the future. With access to new technologies, "LIBERTY" became a more exportable concept than ever before.

Itinerant Presses

As they embarked on their expeditions, revolutionaries packed an extensive arsenal of weapons that, they hoped, would strike fear into the hearts of their opponents and inflict some lasting damage. Among this arsenal were swords, pistols, rifles, muskets, and printing presses. The latter became an essential staple of revolutionary expeditions in the late eighteenth century. Printing technologies changed very little in the 250 years after Johannes Gutenberg first constructed a wooden press that used a movable type. Hand-operated Gutenberg-style wooden presses remained the norm for most of the eighteenth century. Ben Franklin, for example, worked on such a press during his time as a journeyman in London in the 1720s. Franklin occasionally supplied printers in the British colonies of Jamaica, Antigua, and Barbados with paper. In the Caribbean, most of the paper came from Europe, and printing equipment was limited to letterpress printing.[11] However, technological innovation in the late eighteenth century was a gamechanger.

Technological innovations had recently created portable presses. A couple of men could easily carry portable presses on board ships and chariots. Such presses were worked by hand and ranged from five to seven feet long, three feet wide, and seven feet tall on average. In the early nineteenth century, new cast iron presses rivaled wooden presses. The earliest iron hand press was the Stanhope, built in England and adopted by newspaper shops in the United States by the mid-1810s. Although iron presses were more durable, they were also heavy and cumbersome. Most expeditions still carried the wooden hand presses because of the ease of transportation and repair.[12] Lithographic printing was also becoming popular at the time. Invented at the end of the eighteenth century, lithography was a cheap method of printing texts or artworks: this technique required only a lithographic plate to reproduce an image etched into a coating of wax or an oily substance. This type of printing was ideal for the genesis of short and often-ephemeral documents printed on one or two pages to spread the word of revolution.

Different elements of the wooden presses and lithographic plates traveled across lands and seas: once headquarters were set up, they could be reassembled. Most revolutionary leaders acquired printing presses in regions that had proclaimed their neutrality in the conflicts between Spain and its colonies—Britain, the United States, Saint Thomas, and Saint Barthélemy. Understandably suspicious of these small and portable presses, Spanish authorities attempted to obtain information about the buyers, hoping to track these transactions. The Spanish government activated mechanisms of control and vigilance, instructing their consuls and other agents and spies to keep an eye on who was selling and purchasing these presses.

It would be technological determinism to claim that the arrival of the printing press marked the beginning of social and political changes. After all, oral sources of information such as rumors, gossip, and songs had long played—and continued to play—a major role in the creation of political networks. People learned, exchanged, and shared ideas in one-to-one inter-actions. They obtained news from visitors, sailors, and travelers and shared them with one another. The printing press built on these other forms of com-munication.[13] The portability of printing presses, however, was relatively new when the age of revolutions swept up the Atlantic world. Revolutionaries quickly embraced this new technology. That they saw the printing press as an essential tool of war shows the place this technology occupied in their politi-cal consciousness. For small revolutionary expeditions, printing presses were necessary assets: they served to legitimize these expeditions. Not only did these presses produce revolutionary propaganda for the outside world, but they also manufactured the foundational documents of autonomous govern-ments: military titles, naval commissions, and sometimes currency. Without them, these attempted republics would have disappeared from the archives, leaving no trace behind them.

Access to a printing press was the first step toward a revolution. Revolu-tionaries took advantage of entangled sovereignties in the Caribbean to get their hands on these desired objects. In 1797, a Swiss captain informed Span-ish authorities that he saw a Frenchman from the Swedish colony of Saint Barthélemy trying to buy a printing press in Danish Saint Thomas. Both col-onies were neutral in the wars between Spain and the colonies and adopted a lucrative free trade policy, attracting many foreigners to their shores. The captain conjectured that this suspicious buyer was conspiring with Manuel Cortés Campomanes, who was also in Saint Thomas to buy guns and recruit followers to attack the Spanish mainland.[14] Having barely turned twenty, a thin man with piercing black eyes, a large forehead, and dark hair, Cortés Campomanes was no revolutionary neophyte.[15] A year earlier, in Madrid, he and Juan Bautista Mariano Picornell attempted to overthrow the Bourbon monarchy and establish a republic in its place. The plot took the name of the San Blas conspiracy when it was uncovered in February 1796. The government deported the conspirators to La Guaira in Venezuela. While in jail, Picornell "constantly wrote inflammatory papers."[16] He escaped to Curacao with Cortés Campomanes. Both men sought refuge in the French colony of Guadeloupe and often traveled to other islands in the Lesser Antilles.

In the Caribbean, Cortés Campomanes and Picornell continued to work toward exporting revolution to the mainland. They were in good company. Another believer in the power of the printed word was the Venezuelan revolutionary Francisco de Miranda, who led an expedition against his homeland in 1806 from Jacmel in southern Haiti. While in Haiti, he installed a printing press on the quarterdeck of one of his ships. A few members of the expedition, including a young printing apprentice from Massachusetts, Henry Ingersoll, spent three full days printing 2,000 proclamations in Spanish and setting the type for military commissions. Exhausted, Ingersoll took comfort in envisioning the future of these proclamations: "as soon as we arrive at our destination," he rejoiced, they "will be distributed to all parts of the world."[17] When the expedition left Haiti, it ran into two armed Spanish vessels and never reached its destination. Spanish colonial authorities took Ingersoll prisoner but eventually pardoned him. He returned to the United States. Miranda escaped and took refuge in the British colony of Trinidad. Other members of the expedition did not have this luck: ten were sentenced to death.[18]

Revolutionaries needed experienced personnel to operate the presses. They hired printers from the United States or England. Manuel Cortés Campomanes honed his knowledge of print culture as well as his editorial skills when he joined Spanish American patriots, including Miranda, exiled in London. The group—historian Karen Racine called them a "newsprint nation"—attempted to influence public opinion and recruit volunteers and investors. They also lobbied the British government but to no avail since Spain and Britain were allies at that time.[19] In 1810, Cortés Campomanes became a writer for Miranda's paper *El Colombiano*. The paper launched a fierce attack against Napoléon's ambitions, claiming that the French emperor gave the world "the most oppressive system that could ever affect mankind!" With the French invasion of the Iberian Peninsula in 1808, sovereignty had devolved to the people of the Americas, and *El Colombiano* encouraged municipal authorities to declare independence from the French despot. Otherwise, the writers warned, "you are destined perpetually to remain slaves!" The paper included translations of French and U.S. newspapers to share information about current events.[20] The enterprise was short-lived: only five issues appeared before funding dried up. Despite the ephemerality *of El Colombiano*, it had an illustrious career overseas. Several of its articles were reprinted in the secessionist papers *Gaceta de Caracas* and *Gaceta de Buenos Aires*. The paper circulated in Peru and in Mexico despite the vigilance of local authorities.[21] In late 1810, Cortés Campomanes and Miranda crossed the Atlantic Ocean and sailed toward Venezuela once again.[22] Picornell joined them soon after.

The experience of the revolutionary wanderers in the first Republic of Venezuela (1811–1812) was short-lived. The republic fell after a devastating earthquake and the arrival of Spanish royal forces. The friends parted ways once again. Miranda ended in the hands of the Spanish army and died in a prison cell near Cádiz in 1816. Cortés Campomanes sought refuge in the Republic of Cartagena and Picornell traveled to Philadelphia. The former U.S. capital was a hotspot for revolutionary activities. Picornell became familiar with the political ideas and debates of the young U.S. republic but also remained abreast of developments in Europe. Walking the streets of Philadelphia, he rubbed shoulders with other exiles from Europe and Spanish America and overheard conversations in Spanish, French, Dutch, and German. The concentration of printers in the city provided a vibrant multilingual and international atmosphere. Shortly after his arrival in the city, Picornell met José Alvarez de Toledo y Dubois. Born in Cuba and educated in Spain, Toledo had fought Napoléon in the Peninsula War. In Philadelphia, Toledo used his education and contacts to promote Spanish American independence. He notably sent a series of articles to U.S. newspapers and published a Spanish-language memoir. These materials reached not only Europe but also Cuba, Mexico, and Colombia.[23]

Lobbying public opinion in favor of independence was not enough for Picornell. He yearned to start another revolution. The arrival of Mexican blacksmith José Bernardo Gutiérrez to the East Coast provided him with such an opportunity. Working as an envoy of the independent government of Mexico, Gutiérrez hoped to convince U.S. authorities to support his cause. Failing to achieve this goal, he convinced a few exiles, including Picornell and Toledo, to join him in a coup against Texas. Toledo even flattered Picornell by asking him to join the expedition as "a Pamphleteer, or fabricator of proclamations, to the Province of Texas where he was going to found the Mexican Republic."[24] Gutiérrez traveled to the Texas-Louisiana border and gathered the Republican Army of Northern Mexico near New Orleans. The armed troops were a motley assemblage of U.S. Americans, Spanish Americans, European exiles, and free men of color, mostly exiles from Saint-Domingue. When Toledo and Picornell joined the armed expedition in April

1813, they brought a printing press and a printer with them—the first introduced to Texas. Printing presses were widespread in Europe and on the U.S. eastern seaboard, even in small towns, but they remained scarce in Spanish America, where they only operated in large cities and were controlled by local authorities.

The Spanish governor of Texas lamented that the contagion of revolution was imminent. With their press, the revolutionaries were able to "print proclamations and lies in order to provoke an insurrection."[25] Gutiérrez and his followers were initially successful and declared Texas independent from Spain. In April 1813, in San Antonio, Gutiérrez organized a provisional government and issued a constitution. The republicans hoped to recruit more volunteers and drum up support for their republic. They relied on newspapers in Louisiana to relay their messages. Other papers, in turn, reproduced these declarations across the United States.

The portable press and Picornell's literary skills were put to work right away. On March 25, 1813, the first and last issue of the *Gaceta de Texas* appeared in print. The editors of the *Gaceta* proudly announced that "not only is it the first time that Texas prints in its territory," they continued, "but it is also the first time throughout all of the Mexican continent one may write freely." The location of the issue was Nacogdoches, Louisiana, where the Cuban Toledo, the Spaniard Picornell, and the U.S. American William Shaler had erected a press with no inkling that the Republic of Texas would be short-lived. The editors of *La Gaceta* proudly proclaimed, "Mexico now has also freedom of the press: it is the strongest fortress against the violence and the tyranny of despots, and one of the most precious and sacred rights of man. The right to think and to communicate the principles and most sublime ideas of philosophy, can only be attained through the medium of the freedom of the press."[26] *La Gaceta* was short, only two separate sheets. Printing appeared only on one side. Each page had two complete columns. While the first page was a summary of the principles underpinning the Republic of Texas, the second page looked outward to the political events in the United States and in Spain, implying that European and U.S. powers were ready to support the revolution. Despite this optimism, the Texas republicans proved unwilling to support one another: rumors ran wild, and each leader accused the other of being double agents for Spain or for Napoléon.

Freedom of the press also meant freedom of expression, and members of the expedition expressed their discontent openly. Shaler, Picornell, and Toledo turned against Gutiérrez and used the same printing press to publish another paper, *El Mexicano*, in June 1813. The articles and editorials played on the fear that Gutiérrez's foreign followers, who were mostly French and free men of color, could be "Napoleonic agents." The editors leveled the accusation that many of them were planning to use the unrest in the region to set the stage for a Napoleonic invasion. Using *El Mexicano* as a weapon in their defamation campaign, the editors eventually forced Gutiérrez to give up command of the army to Toledo. The victory was short-lived: the Republic of Texas soon fell with the arrival of royalist troops in August 1813. Two years later, revolutionary agents sent another press from New Orleans to the insurgent port Boquilla de Piedras, near Veracruz, alongside boxes of proclamations, two thousand weapons, and a large number of saddles.[27]

Spanish-born revolutionary Xavier Mina brought another printing press to Texas in 1817. This press had come a long way: purchased in England, it traveled across the Atlantic with Mina and transited through the U.S. East Coast and Haiti as Mina bought guns and recruited volunteers. The voyage from Haiti to Texas was not smooth: the ships ran into bad weather and an epidemic of yellow fever ravaged the crew, doubling the amount of time it normally took to sail from Haiti to the Texas coast.[28] Seeing to the well-being of the press was eighteen-year-old Samuel Bangs from Baltimore. Bangs set up itinerant printing centers at every stop of the expedition. Mina's forces stopped first at Galveston Island, off the coast of Texas, then controlled by the French privateer Louis-Michel Aury. A few miles eastward, in New Orleans, Cortés Campomanes had reunited with his "companion in misfortune," Juan Bautista Mariano Picornell. Cortés Campomanes soon left his friend and joined the Mina expedition in Galveston. Thanks to his revolutionary résumé, he became Mina's secretary.[29]

Three months after their arrival in Galveston, the revolutionaries used the printing press to issue a proclamation announcing Mina's intention to revolutionize Mexico. Mina left Galveston Island with a force of eight ships and 235 men and stopped at the mouth of the Rio Grande, where the printing press churned out another proclamation. Pushing further north, his forces turned Soto de la Marina, in the province of New Santander, into a military, naval, and printing post. Soto de la Marina was a port halfway between the mouth of the Rio Grande and Tampico, about fifteen leagues off the coast of the Gulf of Mexico. According to a U.S. volunteer, "a printing press was immediately established . . . under the direction of Doctor Infanté, a native of Havana; and the general's Manifesto was published."[30]

Composed mostly of foreigners, the expeditionary force looked highly suspicious in Mexico, especially with a Spanish general at its head. The core of the revolutionary propaganda was therefore devoted to reassuring local

populations. Mina articulated his ideas of a transatlantic republican fraternity in a proclamation printed in Soto de la Marina in April 1817: "Mexicans, allow me to participate in your glorious struggles, accept the services
I offer to you in favor of your noble enterprise and count me among your
patriots. . . . Then, in recompense, say to your children: 'This land was twice
flooded in blood by servile Spaniards, abject vassals of a King; but there were
also liberal Spaniards and patriots who sacrificed their tranquility and lives
for our welfare.'"[31]

Copies of Mina's proclamations traveled inland along with the catchy tune
of the "Canción patriótica," a song written by Joaquín Infante and printed on
a book-sized broadside. Infante was a Cuban lawyer who had hatched a plot
to separate his native island from Spain and create the independent republic
of Cuba in 1809. Infante escaped jail and joined the patriots in Venezuela
in 1811. While in Caracas, Infante wrote a constitution for an independent
Cuba fashioned after the French Constitution of 1791. Infante had already
established his credibility as a political writer in exile when he met Mina in
Philadelphia and joined his revolutionary project against Mexico. In "Canción patriótica," Infante called for an international republican brotherhood:

Join, then, Mexicans
Our battalions
We will all be brothers
Under equal flags
We will form a nation[32]

Papers in the United States printed the song and different proclamations.
They reached European papers three months later. The *Morning Chronicle* in
London translated some portions into English.[33] Songs were part of a wide
circulation of news and information back and forth in the Atlantic basin.
The deployment of royalist troops to the region cut the revolutionaries' ambi-
tions short. While Cortés Campomanes was able to escape unharmed, the
army captured and executed Mina. Spanish authorities sent Infante to jail in
Veracruz and later deported him to Spain. There he continued to add to his
revolutionary legacy by publishing proindependence pamphlets, including
Solution to the Question of Rights in the Emancipation of America in Cádiz in
1820. Within a year, this ten-page brochure was reprinted across the Atlantic
Ocean in Mexico, Buenos Aires, and Caracas.[34] The printer of the expedition,
Samuel Bangs, fared better. The technical expertise of printers was highly
valued by insurgents and royalists alike, and Bang's ability to operate a press

saved his life. He worked for the royalists in Monterrey until the end of the wars when he began printing for the newly independent Mexican government.[35] The next printing press in Texas arrived with the James Long expedition in 1819 and fabricated the short-lived newspaper the *Texas Republican*.

The reliance on portable presses and the conditions of production of these documents certainly influenced their contents. Because the revolutionaries depended on rudimentary printing presses or lithographic plates, the documents had to be short. Most of them, newspapers included, did not go over two pages. In such a short amount of space, the revolutionaries often recycled the language of other revolutions' own ideas and sometimes adapted them to local conditions. In order to be efficient, revolutionary propaganda had to be accessible to different audiences by foregrounding such keywords as "oppression," "tyranny," "freedom," and "independence." Technology was not the only factor in shaping the contents of these documents. The environment in which they appeared—printed on a press lugged from the United States, England, or Haiti; operated by a printer from Philadelphia or Saint Thomas; composed by a philosopher from Cuba or Spain with the help of exiles from Saint-Domingue, France, and Italy—shaped the emergence of a cosmopolitan political philosophy.[36]

Inflammatory Ideas in Translation

A key feature of this revolutionary propaganda was its multilingualism. French was the international language of the day to which many revolutionaries added English and even Dutch. The presence of diplomats and intellectuals from Spain and Latin America also created a thriving Hispanophone printing world in the United States. Language was as fluid as imperial and national affiliations. Writing, printing, publishing, and communicating back and forth between French, Spanish, and English, revolutionaries produced programmatic documents that fleshed out their motivations and goals. They developed a modus operandi that they repeated in different locations, hoping to convince local populations that the future of the Americas was independent and republican. Revolutionaries brought not only printing presses and printers on their expeditions but also translators and secretaries.

Translation was an essential aspect of the circulation of words and ideas in the Atlantic world.[37] It presumed the crossing of borders, not only linguistic ones, but also cultural, social, and historical. Revolutionaries honed their cultural translating skills as they moved from one region to the next. The literary work of Manuel Cortés Campomanes illustrates how he adapted words and ideas to different environments. He composed two songs, the "Soneto Americano" (American Sonnet) and "Carmañola Americana" (American Carmagnole), after he and Picornell escaped from La Guaira and sought refuge in Guadeloupe in 1797.[38] The two men were familiar with the ideas and the language of the French Revolution. Not only had they devised a conspiracy in Madrid in 1796 modeled after this revolution, but they were also staying in Guadeloupe where the governor, Victor Hugues, had proclaimed the principles of the revolution.

The popularity of French revolutionary songs was at an all-time high in the 1790s. The *Gazette of the United States*, for example, claimed that French revolutionary songs accompanied the toasts for Jefferson's inauguration, including "Ça ira, The Rights of Man, Marseilles hymn, &c." A French privateer, named the *Carmagnole*, operated from Saint-Domingue in the early 1790s and crisscrossed the Gulf of Mexico.[39] The "Carmagnole" was a sarcastic and antimonarchical song with lyrics anyone could easily learn and understand. "Let us dance the Carmagnole," the chorus instructed, "Long live the sound of the cannons!" It was the perfect song for Cortés Campomanes's revolutionary project against the Spanish monarchy. "All the Kings of the World," his "Carmañola Americana" insisted, "are the same Tyrants."

However, Cortés Campomanes did not merely translate the "Carmagnole"; he reinterpreted and adapted it to the particularities of the Spanish colonial world—a world he had experienced only briefly in the La Guaira jail before escaping to Guadeloupe. He composed an *American* carmagnole. He quickly realized that the political and economic circumstances in Venezuela differed from those in Europe and more closely resembled what he saw in Guadeloupe. While Picornell and Cortés Campomanes's propaganda for the Madrid conspiracy had denounced social and political divisions, the documents for the La Guaira revolution promoted free commerce and the abolition of the ethnicity-based *casta* system.

While the homage to the French Revolution was unmistakable, Cortés Campomanes's "Carmañola Americana" differed from its French model in many regards. He purged the song of the bawdy puns and radical calls for mob violence that characterized the original. The brevity and the simplicity of Cortés Campomanes's songs hint that he targeted nonliterate audiences. The promises of emancipation and racial equality and the references to the French Revolution were a way to reach out to populations of African and indigenous descent. Like Picornell, Cortés Campomanes openly disagreed with many French revolutionaries on the matter of religion: "God protects our cause," Cortés Campomanes wrote, "He directs our arm." The lyrics encouraged its audience to unite against tyranny and to claim their rights based on equality, liberty, fraternity, and justice. "The war will make a hero of every one of us," Cortés Campomanes promised, "The *sin camisas* are dancing, and long lives the sound of the cannons!" While Cortés Campomanes reimagined French revolutionary songs, Picornell translated the radical and egalitarian 1793 version of the French *Rights of Man and Citizen* into Spanish.[40]

Neither Picornell's *Rights of Man* nor Cortés Campomanes's "Carmañola Americana" ever harmonized with the sound of cannons in La Guaira. The conspiracy was discovered before any uprising ever occurred. About two thousand copies were printed in Guadeloupe in 1797 under a fictitious imprint (*imprenta de la verdad in Madrid* [the press of truth in Madrid]). The authors not only disguised the place of publication but also hid their identity, presenting themselves simply as "well-known patriots."[41] The revolutionary materials of Picornell and Cortés Campomanes circulated throughout the Americas. Spanish spies found copies scattered in Guyana, Cartagena, Puerto Rico, and Cuba.[42]

A few years later, these texts received a second life when the Caracas junta convened in April 1810. According to various reports, Cortés Campomanes's "Carmañola" was sung in the streets of Caracas. Insurgents reprinted the "Canción Americana."[43] This radical reversal of situation encouraged Picornell and Cortés Campomanes to return to Venezuela. The Congress of Caracas proclaimed the *Rights of Man* in its formal declaration of the independence of Venezuela in July 1811.[44] If the two wandering revolutionaries had failed to ignite the fires of republicanism in La Guaira fifteen years earlier, they did not want to miss the opportunity to play a role in the new republic. The Venezuelan Constitution in December 1811 recycled many of the principles put forward by the programmatic documents of the 1797 La Guaira conspiracy: racial equality, the abolition of censorship, and freedom of expression, among others. There were, however, some crucial differences between the two political projects: Picornell and Cortés Campomanes had imagined a republic without slavery back in 1797, but the Republic of Venezuela maintained its existence.[45]

Like the men who printed them, words, images, and metaphors traveled back and forth around the Atlantic world. Upon arriving in New Orleans in the summer of 1813, a man, Jean-Joseph Amable Humbert, experienced a revolutionary déjà-vu. A veteran of the French Revolution, he had launched a revolutionary invasion of Ireland in 1798. His ambition was rekindled when Gutiérrez, Toledo, Picornell, and their followers proclaimed the Republic of

Texas in 1813. Humbert immediately offered to raise a regiment of volunteers and started his own advertising campaign. While most of the volunteers disbanded after the fall of the Republic of Texas in August 1813, Picornell and Humbert joined forces and remained in the region. The revolutionary leader José Alvarez de Toledo y Dubois forbade them from using the name of "independence . . . [and of the] Mexican republic."[46] Picornell and Humbert promptly ignored him, conjured up a "provisional government of the internal provinces of Mexico," held elections, and elected Picornell as president. While they publicly stated that they could turn to 3,000 American, French, and Irish troops and 1,000 "Indian" warriors, this government was only made of a handful of individuals.[47]

Humbert and Picornell wrote and printed multilingual proclamations as they formed their own government on the banks of the Sabine River. Humbert dreamed of a free Mexico. He sent letters to Spanish American leaders, including the presidents of the republics of Venezuela and of Cartagena, asking them for financial support in the name of transamerican republican solidarity.[48] While camping near the Sabine River in December 1813, the revolutionaries printed a five-page broadsheet stating the ambitions of the new government. The intended audience was the residents of New Orleans and Louisiana or, more broadly, the "freemen of all nations." The broadsheet was printed in English and French. The awkwardness of the English version suggests that the revolutionary authors originally wrote in French and then translated the work into English. They even translated financial amounts: the eleven million piasters in French became $55,000,000 in English. The translation was not identical. Picornell attacked the "iron-hand of foreign despotism" in the English version when referring to the Napoleonic occupation of the Iberian Peninsula but did not include this inflammatory expression in the French one—maybe because many French-speaking New Orleans residents supported Napoléon. The broadsheet reserved its ire for the "Spanish tyrants" and stated emphatically that the goal of the government was the "regeneration" of Mexican provinces.

The theme of regeneration, or breaking away from the past and propelling forward to a revitalized society and population, was a leitmotiv in the revolutionary Atlantic.[49] Picornell fused political regeneration with mass mobilization and fundraising. Picornell's government was strategically cosmopolitan. To attract volunteers, the revolutionaries promised citizenship and equality: "It has also thought it necessary to honour all the soldiers with the title of citizens that they may join interest with those of the public." To attract merchants, they promised free trade with Mexico. To attract funding, they opened a subscription for gifts and loans and appealed to "friends of humanity." After all, Picornell noted, the success of the U.S. revolution had rested on the financial and material aid of France and Holland, so why should this new revolution not benefit from "similar succors, both from individuals and foreign powers interested in our independence?"[50] In January 1814, the manifesto appeared in the New Orleans paper *L' Ami des Lois* and gave a platform to Picornell and Humbert's quixotic plans.

Humbert's proclamations for this imagined republic mirrored those he created in 1798 during his expedition to liberate Ireland with French revolutionary forces. Humbert had pledged independence, careers open to merit, and religious freedom. He made the exact same promises thirteen years later in Texas. A product of the universal ambitions of the French Revolution, Humbert contended that the sacred cause of liberty thwarted national differences. Humbert promised the Irish in 1798: "Brave IRISHMEN, our cause is common. Like you, we abhor the avaricious and blood-thirsty policy of an oppressive government. Like you, we hold as indefeasible the right of all nations to liberty." He promised the Texans in 1814: "MEXICANS, you used to be under your Tyrant's yoke, whimpering under your chains; now that they are broken, your destiny must be fulfilled. . . . Welcome the foreigners who have espoused your cause: treat them like friends and brothers. They came to share your turmoil and dangers, they must also share your glory."[51]

It was revolution redux in Humbert's geopolitical imagination. The cause was the same in Ireland or in Texas: the fight against tyranny and the quest for liberty. The promises were also the same: equality, justice, and meritocracy. The strategy was the same: a foreign legion liberating a territory and a people. Humbert traveled with these ideas in his head, slightly adjusting them to local conditions. In both cases, Humbert failed in transforming these dreams of a worldwide revolution into a reality. When the manifesto for the imagined Republic of Texas came out in the press in New Orleans, President Picornell had already jumped ship. In February 1814, barely two months after Humbert and Picornell announced the launch of their revolution, the *Moniteur de la Louisiane* publicly announced Picornell's resignation from the project. Picornell secretly penned a petition for royal pardon with the Spanish consul—serving as a double agent for a while and making his conversion public a few months later.[52] Humbert clung to his republican convictions until the end. He launched another expedition against Mexico from the Sabine River with fifty men in November 1815.[53] Picornell and Humbert both remained in New Orleans, and one can only imagine how the two former collaborators saluted each other every time they crossed paths.

Jean-Joseph Amable Humbert's grandiosely romantic determination eventually got him into trouble. He led three more expeditions against Texas until U.S. authorities arrested him for accessory to piracy in the summer of 1820. They charged him with issuing commissions to "brigands of every country and every color," by virtue of "the fictitious title of chief of the imagined republic of Mexico" he had set up in Galveston with a former U.S. army surgeon and veteran of the Battle of New Orleans, James Long.[54] In New Orleans, the editor of *L' Ami des Lois* launched a campaign on his behalf and pressured the French consul to get involved and protect the honor of one of France's former officers.[55] Louisiana authorities eventually released Humbert. His time in jail combined with the independence of Mexico in 1821 put an end to his revolutionary activities, and he became a teacher. Aimless, Humbert drank more and more heavily until he died in 1823 at the age of fifty-five.[56]

Circulation of Print

Two circuits of communication coexisted and overlapped: on one hand, a local circuit allying technological expertise and a multilingual network of ideologues, printers, translators, and deliverers and, on the other, a broader hemispheric circuit that mobilized a network of support from ship captains, newspaper editors, and readers. The form and content of these documents evolved as they traveled from one place to another. Even the consular agents and spies who monitored the circulation of these documents unwillingly became a part of this creative process as they copied, edited, and translated these documents in their correspondences with the metropole.

The turn of the century saw the rise of cheap, readily available newspapers on both sides of the Atlantic Ocean. This explosion of a commercial news market transformed the ways people gained information but also changed their patterns of political participation.[57] Newspapers increased a sense of what literary scholar Mary Louise Pratt called "planetary consciousness," an increasing recognition of the world's interconnectedness.[58] Newspapers shared, translated, and commented upon each other's stories. A paper in New Orleans reprinted and edited articles from Parisian, Bogotano, and Madrileño gazettes while also drawing from the private and commercial correspondence that arrived with boxes of merchandise from ships in the harbors. The extent to which newspapers shaped public opinion is not easily determined, but they certainly mirrored contemporary concerns.

Latin American exiles in the United States and in England used both the freedom of the press and the availability of printing presses to foment independence from Spain. Between 1800 and 1830, printers in London, Philadelphia, and New Orleans published a significant number of Spanish-language items. The U.S. press teemed with reports, commentaries, and debates over what was happening south of their borders.[59] Newspapers were decidedly political organs, benefiting from partisan associations and rarely maintaining the guise of impartiality. Revolutionary leaders took full advantage of this print culture. They scripted proclamations, decrees, and memorials to ensure that newspaper readers would read their arguments. They tried to control the narratives around their political projects. Port cities such as Philadelphia and New Orleans were bustling with men occupied in both business and politics, and many of them took their chances by funding revolutionary expeditions and arming privateers.

Like many revolutionaries at the time, Cortés Campomanes and Picornell had ties to freemasonry. Masonic credentials facilitated their access to transatlantic networks of editors and printers. At the time of the Atlantic revolutions, freemasonry was an important element of political and civic culture in Western Europe, the United States, and the Caribbean.[60] Membership in freemasonry became a way for men to gain access to social networks as they moved across locations. Masonic lodges, especially in port cities, were hubs of sociability alongside cafés, boarding houses, and taverns. Revolutionaries used them to gather news and information, to socialize, and to reminisce about past military exploits. Masonic lodges were meeting places that brought together merchants, sailors, and administrators. They were also recruiting offices where revolutionaries organized political activities with people of different social backgrounds. Individual relationships and friendships were in turn generative of wider collaborative networks via mutual acquaintances. In a world characterized by constant movements and fluctuating fortunes, friendships enabled collaboration and cooperation.

Freemasonry not only fostered connections among men uprooted from their households and their homelands but also contributed to the ideology of cosmopolitan fraternalism. The rhetoric of many revolutionary documents echoed Masonic philosophies, deploying tropes about worldwide male fraternity. The rise of freemasonry on both sides of the Atlantic helped its members conceive of an interconnected world more easily. Promoting the ideals of universal freedom and equality, lodges were places for men to become "citizens" where they wrote constitutions, gave orations, elected leaders, and viewed each other as social equals.[61] Although they were often segregated along racial and ethnic lines, fraternal associations also provided alternative frameworks for conceptualizing relations.[62] Picornell and Cortés Campomanes fueled freemasonry's commitment to cosmopolitan fraternalism into universalist revolutionary projects. They imagined republics open to everyone and tried to galvanize supporters with a shared language. In 1797, Cortés Campomanes's "Soneto Americano" extolled the fraternity and equality of the upcoming republic in Venezuela:

> Let's unite as good brothers,
> Friendly fraternity,
> Embrace the arms of
> The new neighbors:
> Indians; Blacks, and Pardos,
> Long live one Pueblo.[63]

The multiplication of printing presses and the increase in periodicals were just two elements of much wider information networks. Once revolutionaries had drafted and printed their documents, they needed to place them in the hands of the public. If portable printing presses reduced the distance between authors and audiences, they did not completely dissolve it. In addition to local audiences, these documents targeted various groups all around the Caribbean basin. Attracting volunteers was a significant objective. Free men of color, in particular, were a coveted audience. Obtaining the support of people of African descent—the majority in the Caribbean region—was vital for the success of revolutionary movements. Perhaps the work of French sailors of African descent who traded back and forth between Guadeloupe and the mainland, Cortés Campomanes and Picornell's works were smuggled into Venezuela. In June 1797, Juan José Chirinos, a militia *pardo* who worked in a barbershop in La Guaira, received a copy of Cortés Campomanes's "Soneto Americano" from the hands of a local merchant who asked him to copy it and pass it to others. The song failed to kindle Chirinos's revolutionary zeal. Together with two other barbers and militiamen, he decided to report the conspirators to the authorities.[64]

Because of their mobility and their intermediary position between enslaved and free white communities, free men of color were often crucial agents in these advertising campaigns, either supporting or reporting them. Some of them learned to read and write through informal means, and others turned to oral vectors of communication, including word of mouth, to acquire and diffuse information.[65] The correspondence between

French authorities in the West Indies teemed with warnings about free men of African descent. The French government even commissioned an agent for a reconnaissance mission in the Danish colony of Saint Thomas. His instructions were to record the whereabouts of free men of color, especially those working on ships and traveling between the French colonies, Haiti, and the neutral islands of Saint Thomas and Saint Barthélemy, since the last two islands were "swarming" with European adventurers. The danger lay, the French agent knew, "not only in actual attempts, but also in dangerous and even more threatening doctrines that they [individuals of color] could spread in the shadow." Once these seditious doctrines spread around the Greater Caribbean, the agent noted, it would be too late.[66]

Counterrevolutionary Print Culture

Revolutionaries were not the only ones who believed in the power of the printed word. Freedom of the press in the United States and Britain meant that Spanish authorities regularly and vainly lodged complaints against proinsurgent propaganda, especially in cities sympathetic to the insurgent cause such as Philadelphia, Baltimore, New Orleans, and London. In this last location, newspapers such as the *Morning Chronicle*, the *Time*, and the *Caledonian Mercury* published articles and editorials in favor of independence that prompted the Spanish ambassador to express his stern disapproval to the Foreign Office, with one side citing the two countries' alliance and neutrality acts and the other brandishing the country's laws on free press.[67]

The revolutionary advertising campaigns forced Spanish authorities to start a counterrevolutionary print campaign in the Greater Caribbean and invent new ways to establish the legitimacy of the Spanish monarchy in the Americas. Until then, the Church and the Inquisition had controlled and confiscated prohibited books and seditious papers. After the revolutions in France and Saint-Domingue, the Spanish crown prohibited the importation of newspapers, texts, and even objects that contained revolutionary and anti-religious ideas and restricted the use of information from or about France. Printers and publishers, however, did not always respect these restrictions. The lack of printing presses did not prevent informal circulation networks from borrowing and lending news, pamphlets, and books. In reaction, Spanish colonial authorities honed control and surveillance strategies. They attempted to monitor ports, spy on foreign visitors and inhabitants, and confiscate subversive materials.[68]

Spanish authorities in the United States quickly understood how to play the game and adapted their resistance strategy during the surge of independent movements. They demanded government funds to operate counterrevolutionary propaganda and hoped to create a proroyalist print community. They centered their efforts on a few key cities. In Philadelphia, Spanish foreign minister Luis de Onís managed to convince a few editors to support the royal government. The editor of a French journal also contacted Onís, asking him for money to take up the Spanish cause. Although Onís had no illusion about the editor's ideological convictions, he still insisted that money be given to this potential ally to prevent him from supporting the other side.[69]

New Orleans' location made it a privileged site for the preparation of expeditions against Spanish colonies. In 1815, Luis de Onís noted that "the revolutionary flags of Cartagena of the Indies and of the Mexican Republic" were a common sight.[70] The Spanish consul José Vidal decided to work with an editor in New Orleans to print the bilingual *El Misisipi* in 1809 in order to circulate proclamations and other imprints from Spain.[71] Ironically, the pro-Spanish *El Misisipi* was printed on the same press as anti-Spanish propaganda.[72] In a letter to the Spanish minister in Washington, the consul listed all the papers of New Orleans and the parties they served: he lamented that out of ten periodicals, four were pro-French, five were either neutral or pro-U.S., and only one was pro-Spanish: *El Misisipi*, the one he sponsored.[73] The consul's efforts proved futile: public opinion overwhelmingly favored the insurgents. Even after most Spanish American republics secured their independence in the early 1820s, Spanish authorities persisted in their efforts to win the hearts and minds of the inhabitants of the Crescent City, and in 1829, they gave thirty pesos a month to an editor to protect a paper, *El Español*, with the instruction that the involvement of Spanish authorities was to remain under wraps.[74]

The conviction that the printing press could be mightier than the sword appeared in the petition Picornell sent to the Spanish crown in 1814. Then fifty-five years old and with a body bearing the marks of his different incarcerations and constant peregrinations, Picornell yearned to be pardoned by the Spanish crown. His hatred for despotism had made him "appear as a traitor in the eyes of the nation," the revolutionary veteran explained, but the recent adoption of the liberal Cádiz Constitution in Spain had sated his liberal fever. The constitution dated to 1812, when juntas met in the southern Spanish city of Cádiz to resist the French occupation of the Iberian Peninsula. Metropolitan and American representatives drew up a constitution that would serve as a touchstone of Spanish liberalism. Among other political and civil rights, it enshrined popular sovereignty, universal male suffrage, constitutional monarchy, and freedom of the press. Picornell was more liberal than republican, and a constitutional monarchy satisfied his political ambitions. His ailing health might have also played a role in the decision to abandon his revolutionary quest.

Picornell's petition presents some unusual rhetorical features for a confession. He never condemned the insurgent movements or the insurgents themselves. He never presented himself as ignorant or led astray. He never apologized for actively taking part in different revolutionary coups. However, he did apologize for translating and publishing the *Rights of Man*, an act designed to incite Americans to "overthrow the yoke of Spanish despotism and achieve their independence."[75] He filed his petition in February 1814 as Ferdinand VII was making his way back to the Spanish throne. Three months later, Ferdinand VII reestablished absolute monarchy and declared the Cádiz Constitution illegal.[76] Despite this volte-face, Picornell apparently remained faithful to the Spanish crown.

It is difficult to assess whether these ephemeral revolutionary prints actually converted or even influenced their audiences. An anecdote by French traveler J. J. Dauxion-Lavaysse reveals the intense ideological competition to win hearts and minds. While in Cumaná, in eastern Venezuela, Dauxion-Lavaysse saw a grocer making cones and bags with copies of the *Declaration of the Rights of Man* and Rousseau's *Social Contract*. The grocer informed the traveler that he obtained these "wrapping papers" from a mysterious M . . . on a trip to Trinidad. These materials were given to every interloper going through the ports of the British colony. Fully aware that he was at the center of a geopolitical game, the grocer complained that the British were now sending them some "democratic writings to inspire this spirit in us," while they had just finished waging war against France and its revolutionary government. The grocer had reservations: "Truthfully, they have to believe that we are quite a stupid race of men if they believe we are going to fall in such traps."[77] The reaction of the Venezuelan grocer reveals the competitiveness of the information marketplace.

Loyalty was not a zero-sum game. The Spanish Empire and the republican insurgents might have seen themselves as fundamentally antagonistic forces competing for Americans' allegiance, but people did not always define their political identities in binary terms. This either/or assumption is even more difficult to apply to border regions in the Greater Caribbean, whether these borders were defined by land or sea.[78] Residents lived with a multilingual print culture that was teeming with opposing politics. Men like Picornell could claim to be the president of a newly formed republic only to embrace the Spanish crown a few months later. People around the Greater Caribbean exposed themselves to various sources of information and encountered diverse viewpoints, which they then could filter according to their own biases.

*   *   *

As Spanish American countries secured their independence in the 1820s, the two former professors Manuel Cortés Campomanes and Juan Bautista Mariano Picornell began their professional reconversion. They boasted impressive revolutionary credentials. Each participated in at least five republican attempts in over twenty years. They attempted to foment revolutions in Spain, Venezuela, Texas, and Mexico. They crisscrossed the Atlantic Ocean and carried ideas, ideals, and words along with them. They not only borrowed ideas and idioms from other revolutions but also invested them with a new totalizing and universalizing meaning. It was maybe no coincidence that both Cortés Campomanes and Picornell were professors-turned-revolutionaries. Others—for instance, Picornell's collaborator in New Orleans, Jean-Joseph Amable Humbert—turned to teaching when revolutions became scarce. Both activities—teaching and revolutionizing—required similar skills: an ability to synthesize different influences, to produce an efficient and convincing message, as well as a tendency to pontificate. The revolutionaries had also acquired such valuable knowledge of foreign languages—knowledge that prove recyclable when revolutionary opportunities dried up.

The two friends' political paths, with Manuel Cortés Campomanes remaining committed to republicanism and liberalism and Juan Bautista Mariano Picornell embracing Spanish constitutional monarchism, may have diverged and broken their friendship, but their commitment to the printed word endured. In 1819, after the failure of Mina's expedition, Cortés Campomanes wrote a history of the revolutions in Venezuela and Colombia for French officials in Martinique in exchange for a passport and a recommendation letter.[79] Armed with these documents, he returned to Europe. He reinvented himself as a literary agent in Brussels and promoted Spanish American writers, including Venezuelan poet Andrés Bello, whose work he helped translate and publish in Europe. Moving away from a clandestine to a commercial printing world, Cortés Campomanes applied the lessons learned in the Greater Caribbean. He set up his own editorial network and mailed a hundred copies of Bello's *Cartas* to an agent in La Guaira.[80] Yet his memories were tinged with bitterness. "After thirty years of perseverance and suffering for the cause of America," he pondered, "my reward is to be forgotten and abandoned." The hero worshipping of postindependent Gran Colombia bothered him; "the cause of America was and is for me the cause of humanity and reason," he insisted, "and absolutely not the cause of Bolívar, Marino, Miranda etc."[81]

Having reconciled with the Spanish crown and recovered from revolutionary fever, Picornell wrote an essay on another kind of infection: the yellow fever and its ravages on public health in New Orleans.[82] He then moved to the colony of Cuba, where he lived to see the rest of Spanish America secure its independence from Spain, eventually dying there in 1825. A man of letters until the end, he left two boxes of books as his most valuable possessions—some of these books had probably traveled with him and Cortés Campomanes on all their adventures to bring revolution to the world.[83]

While it is easy to focus on cities as the centers of print production from which pamphlets, books, and translations traveled to the border regions, the revolutionary advertising campaigns studied here upend this circulatory map. They encourage us to think in terms of not only fixed urban print centers but also very mobile print centers that followed the peregrinations of the revolutionaries. The center-periphery model of print culture does not hold. There existed a multitude of smaller and intermittent print centers in places such as Amelia Island, Galveston Island, and Soto de la Marina. The influence of these "centers" radiated in both hemispheres thanks to the reproductions and translations of these documents in newspapers.

With the proliferation of information-sharing networks, confusion ran rampant. News arriving by ship, newspaper, or correspondence contradicted the news of the previous week. The editor of an English paper in Oxford expressed his frustration to his readers: "the American Papers contain accounts from the Patriotic Armies in South America, which are at considerable variance with those previously received through the same channels."[84] The rise in relatively inexpensive and easy ways to print and distribute materials, combined with the persisting importance of personal exchanges, created a vibrant and cacophonous age of information.

CHAPTER 3

American Freedom Fighters

The Struggle for Equality

The journey to Angostura on the banks of the Orinoco River was a perilous one. Colonel Gustavus Hippisley and his troops sailed from England to assist the independence movement in Venezuela in December 1817. One of the ships foundered in a gale. When the other ships arrived in the West Indies, the volunteers found that no arrangements were in place. Those who did not die of smallpox, malaria, or dysentery or who did not desert finally reached the mainland in the summer of 1818. They met with crocodiles, snakes, yellow fever, and scorpions. Their uniforms—dark green jackets and trousers with scarlet collars and gold-scaled epaulets discarded from the Napoleonic wars—disintegrated into rags. When Hippisley quarreled with local leaders, "a line of almost naked blacks with muskets" approached him and "a dark-looking fellow in uniform came up to [him], and in French demanded [his] sword." These men were also foreign volunteers who had traveled through the swampy forests of the Orinoco River in the name of independence and freedom. Unlike the British forces, they came from a country where slavery and racial hierarchy no longer existed: Haiti.[1]

Thousands of foreign volunteers, mostly British like Hippisley, served in the insurgent militaries in Spanish America. Haitians, including members of the Saint-Domingue diaspora, also contributed to independence movements across the Americas. Yet we still know very little about these participants.[2] The British colonel's anger at receiving orders from these "almost naked black men" reveals that color prejudice defined the revolutionary experiences of free people of color. Their presence made an impression on Hippisley but not enough for their names to enter the historical records.

The Haitian Revolution was unique in the early nineteenth century Atlantic world. As a war that overthrew slavery, white supremacy, and European

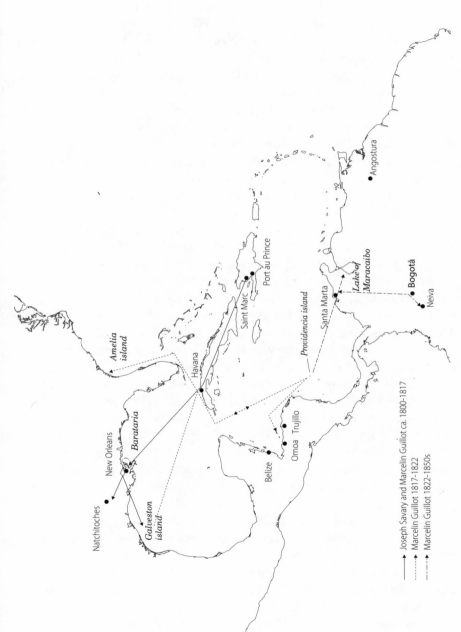

Map 4. The voyages of Joseph Savary and Marcelin Guillot, 1800–1850.

Natchitoches

New Orleans

Amelia island

Barataria

Havana

Galveston island

Belize

Omoa Trujillo

Saint Marc

Port au Prince

Providencia island

Santa Marta

Lake of Maracaibo

Bogotá

Neiva

Angostura

Joseph Savary and Marcelin Guillot ca. 1800–1817
Marcelin Guillot 1817–1822
Marcelin Guillot 1822–1850s

colonialism, it shocked the Western world and ideologies that condemned people of African descent as naturally inferior. Memories of the Haitian Revolution fell into two competing narratives: horrendous or heroic.[3] Officers, soldiers, and sailors from the Saint-Domingue diaspora and Haiti personified these polarizing narratives. However, this chapter does not envision them as merely symbols of hope for free and enslaved groups or of tremulous fear for slaveowners across the Americas; it posits that they were active participants in the military, political, and intellectual movements of the time. Commitment to racial equality meant negotiating different systems of discrimination across the Greater Caribbean. Either free people of color advocated for the complete dismantlement of the system, running the risk of being labeled radicals who fanned the flames of racial dissension, or they asked for regimes of exception that protected their own interests while leaving the system of discrimination intact.[4]

This chapter reconstructs the quest for equality of Joseph Savary and Marcelin Guillot, both freeborn Saint-Dominguans of mixed Afro-European descent.[5] Advocating for their human and civil rights, they joined various revolutionary movements in Spanish Texas and on the islands of Galveston, Amelia, and Providencia before settling in Louisiana (Savary) and in Colombia (Guillot). They even briefly joined the U.S. army in the Anglo-American War of 1812. Guillot served in the decisive battle between royalists and insurgents in the Battle of Lake Maracaibo in Venezuela. Their trajectories reveal that key events of the era, often read through a national perspective as foundational moments (the War of 1812 is called the United States' second war of independence, and Venezuela celebrates Navy Day on the day of the Battle of Maraicabo), also need to be understood as part of a broader anticolonial hemispheric effort to achieve full equality.[6] Military careers were one of the more promising avenues for ambitious men of African descent. Bearing arms gave them the opportunity to gain political and social prominence and eschew legal and social constraints attached to color prejudice.

While they moved around the Greater Caribbean in the name of freedom, Savary and Guillot never stopped trading or owning human beings—a reminder that revolutions were as often unequal and exploitative as they were liberating and egalitarian. The two men's commitment to equality ironically included disavowing the rights of enslaved people. Born in a colony erected on enslaved labor, Savary and Guillot grew up in a world where colonists of mixed ancestry had often owned enslaved workers and domestics. The creation of Haiti as a free country did not alter their ambitions. They wanted to achieve the same rights as other (white/free) men in the Atlantic world, and these rights included owning, buying, and selling other human beings.

Bearing Arms and Gaining Rights

In a colonial world centered on racialized slave labor, free people of color developed strategies to counter race-based hierarchies and prove their respectability. One strategy was to be a slaveowner. Another was to join the military. Savary and Guillot adopted both. Eighteenth-century rivalries led to a series of wars and conflicts between France, Britain, and Spain. Militias across the Americas increasingly recruited enslaved and free men of African descent as the first line of defense.[7] Military service provided certain privileges and distinctions. Upon retirement, members received pensions, which their widows inherited. They forged a network of relationships that enable social mobility. For those of African descent, militia service also demonstrated equality with their white counterparts and loyalty to the empire. About two-thirds of the militia units in Saint-Domingue were free people of color, as was the rural police, responsible for hunting down maroons. Militiamen of color started to express their resentment over the racial restrictions put in place in 1769 to reform the colonial militia and control their ambitions—no free man of color could earn a rank higher than sergeant or quartermaster.[8]

In spring 1779, the Chasseurs Volontaires, an expedition of almost 600 free Saint-Dominguans of African descent, sailed to Savannah, Georgia, to support the North American insurgents with whom France, a rival of the British Empire, had signed a treaty of alliance. The French attack failed. Some in the expedition went to the metropole, others to South Carolina, and the rest to Granada in the eastern Caribbean. Wealthy people of color adopted a new strategy in the mid-1780s and appealed to the metropolitan government directly. Julien Raimond, an important slaveholder, property owner, and a sergeant in the militia, requested new laws to reduce racial discrimination. He complained that free men of color in the royal service had to serve for long periods away from their families, plantations, and occupations while their white counterparts did not.[9]

Joseph Savary and Marcelin Guillot grew up in an environment in which ambitious free men of color were increasingly frustrated. The former was born in 1788 in Saint-Marc in northern Saint-Domingue; the latter was born two years earlier, probably in the Northern Province as well.[10] When the revolution erupted in both the metropole and in the colonies, military training proved essential. As they did during the colonial period, free men of color turned military service into a significant means of demonstrating their patriotism, using the French Republic's rhetoric to secure their civil and political rights. With the official end of slavery and racial discrimination in 1794, many rose through the ranks and reached positions that were previously closed to them.[11]

In 1802, peace between France, Spain, and Britain eliminated the military advantages provided by policies of slave emancipation and racial equality, paving the way for Napoléon to reestablish slavery and legal segregation. The same year, Napoléon sent a military expedition to restore prerevolutionary rule in the Caribbean, and new waves of rebellion erupted in Saint-Domingue, leading to the removal of French troops in late 1803 and the independence of the former colony on January 1, 1804. The Haitian Revolution not only set the Atlantic world on fire by spreading ideas and images of abolition, equality, race wars, and black leaders but also resulted in a refugee crisis. Some 30,000 men, women, and children left the colony's shores to escape armed conflicts, political rivalries, and foreign invasions, in search of a temporary or a permanent home. Many sought shelter in neighboring Cuba.[12] Savary and Guillot were probably among them and lived in the Spanish colony for five to seven years until Napoléon's invasion of the Iberian Peninsula in 1808 led Spanish authorities to expel nonnaturalized French colonists. Almost ten thousand Saint-Domingue refugees, about 70 percent of them free and enslaved people of African descent, sold their belongings, packed up their houses, and moved again—this time to Louisiana.[13] Although Louisiana prohibited the entrance of people of African descent, many nonetheless eluded immigration authorities by slipping into the U.S. territory through Barataria, a coastal settlement west of the Mississippi River, where the governor of Louisiana noted the presence of "St. Domingo's negros of the most desperate characters." The newcomers doubled the size of New Orleans.[14]

Familiar with the French and Spanish colonial systems, Savary and Guillot discovered a new legal and racial system slowly implemented by the United States since the Louisiana Purchase of 1803. In an effort to curtail the liberties of the population of African descent in New Orleans, the territorial legislature in 1806 suppressed the militia of free men of color, which had thrived under Spanish rule.[15] The arrivals of thousands of refugees from Saint-Domingue troubled the governor of Louisiana, who feared revolutionary contagion. He noted that "the free men of color, in and near New Orleans (including those recently arrived from Cuba), capable of bearing arms, cannot be less than eight hundred." He wrote, "Their conduct has hitherto been

correct, but in a country like this, where the Negro population is so considerable, they should be carefully watched."[16] These fears about the refugees were
unfounded. A large slave revolt in 1811 in the sugar plantations near New
Orleans was defeated with the help of some Saint-Dominguans and the governor praised their "bravery and patriotism."[17] The sugar cane industry was
growing and the U.S. decision to close the international slave trade in 1808
turned slave trading into a prosecutable but profitable enterprise. Louisiana
planters' need for enslaved workers was insatiable. In 1810, the French privateer Louis-Michel Aury engaged Louis Crispin, described as a "subject of the
Empire of Hayti," to capture a Spanish slave ship off the coast of Cuba and sell
the cargo in Louisiana.[18]

Savary soon seized his chance to exert revenge on the Spanish Empire
that had expelled him from Cuba. In November 1813, he collaborated with
Jean-Joseph Amable Humbert, a former French republican general who had
participated in the Leclerc expedition in Saint-Domingue. Savary offered to
send 500 Saint-Dominguans to fight with Mexican insurgents in neighboring Texas.[19] Spanish authorities were greatly worried and noted that more
than 2,000 white and black Frenchmen had come from Louisiana; they had
been "thrown out from the Island of Cuba, [and] will take up arms to provide
themselves with a new Patria and take revenge on the Spanish government."[20]
Savary participated in a short-lived republic in Texas in 1812–1813, but the
presence of foreigners, "Napoleonic agents," and men of color like Savary
made some U.S. volunteers uncomfortable. Internal divisions and the arrival
of the Spanish army accelerated the demise of the Republic of Texas. Savary
returned to New Orleans.[21]

While Savary supported the emancipation of the New World in Texas,
the United States started an anti-European war of its own. In 1812, war broke
out between the United States and Great Britain, and the latter attacked
New Orleans in late 1814. In a dire situation, Army Major General Andrew
Jackson penned an address to the "Free Colored Inhabitants of Louisiana,"
promising to pay them the same pay as white volunteers and assuring that
they would "receive the applause, reward, and gratitude, of [their] Countrymen."[22] Many answered the call to arms. An influential figure in the region,
Savary organized the Second Battalion of Free Men of Color in December
1814, recruiting about 256 volunteers from Saint-Domingue. New Orleans
authorities and elites expressed their fears around such an assembly of black
officers and soldiers, and D'Aquin, a white refugee from Saint-Domingue,
commanded the battalion. Savary was the second major in command.
Guillot enlisted as a captain. Since both men were appointed officers, their

ranks indicate that they had previous military experience from either Saint-Domingue or Cuba.[23]

When New Orleans ceased to be under imminent threat, racial prejudice resurfaced vigorously. Jackson ordered the battalion to repair fortifications to a remote site in the marshland east of the city in February 1815. Officers and soldiers felt disrespected. Laying up bricks was not why they had risked their lives. They organized a two-thronged protest resistance tactic. The first was to walk out. A week after receiving their marching order, sixteen volunteers deserted; twenty-one left ten days later.[24] The second was to use official avenues of protest. Publicly defying military orders, Savary relayed a message that his men "would always be willing to sacrifice their lives in defense of their country as had been demonstrated but preferred death to the performance of the work of laborers."[25] Implied in the volunteers' protest was the fear of being equated with enslaved men. Performing manual labor in a swamp blurred the line between free and enslaved status in a slaveholding country. Defending their status as free men of African descent was essential to their futures.

Such a rapid fall from grace destabilized the officers of the battalion only very briefly. Keenly aware of their precarious status, Joseph Savary and Marcelin Guillot asked Jackson to intercede in their favor with the state of Louisiana. This petition reveals how Saint-Dominguans foregrounded their identities as refugees. Despite being foreign born, they contended they had proved their loyalty with their service in the Anglo-America War. Arguing that they had been "zealous in serving the United States . . . a country which has given them an asylum," they demanded "a protection which will put them beyond a prejudice which allways excised in this country twards them." This act, the officers claimed, would "save them from future insult."[26]

The petitioners drew on the Spanish colonial practice of the *fuero militar* they had likely learned in Cuba. This was a privilege granted by the king to his soldiers, conferring upon them protection, respectability, and particular rights.[27] Savary and Guillot had risked their lives and successfully defended their adopted country—the country that had granted them asylum. The strategy failed, and the army never answered the officers' petition. By mid-February, more than two-thirds of the battalion had abandoned the U.S. service. As the highest-ranking officer, Savary held on the longest and served until March 20, 1815. Enslaved members of the Saint-Domingue diaspora also used the War of 1812 to seize their own opportunities for freedom. Louisiana planters submitted claims for 163 individuals who fled with the British: five of them were from Saint-Domingue.[28]

Often considered the United States' second war of independence, the War of 1812 was also an Atlantic war for independence and equality. The activities of many participants before and after the Battle of New Orleans reveal that this war was but one moment in their transnational military and political careers. Their attachment to the United States was provisional. When U.S. authorities failed to grant them the rights they desired, they exported their military expertise elsewhere. Savary and Guillot's actions demonstrate how an individual could be committed to local laws promising equality but could abandon that local loyalty if rights were not forthcoming.[29] During wartime, authorities repeatedly turned to men of African descent for military assistance, who, in turn, leveraged these opportunities for rights. However, as with the War of 1812, these strategies were often unsuccessful once peacetime returned.

Without leverage, Saint-Dominguans ended up at the mercy of the U.S. federal and state laws that privileged whiteness. Legislators passed laws designed to control free nonwhite residents. In 1790, a federal law limited naturalization to white foreigners.[30] Citizenship remained largely under state control. Louisiana's state constitution of 1812 limited suffrage to white men. Other measures included the prohibition of interracial marriage and the obligation to treat white people with deference. In 1817, the Louisiana legislature passed a law limiting the migration of free blacks into the state.[31] Possibly alienated by these measures, Guillot joined Savary in defending the cause of Spanish American independence. Both men joined the French privateer Louis-Michel Aury's headquarters on Galveston Island.[32] After some of Aury's collaborators rebelled, Savary, who was in New Orleans at the time, traveled to reinforce the revolutionary headquarters with forty other Saint-Domingue refugees.[33] Marcelin Guillot was among them. Savary and Guillot grew close to Aury. Savary "was a man in whom Mr. Aury has complete trust."[34] Guillot's alliance with Aury continued as the republicans moved on to Florida and then to Providencia. An army captain against the British, Guillot reconverted himself into a ship captain at Galveston. He rose through the ranks and became a cavalry colonel in Providencia.

The Appeal of the Monarchy

Living in the penumbras and interstices of colonial and postcolonial states, diasporic Africans and their descendants developed strategies to secure opportunities for themselves and their families. While some embraced the republican cause, others placed their bets elsewhere. As governments appeared and disappeared around them, some decided to align themselves with what appeared to be a more stable force: the monarchy. It stood as viable alternative to republicanism and independence in the Americas. Britain had lost thirteen continental colonies in 1783 but held strong in Canada and the West Indies and prevailed over France during the Napoleonic wars. Spain might have lost its monarch thanks to Napoléon, but this loss was temporary: King Ferdinand VII returned to his throne in 1814 and launched a reconquest of the Americas.

The republicans in Providencia launched two revolutionary expeditions against the coast of Spanish Honduras, a contested space where the two rival empires of Britain and Spain vied for control of the region alongside the Miskito Indians on the coast.[35] Guillot's revolutionary activities there reflect the constellation of political ideologies circulating in the Greater Caribbean at the time—independence, revolution, counterrevolution, absolute monarchism, constitutional monarchism.[36] Like republicanism, monarchism was not a homogeneous historical force but was shaped and interpreted locally. Historical actors embraced and adapted political ideologies according to their interests.

Coastal Honduras was connected to the revolutionary Atlantic long before Aury and Guillot set up their republican headquarters in Providencia some 370 miles away. One of these points of connection came from the Haitian revolution. During the slave insurrection in Saint-Domingue in 1791, Spain invaded the French colony, enticing enslaved and free men of color to their cause by promising them freedom, lands, and titles. After the defeat of Spain, the new conscripts evacuated with the royal troops to the neighboring Spanish colony of Santo Domingo. The so-called French black auxiliary forces became a thorn in the Spanish side. Local authorities wanted them out of their colony. Cuba's captain-general refused to welcome them, fearing the contagion of revolutionary ideas. Spanish authorities decided to split them across different Caribbean colonies, and 307 went to the Honduran coast. In 1796, they landed in Trujillo. Some resettled to Omoa, a coastal town in the northern border close to British Honduras.[37] Around the same time, another group arrived on the Honduran coast. Like the Saint-Domingue auxiliaries, this movement of population originated from the revolutionary Atlantic. Black Caribs waged an ill-fated revolt in 1795 against British rule on the island of Saint Vincent with a coalition of French forces and self-liberated, formerly enslaved Africans, which led to their deportation to Roatán Island off the coast of Honduras. About 2,000 rebels convinced the Spanish crown to let them move to Trujillo, where they spread along the Atlantic coast.[38] The immigrant groups gradually merged to become known today as the Garifuna.[39]

Local authorities warily acknowledged the newcomers: many of them had valuable but potentially dangerous military experience. The 1802 peace between the British and Spanish empires decreased the need for military protection. A few months after the independence of Haiti, the intendant governor of Honduras counted 4,500 blacks in Trujillo, noting that many of them were free and originated from the British or French Caribbean. "Within a few years," he predicted "with so many blacks who practice polygamy . . . they will not fit on the North coast; and in that case, they will rise up, [and] the Kingdom's ports will be lost."[40] During the anti-Napoleonic years from 1802 to 1815, Honduran authorities prevented any free person of color suspected of having French connections from entering the settlements.[41] After the fall of Napoléon, the fear of anticolonial revolts in the Spanish colonies replaced the fear of the French. With limited military resources, British and Spanish authorities complained that Spanish American privateers disrupted trade on the coast of Honduras with impunity. They also feared that free and enslaved people of African descent would decide to rebel or join insurgent ships.[42]

Tensions between colonial authorities and their unruly subjects boiled over when the revolutionaries Aury and Guillot conducted two attacks against the Spanish Honduran coast. The success of a first expedition in 1819 encouraged Aury to lead a second attack against Spanish Honduras the following year. He faced more resistance this time. The troops led by Guillot arrived offshore at Trujillo in April 1820. About 20 percent of the population of the city at the time was made up of free blacks.[43] The people of Trujillo rejected Guillot's demand that they join the independence movement.[44] The royalist commandant cited two Carib lieutenants for their loyalty to the crown.[45]

After two days of fighting, Aury withdrew his troops and redirected them to Omoa. The port city boasted a massive eighteenth-century fortress. Guillot, as the representative of the republican forces, disembarked with sixty men and met the representative of the royalist forces, Colonel Guillermo.[46] Another Saint-Domingue transplant, Guillermo had arrived with the French black auxiliaries in 1796, probably as a child. Guillot might have appealed to a sense of diasporic solidarity. Both men had been forced to leave their native homes. Events in Saint-Domingue had prompted Guillot and Guillermo along paths that eventually crossed in this fortified town on the Honduran coast in the last days of spring 1820. Both men also used the military as a means of social ascension. However, they each placed their bets on a different system of government. Despite Guillot and other republicans' promises of equality, Guillermo and other people of African descent remained loyal to the Spanish crown. The republicans laid siege to the small town for eleven days, but the use of force was in vain. Aury remembered, "All had guns in their hands; blacks and Caribs, Creoles of all classes and colors, none tried to approach us."[47] Aury and Guillot's expedition returned to Providencia.

Promises of equality were not exclusive to liberal and republican projects. Men like Guillermo appropriated rights and privileges found in other forms of governments, including monarchism.[48] Guillermo's own words made their way to the written record via Aury, who recorded his response. His loyalty, Guillermo declared, was to the Cádiz Constitution; the "inhabitants and troops that [he] has the honor to command will not accept any other Government."[49] A few months earlier, Spanish troops waiting to be shipped to the Americas revolted. Liberal army officers initiated a mutiny and forced the king to restore constitutional monarchy in March 1820.[50] The constitution was ratified in Havana on April 17, 1820. News traveled fast between Cuba and Honduras. A mere ten days later, Guillermo declined the republican Guillot's offer of independence and pledged allegiance to a constitution that, according to him, "declares all of our Rights."

Military service shaped Guillermo and other free people of color's adhesion to liberal monarchism and, more broadly, their relationships with race, allegiance, and citizenship. The ostensible loyalty of Guillermo and others to the Cádiz Constitution's declaration of "Rights" shows that they believed that a reformed liberal empire could be a reality. However, this empire did not guarantee equality to all. The constitution restricted the rights of citizenship to exclude free Africans and their descendants. That Guillermo pledged loyalty to a document that legally disenfranchised him, his troops, and his family may appear puzzling, yet Guillermo's actions in Omoa reveal how a subaltern group reinterpreted this document. The Cádiz Constitution left open a possibility for people of African ancestry to gain citizenship. Guillermo implied as such when he called the rights contained in the constitution "all of our Rights." Article 22 provided an exception for free blacks who distinguished themselves by their "merit and virtue," which could include property ownership, free parentage, and service to the crown. Guillermo's identity as a military man shaped his relationship to political projects and forms of governments. In regions where militias included high numbers of descendants of diasporic Africans, free people of color felt included. Grant titles and other special rights often rewarded exemplary defense of the king thanks to the imperial practice of the *fuero militar*.[51]

Interpreted within a local framework, Guillot's decision suggests that we might be mistaken in using legal citizenship as our main frame of reference to define affiliation. Caribs and Saint-Domingue refugees may have had little interest in the title of citizen. Citizenship had little or no precise legal meaning at the time. It excluded more people along lines of class, gender, and race than it included. Free men of color achieved de facto citizenship rights notably through military service. Local conditions—namely, isolation from the centers of power, sparse colonial population, and rivalries with British and French neighbors—made them indispensable to colonial authorities. Furthermore, seen through a regional Greater Caribbean framework, monarchism may have appeared as a safe option. Most states around Spanish Honduras had fallen, and independence appeared to be but a temporary project. When Aury and Guillot came from Providencia to Omoa to extoll the principles of independence, liberty, and equality, they had already participated in three failed republics in Cartagena, Texas, and Florida. Bolívar was on his way to construct a form of authoritarian republicanism in Gran Colombia. Any choice was a gamble.

As evidence of the highly contingent nature of the era, Honduras gained formal independence from Spain in September 1821—a year after defending its territory against Guillot's republican troops. After joining Mexico briefly, the territories of the former captaincy general of Guatemala were included in the new state of the Federal Republic of Central America.[52] Despite the principle of equality among all citizens, the relationship between the republic and the Saint-Domingue diaspora was contentious. The militia's attachment to Spanish constitutional monarchism meant that they did not readily embrace independence. An official in Omoa described the government's precarious hold on the coast. The "black veterans from Santo Domingo," he lamented, "could make a revolution, and they threaten to do so at every turn." He imagined that "if they seize [Omoa] it will always be up for sale to whomever wishes to occupy it, because [they] are complete barbarians and only pursue their own self-interest, without adherence to Guatemala, Comayagua, or Spain, but rather to whoever gives them more."[53]

People of African descent might have received full citizenship and equality on paper, but when they complained, their legitimacy was immediately questioned. The official in Omoa implied that their loyalty was for sale; he coded them as foreign when he described them as "black veterans from Santo Domingo" and used the racially loaded expression "complete barbarians." In retrospect, the new republic and its claims of universal equality probably reinforced Saint-Dominguans' attachment to the Spanish crown. The

Comisión de Guerra observed, "Once the Spanish flag no longer waved in the port, some grumblings and [expressions of] displeasure were heard." They may have experienced some discrimination under the colonial system, but at least discrimination came with a paycheck. The troops in Omoa had not been paid since independence a few years earlier.[54]

The Specter of a "Saint-Domingoise"

As an example of black self-determination born out of a slave revolt, Haiti became the symbol of slaveowners' worst fears. From their point of view, it cast a dreadful shadow over the Americas, where images of the revolution tied independence to racial violence and destruction of property. Thus, a slave insurrection in southern Puerto Rico in 1826 worried the French agent in Saint Thomas, who reported that the goal "was to kill all the Whites and to do a Saint-Domingoise."[55] Haiti remained a dangerous example in a region whose wealth depended on enslaved labor.[56]

Although foreign powers refused to recognize its independence for over twenty years, Haiti functioned as a sovereign state, weaving economic and diplomatic links with the outside world.[57] Haiti was a key player in Caribbean geopolitics and actively supported independence movements: Dessalines supported Francisco de Miranda's expedition against Venezuela in 1806; Pétion's Republic of the South sustained various expeditions against the Spanish crown between 1815 and 1817, including Francisco Xavier Mina against Mexico, Bolívar against Venezuela, and Gregor MacGregor against Amelia Island and Portobelo.

Haitian leaders relied on the members of the Haitian diaspora to support their proinsurgent and anticolonial diplomacy. However, these actors' own interests and principles did not always align with those of the Haitian government, notably on the issue of slavery. Savary's ambivalent relationship with the place of his birth illustrates this point. After his brief stint with the U.S. army in 1815, Savary resumed his involvement with Mexican revolutionaries. In New Orleans, he met José Manuel de Herrera, a minister from Mexico, who commissioned him to Haiti. The U.S. government had refused to help the Mexican insurgents, and Herrera hoped that Haiti would prove a friendlier ally. Crossing the Gulf of Mexico, Savary returned to his native land at the beginning of 1816.[58]

When he arrived at Les Cayes in southern Haiti, Savary held in his hands twelve blank privateer commissions in the name of the Mexican republic.[59]

As he stepped off the ship onto the bustling harbor, he encountered a real Tower of Babel with soldiers, sailors, and merchants speaking French, Creole, but also English and Spanish. Casks of claret arrived weekly, and bales of coffee and indigo were sent out to other islands and to France.[60] The Republic of the South sheltered Latin American independents driven out of the continent after several Spanish victories, including 400 refugees after the defeat of the Republic of Cartagena in December 1815, many of them originally from Spain, Guadeloupe, France, the United States, and Saint-Domingue itself. In total, around 2,000 residents from Colombia and Venezuela lived across southern Haiti, including, most famously, Simón Bolívar.[61]

Bolívar's sojourn in Haiti secured his place as the leader of the independence struggle and guaranteed the abolition of slavery in the territories to be liberated. Pétion insisted that Bolívar push for abolition as a condition of his support of Latin American independence.[62] Bolívar would eventually rescript his promise. The Republic of Gran Colombia later adopted gradual, not immediate, emancipation. Gradual or not, emancipation was not one of Savary's priorities. He met Pétion as an agent of the Mexican republic. The meeting went well. The Haitian president told Savary that "all those from the Republics of the World" were welcome in his republic. He allowed him to recruit soldiers and sailors to attack Texas.[63] Savary found a sympathetic ear in Louis-Michel Aury, whose feud with Bolívar made him persona non grata among the insurgents.[64] The two men moved to Galveston on the Texas coast where they created an egalitarian government in the name of the Mexican republic.

Ideologies and practices of freedom coexisted with slave trading and enslavement. Joseph Sauvinet, a native of France and a Saint-Domingue refugee in New Orleans, owned the ship that carried Savary to Haiti. The same ship transported many enslaved Africans from Galveston who were sold on the mainland.[65] While Haiti's support of the Spanish American insurgents came with the expectation that they would abolish slavery in the new republics they planned to create, Savary and Guillot traded enslaved Africans to fund their revolutions. Their commitment to the slave trade superseded the antislavery principle of the Haitian state from which they received support. It also contravened the principles of the Mexican republic to which they had pledged allegiance. The 1810 Hidalgo rebellion, which started the Mexican independence movement, passed a decree abolishing slavery.[66] When Aury accompanied Spanish revolutionary Xavier Mina to fight for the Mexican independence movement, the thirty to forty men left in Galveston formed a new government.[67] Among them were several Saint-Dominguans of African descent, including Savary and Guillot.[68] They oversaw the transit of over 600 enslaved Africans to planters along the Mississippi River.[69]

That Savary traveled on a slave ship to and from Haiti while holding in his hand commissions to export revolution in the name of the Mexican republic illustrates the explosive contradictions of the revolutionary Atlantic. Central to all these revolutions and their contradictions was a vortex swirling around redefinitions of freedom and necessity based on the enslavement of Africans. For Savary and Guillot, liberty and equality meant the freedom to climb military and political ladders. It also meant the freedom to seize and sell enslaved Africans in the face of mounting anti–slave trade campaigns; Britain ended the profitable trade in 1807 and pressured European powers into doing the same at the 1815 Congress of Vienna.

Guillot profited from slave trading. While in Providencia, he made over $2,300 from the sale of enslaved Africans captured from Spanish ships as well as indigo and other trade goods produced by enslaved labor.[70] He was also wary of slave emancipation. When another Saint-Dominguan, Sévère Courtois, became the head of Providencia in 1821, he sent Guillot on a mission to Haiti. Courtois planned to launch a revolution in Cuba and wanted foreign assistance. A promise to abolish slavery in Cuba was included in the request—a reference to Bolívar's promise to abolish slavery in Spanish America in return for Haiti's help. Having already clashed with his compatriot a few times, Guillot distrusted his ambitions. Instead of going to Haiti, Guillot revealed the plans to the governor of Cartagena and turned his back on Courtois.[71]

Reinterpreting the disparate values and ideologies of their times, historical actors embraced political principles selectively. Savary and Guillot adopted republicanism, militarism, and racial equality for themselves. Another revolutionary who also received aid from Haiti, Bolívar, only embraced the former two in the long term. He feared the anarchical and violent forces triggered by the struggles for independence. As Spain lost ground in the region, Bolívar proclaimed what was then the fourth Republic in Venezuela in ten years. Racial equality became the law. The Congress of Cucúta adopted a constitution in 1821 that opened suffrage to all male heads of household who lived independently off their rents or labor. When Bolívar secured independence and became president of Gran Colombia, his commitment to emancipation started to weaken while his fear of a race war began to increase. He grew deeply uncomfortable with the racial equality embodied by Haiti. He feared that free people of color (*pardos*) would shift from demanding equality to seizing control of the government from the white elites.[72]

When Guillot officially petitioned the Republic of Gran Colombia to integrate its military, the government recognized him as lieutenant colonel of cavalry—the rank he occupied in Providencia.[73] In July 1824, Guillot fought in the Battle of Lake Maracaibo in northwestern Venezuela under the command of Admiral José Prudencio Padilla. The battle was brutal and gory. After the Venezuelan rebels blew up a Spanish vessel, a thick purple mantle covered the waters while sharks feasted on the corpses.[74] A free man of African descent born to a lower-class family in Riohacha on the Caribbean coast, Padilla started his career as a sailor before joining the Republic of Cartagena in 1811. After its fall, he took refuge in Haiti. He became general of the Colombian navy. The Battle of Lake Maracaibo turned him into a hero, resulting in his commission as commander general of the third department of the navy.[75]

Although Gran Colombian leaders gained the decisive military support of people of African descent with promises of equality, they quickly resented the prestige of nonwhite officers. Guillot followed Padilla through his ascent. Together they squelched a royalist revolt near Santa Marta in January 1823. Padilla's popularity on the Caribbean coast continued to grow. However, the following year, he received a promotion only to general and an annual pension of 3,000 pesos. He was incensed. He compared his reward to that of "a mercenary" and grew irritated at the government for not allowing him "to conclude his career with honour."[76] In November 1824, he issued an incendiary broadside in Cartagena: "The sword that I wielded against the King of Spain, that sword with which I gave days of glory to the homeland, that same sword will sustain me against anyone who tries to overthrow my class, and degrade my person." Padilla claimed that *pardos* had won independence for Colombia and that white elites were now threatening the "holy edifice of people's liberty and equality."[77] He became the commander of the navy in Cartagena, where he clashed with the commander of the department of Magdalena, further fueling Bolívar's concerns: "Padilla will be able to do whatever he wants if he keeps leading his people," he wrote Vice President Santander. "Equality before the law is not enough for them in their present mood. They want absolute equality as a social and public right. They will demand *pardocracia*, which the pardos should rule."[78]

Bolívar opposed a joint Gran Colombian–Mexican expedition against Cuba, fearing it would lead to "the establishment of a new republic of Haiti." Moreover, Padilla would have played a chief role as commander of the navy in this expedition and further overshadowed Bolívar.[79] Padilla briefly took power in Cartagena in March 1828 to defend the republican constitution against Bolívar's intention to impose a new authoritarian constitution.

Bolívar and local authorities accused him of conspiracy and executed him. Padilla's case was one in a series of alleged racial conspiracies in the post-revolutionary period, exposing social and political tensions in the Republic of Gran Colombia. Padilla's treatment at the hands of Bolívar's government sent a powerful message to other men of African descent. It foreshadowed how the Republic of Gran Colombia slowly diminished the standing of Afro-Colombians.[80] The fledging state was struggling to establish and consolidate its authority over its territory and citizens. Any mention of race was now considered unpatriotic, stirring racial tensions unnecessarily.[81]

Petitioning and Belonging

The dilemma for Savary and Guillot was that none of their political projects lasted. Unable to create the countries of their dreams, the two men learned to carve their place in the countries that did survive—countries in which the rights of men of African descent became gradually more restricted post-independence. While in different locations—Guillot settled in Colombia and Savary returned to Louisiana—both men lived under governments that politically disenfranchised or socially marginalized Afro-descendants. They both turned to petitioning as a mechanism of representation. The practice of petitioning illustrates their relationships with the countries in which they lived—their frustration but also their improvisational adaptiveness. They used pension petitions to prove their legitimacy as war veterans and make claims upon their adopted countries.

Across the Caribbean, free men of color of property and wealth turned to petitions to gain political and economic rights, which were often the means to bypass local administrations and ask for protection and enforcement of their rights.[82] In Gran Colombia during the 1820s, the rise of the myth of racial harmony coincided with a slow degradation of military status as well as a debate on the place of foreigners. At the beginning of the decade, military men hoped to obtain pensions and settle down in Colombia while retaining other citizenships.[83] They only formalized their Colombian citizenship when it was convenient. Haitian-born Louis Blanc, for example, obtained his naturalization in 1824 for his "important services in the armies of the Republic."[84] He was lucky to have done so because, in August 1827, a national congress decided to revise the 1821 Constitution, which had granted army members voting rights in recognition of their war efforts. The new congress decided to enforce suffrage requirements more strictly and disenfranchised all ranks below sergeant.[85]

As an officer, Guillot could still vote, but he felt the tide turning. He needed to have his loyalty recorded. In the midst of the racial and social tensions of 1827, he sent a pension petition to the government. Guillot had then parted ways with Padilla and trained local militias in Neiva, in southcentral Colombia. Listing his country as Haiti, Guillot placed his military service in a wider hemispheric context. His first employment, Guillot noted, was captain for the state of Louisiana in the war against Britain. He then listed other stages of his military career, rising to the rank of colonel on Providencia before entering the service of Gran Colombia. Guillot cleverly disguised his services in the unsanctioned privateer forces of Aury by citing instead the military expeditions he led against a common enemy, the Spanish Empire.[86] Aury was a bête noire in Colombia: the *Gaceta de Colombia* republished several communications from the government that lambasted Aury's establishment in Providencia as a "company of corsairs."[87]

Despite this sleight of hand, Guillot's petition request was rejected. Guillot resumed active service. He returned to the Caribbean coast and served as a commandant in Santa Marta. His plan was to acquire more years in the service of the national state and prove his commitment to Colombia. The collapse of the Republic of Gran Colombia, however, exacerbated social and racial tensions even further. Rumors of antiwhite conspiracy circulated in Santa Marta, where inhabitants of African descent were a majority.[88] In July 1831, two battalions rebelled in protest of ill treatment and overdue payment. Guillot's loyalty to the government came under fire, but he claimed that he never "betrayed his republican principles or taken arms against liberty."[89] Lauded as a worthy citizen, he was reinstated as a lieutenant colonel.[90] In 1834, he filed another petition that completely erased his hemispheric military activities in the Caribbean basin. Guillot dated the beginning of his career to his official integration into the national armed forces at the Battle of Lake Maraicabo.[91]

Guillot's two military pension petitions reveal how he revised his past between 1824 and 1837. Cosmopolitan patriotism gradually lost its value; patriotism became associated with a specific country. If a military man like Guillot understood his fight for independence regardless of the flag he carried, the postindependence focus on national memorialization meant that only the specific colors of the flag mattered. His first petition listed his services for the United States, Colombia, and the autonomous governments of Galveston, Amelia, and Providencia, as part of the same hemispheric struggle in the name of republicanism and independence. Having failed to obtain a pension, his second petition a decade later placed him in a purely national

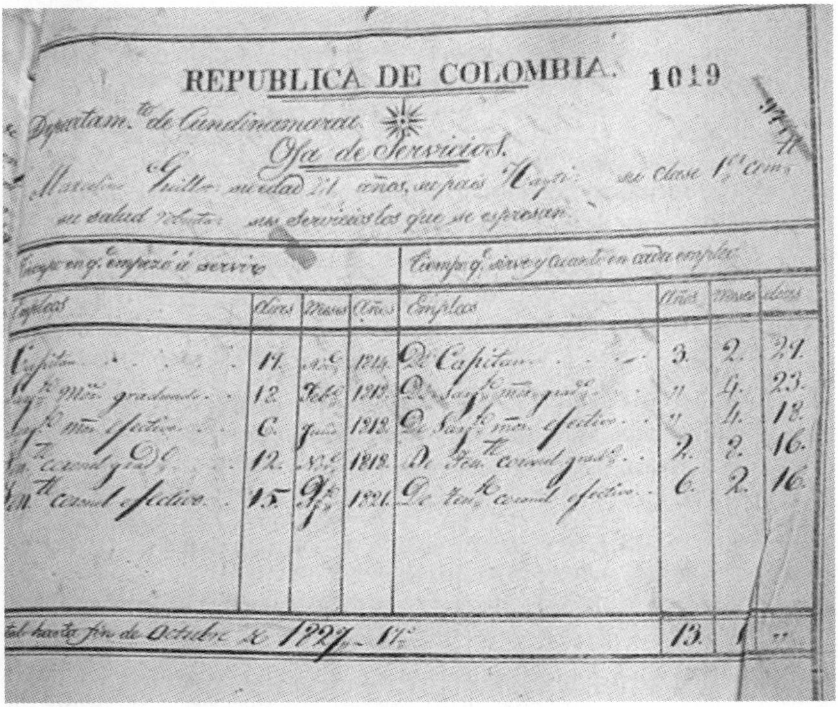

REPUBLICA DE COLOMBIA. 1019

Departam.to de Cundinamarca

Hoja de Servicios.

Marcelin Guillot su edad 27 años, su país Hayti, su clase 1a com... su salud robusta sus servicios los que se expresan.

Empleos	Días	Meses	Años	Empleos	Años	Meses	Días
Capitan	14	Ab.	1814	De Capitan	3	2	29
Sarg.to Mor graduado	12	Feb.	1816	De Sarg.to Mor graduado	"	4	23
Sarg.to Mor efectivo	6	Julio	1818	De Sarg.to Mor efectivo	"	4	18
Ten.te Coronel graduado	12	Nov.	1818	De Ten.te Coronel graduado	2	8	16
Ten.te Coronel efectivo	15	Sept.	1821	De Ten.te Coronel efectivo	6	2	16
Total hasta fin de Octubre de 1827					13		"

Figure 2. Service records of Marcelin Guillot, 1827.
Archivo General de la Nación, Colombia.

framework. Guillot remained in Santa Marta, joining the local conservative party and supplementing his military pension by occasionally running errands. In 1855, at the age of seventy, he traveled to the town of Honda, some 500 miles away, in the heart of Colombia, to carry 1,000 pesos to a merchant.[92]

In addition to inscribing military veterans into a state project, pension petitions also served a more pragmatic purpose: survival. Pensions were often the only source of income for aging soldiers and officers. In 1819, Savary petitioned the Louisiana House of Representatives for his service in the War of 1812. The legislators awarded him a $30 monthly pension and extended it for four years in 1823.[93] No other members of his battalion received pecuniary rewards. The money anchored Savary in New Orleans. He became reluctant to engage in any venture that would have contravened his adopted country's laws on neutrality, piracy, and slave trading and, if caught, would have jeopardized his income. Savary was eager to provide a résumé that fit changing criteria for patriotism. Shortly after he received his pension, Savary bragged to the Spanish consul in New Orleans that the governor of Louisiana had asked him to mount a cavalry corps of 700 to 800 men.[94] Whether the proposition was true or not, this anecdote shows that Savary liked to capitalize on his reputation as a military expert and charismatic leader.

As racial segregation grew, Savary probably realized that his chances of employment in the U.S. army were over and so focused his efforts locally. He developed a transportation business, hiring another free man of color to work as a carter and renting a cart to the city for fifty dollars.[95] Savary also remained intimately embedded within the local community. He sponsored his nephew, described as a fourteen-year-old teenager of color born in the Dutch Caribbean colony of Curacao, to be an apprentice and learn cabinetmaking and carpentry skills with two artisans of African descent.[96] Savary kept a close eye on his nephew's progress, as the cabinetmaking workshop was one block from the house he shared with his wife, Eugenie Pressot, another Saint-Domingue refugee from Saint Marc. The couple lived on Burgundy Street with a thirty-year-old enslaved woman designated as a "quadroon," Sanite, and her son and daughter.[97] Despite Savary's efforts, the couple struggled financially. Savary died in August 1828.[98]

After her husband's death, Eugenie secured her legitimacy as a free woman of color in a slaveholding state. First, she claimed Savary's pension, making sure to exercise her right to a marriage-based entitlement tied to privilege and status. Drawing from a tradition of social provisions for widows of officers in the English, Spanish, and French worlds, Eugenie petitioned the legislature. Her late husband's pension temporarily passed on to her but went from thirty to ten dollars.[99]

After securing her economic survival, Eugenie's second step was to set her enslaved domestics free. Throughout the prerevolutionary Americas, women of African descent used slave ownership to safeguard against discrimination and even challenges to their own freedom.[100] Joseph had not been dead for a year when Eugenie petitioned the parish court to emancipate Sanite and her two young children. Sanite's baby girl had just turned one.[101] The petition did not include Eugenie's motivations. Her husband's death had drastically reduced her income, but her decision to emancipate and not sell the enslaved family indicates some level of closeness between the two women. Eugenie's decision might also reflect an antislavery sensibility that her husband did not share.

In any case, Sanite and her children gained their freedom just in time. Alarmed by the growing population of free people of color, the legislators passed a law in 1830 requiring those wishing to free enslaved workers to post a $1,000 bond to guarantee that the newly freed individuals would leave Louisiana within one month of manumission.[102] Eugenie would have never been able to afford this hefty bond. Conditions also worsened for those born free. In March 1830, the Louisiana state legislature passed a new statute intended to curb the "discontent among free coloured population." Anyone who said, wrote, published, and distributed anything that might encourage such discontent faced three to twenty years of hard labor.[103]

Free people of color were excluded from the political sphere and could not count on the legislative or executive branch of government to protect them or even recognize their claims to legal personhood. However, the courts remained opened to them in Louisiana. They could sue, be sued, and testify.[104] Eugenie appeared in two of the roughly eighty suits for illegal enslavement adjudicated in the Louisiana Supreme Court between 1818 and 1833. Both cases involved members of the Saint-Domingue diaspora and reveal that the courts considered Eugenie a credible witness. The first case dated from 1822, a few years after Joseph retired from his revolutionary career. Both he and Eugenie testified in the trial of Nicholas "John" Tachaud against his owner. Arguing that he had been born free in Saint-Domingue in 1804, Tachaud claimed that he was "unjustly and illegally detained." After the death of Tachaud's mother, another free woman of color took Tachaud to Charleston. When she died, her white companion sold Tachaud into slavery. Counsel for Tachaud called six witnesses, including Joseph and Eugenie Savary.

Although Tachaud was born after the formal abolition of slavery in Haiti, his counsel did not mention Haiti's principle of free soil; instead, he and his witnesses focused on his lineage. Tachaud was free, they argued, because his mother was a free woman of color and his father was a French officer. Eugenie went so far as to swear she had been present at the plaintiff's birth. Tachaud and the Savarys relied on the colonial principle of *partus sequitur ventrem* long in practice and formally adopted by the United States after independence: the status of the child followed that of the mother. The legal strategy of the members of the Saint-Domingue diaspora, emphasizing lineage over the principle of free soil, was successful. The court ruled in favor of Tachaud and set him free.[105]

Eugenie testified in a second illegal enslavement suit involving the extended kinfolk of the Saint-Domingue diaspora. These two cases show the importance of respectability and reputation for free people of color in the Atlantic world. Laws could change, interpretations could vary, relatives could betray their promises, but names carried public recognition.[106] In 1833, a woman named Berard sued her aunt for her and her five children's freedom. Like Tachaud, she claimed to have been born free in Saint-Domingue and to have come to Louisiana as a refugee with her father's sisters. After one of them died, she continued to live with the other until she "conceived the idea of making her and her five children slaves" and "keep them in involuntary servitude."[107] Eugenie was identified in court as a "very respectable woman and is entitled to be fully believed on her oath." As in the Tachaud case, lineage was key. Eugenie claimed that she had known Berard as a child, often visiting the plantation where she lived. She testified that both Berard and her mother were enslaved in Saint-Domingue. The trial court adjudged Berard as enslaved, and the Louisiana Supreme Court affirmed that position.

Rising antislavery agitation across the United States frightened lawmakers into passing draconian measures against nonwhites. In the face of such antagonism, conditions for free people of color in Louisiana grew difficult.[108] In the same way Guillot repeatedly petitioned to have his name inscribed on the list of military veterans in Colombia in an increasingly discriminatory environment, the Savarys secured their reputation in New Orleans society through the memory of Joseph's service in the War of 1812. In turn, Eugenie leveraged her legitimacy to help some members of the Saint-Domingue diaspora obtain their freedom but also condemn others to perpetual enslavement.

*   *   *

The search for equality was hazardous for free people of African descent. A focus on Joseph Savary and Marcelin Guillot shows how power, resistance, and the formation of racialized identities need to be interpreted in local contexts. When they moved across regions, they also moved through different identities—man of color, black, *pardo*, mulatto, refugee, captain, colonel, pirate, and citizen—as categories switched unpredictably. This contingency explains why both men structured their self-presentation around their military identities. Military life gave them the opportunity to become cosmopolitans, crossing borders in the quest of better prospects.

Men like Savary and Guillot fought in many regions throughout their careers and could compare different political systems and social organizations. They learned to navigate the legal and diplomatic structures of different states across the Greater Caribbean and adapted their strategies accordingly. These states often disappeared after a few months or a few years, meaning that they had to start over repeatedly. At the beginning of their careers, military service was a means of gaining legitimacy, including negotiating to expand their rights and moving to locales where opportunities were better. Military skills were valuable assets during wartime, but they became more

burdensome and sometimes threatening during peacetime. Following independence in the mid-1820s, opportunities for people of color to claim equality through military service disappeared quickly. Army enlistment became
increasingly violent and served to punish vagrants, petty criminals, and non-
compliant populations: bearing arms lost its prestige.[109]

Moving from one place to the next might have increased the chances for
political, social, and financial rewards, but options were more limited when
it came to retirement. Living in the countries that survived the tumults of the
age of revolutions meant having to prove one's legitimacy—legitimacy as war
veterans for Savary and Guillot, legitimacy as a war widow and an honorable woman for Eugenie Savary. All three of them could only obtain pensions
from states with the capacity and infrastructure to process these claims. This
dependence on pensions for their survival might explain why none of them
decided to move to their native country of Haiti. Under the threat of foreign
invasions, Haiti was a heavily militarized state that would have welcomed
Savary and Guillot's military expertise. The army was one the main routes to
both landownership and government roles.[110]

Some members of the Savary family did return to Haiti. People of African descent sought to escape mounting racism in the United States, and
mobility became, once again, a way to secure a place in the world. Beginning
in 1858, just before the Civil War, almost 700 people of color left Louisiana
for Haiti. Many of them were second- or third-generation Saint-Domingue
immigrants.[111] They carried their family memories with them. In 1862, Joseph
Colastin Rousseau published a long article, "Souvenirs de la Louisiane," in a
Port-au-Prince newspaper. The son of a Saint-Domingue refugee, Rousseau
was married to Anna, Joseph Savary's granddaughter. Painstakingly sketch-
ing the history of Saint-Dominguans in the United States from the Haitian
Revolution through the 1809 migration from Cuba, he noted that the immigrants fought bravely in the Battle of New Orleans but never received the
recognition they deserved. This silencing was, Rousseau concluded, a taste
of the discrimination to come: "What was done to reward these men who
were so devoted and so disinterested, for the service they performed for the
country? Nothing!"[112] Their descendants were free to leave the United States
and return to their ancestral land in Haiti. They owed the United States no
loyalty.

CHAPTER 4

Revolutionary Dreams

Diplomatic Games and International Politics

In November 1792, the political leader Georges Danton stood in front of the French National Convention and inflamed his audience with a prophecy: the revolution was going to "purge the earth of all tyrants."[1] Three decades later, his cousin, Georges Nicolas Jeannet-Oudin, embarked on a vessel to fulfill this promise. He wanted to bring the revolution to Puerto Rico. The memory of the French Revolution haunted the ship's decks as sailors roared, "To arms, Americans, to arms," alluding to the words "To arms, citizens!" from the revolutionary anthem "Marseillaise."[2] Echoes of the French Revolution followed the careers of most leaders of the expedition against Puerto Rico. Jeannet-Oudin was Danton's nephew, and he served as the republican administrator of the French colonies of Guyana and Guadeloupe in the 1790s. His collaborator was a Prussian French veteran of the Napoleonic armies: H. L. V. Ducoudray-Holstein.[3] Other key figures in this scheme against Puerto Rico were several free men of color—Pierre Binet and Titus and Benjamin Bigard—who had served in the revolutionary privateer fleets of Guadeloupe and lived in the Swedish colony of Saint Barthélemy. "Long live our independence! Long live our liberty,"[4] was the expedition's motto. The name of the future republic was to be the Republic of Boricua. None of the leaders had ever set foot on the Spanish colony.

Seeking reinforcement, the expedition encountered a heavy storm on the way to La Guaira, in the department of Venezuela of Gran Colombia.[5] They requested help in Curacao, where Dutch authorities embargoed and searched the ships.[6] When the local U.S. consul got involved and learned about the expedition's revolutionary dreams, he grew increasingly puzzled: "The most strange part of the affair," he wrote the secretary of state, was that the leaders had "bulletins ready written, in which [they] declare the

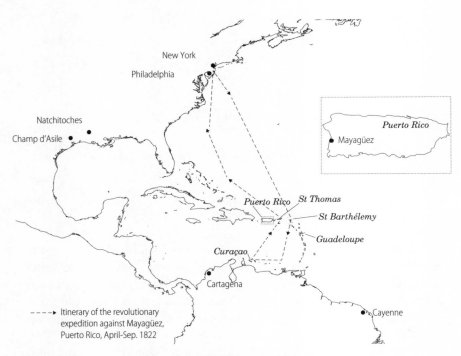

Map 5. Itinerary of the revolutionary expedition against Puerto Rico, 1822.

brilliant success of the expedition . . . the attack and landing are described at large." The revolutionaries had already published so many bulletins that they filled a casket and hid it in the hull of one of the ships alongside a case of cockades and flags.[7] Composed between stops at various ports, the documents reflected the disincarnated intellectual experiment of heterogeneous authors in a politically plural space spanning land and sea.

The expedition against Puerto Rico exemplified the Greater Caribbean's place in global history as a space of experimentation and innovation, a magnet for revolutionary insurgencies. On one hand, the expedition embodied fluid affiliations and a geopolitical imagination outside governmental and state control. The venture not only linked several Atlantic revolutions but also implanted itself in the human, commercial, and ideological sinews of the region. Its leaders filled the decks of their warships with 500 men of every class, color, nation, and religion.[8] Multinational and multiethnic crews had long characterized the seafaring world, but the expedition against Puerto Rico transformed this cosmopolitan environment into a political project.

On the other hand, the failure of the expedition triggered the expanding regulatory reach of modern nation-states. When the Boricua expedition turned into the Boricua affair and grabbed international headlines, the need to control an unfettered right to revolution became urgent. Governments across the Greater Caribbean feared that this kind of expedition would upend the fragile geopolitical balance in the region. It created a diplomatic crisis as governments around the Atlantic world debated who had the authority to prosecute these men, what crimes they had committed, which governments or state agents were involved in the expedition or had let it happen, and how to prevent this kind of expedition from happening again.

The diplomatic crisis around the Boricua expedition represented a pivotal moment in the history of the revolutionary Atlantic: the sorting out of legitimate revolutions that occurred in the 1820s when diplomatic recognition became the main way to legitimize new states and turned into a central instrument in the new international system. In March 1822, the U.S. government recognized the independence of Chile, Peru, Colombia, and Mexico. Fearing hostile reactions from European powers, Congress debated the matter until the first formal act of recognition in June, when the government officially received Colombian diplomatic agent Manuel Torres.[9] During the same time, the leaders of the Boricua expedition busied themselves gathering money, men, and supplies along the U.S. East Coast in all impunity. To respond to the critiques that the United States was a weak enforcer of its own laws, the government promptly sent a naval squadron to police what it depicted as the chaos and lawlessness of Caribbean waters. It was one of the first military interventions by U.S. forces in the Caribbean.

The Caribbean Sea might have been a complex entanglement of overlapping jurisdictions where the interests of various authorities, merchants, and enslaved and free residents overlapped and competed, but it was not a space outside state control.[10] As they did during slave revolts, world powers put their rivalries aside to end the kind of political subversion represented by the expedition against Puerto Rico.[11]

All Roads Lead to Puerto Rico

The grand scheme launched in Philadelphia in the summer of 1822. H. L. V. Ducoudray-Holstein had just arrived in the city and wasted no time planning a revolution against Puerto Rico. As "a person of some celebrity," with impressive military credentials in Europe and northern South America, he was not a man who kept a low profile.[12] French and Spanish consuls raised the alarm, noting that neutrality laws prohibited anyone on U.S. soil from participating in an attack against a country at peace with the United States. Yet local authorities never intervened. Ducoudray-Holstein was free to sell his revolutionary dreams to anyone who would listen. But Ducoudray-Holstein was just one node in the multiethnic and multinational network that engineered the Republic of Boricua.

The expedition was at the center of three overlapping areas of circulation of people and ideas: the first stretching up an Atlantic corridor that linked the United States and northern South America, the second connecting France and the Greater Caribbean, and the third spreading across the Lesser Antilles. These three circuits created a connective political culture that reveals how seemingly disparate actors—a veteran from Europe, a French administrator, a U.S. journalist, and Afro-Caribbean merchants—planned a revolution across multiple borders.

A first thread connected the revolutionary expedition to Colombia, Venezuela, and the United States through two of the revolutionary leaders: H. L. V. Ducoudray-Holstein and Baptis Irvine. The two men ran in the same liberal and revolutionary circles. After leaving Europe in 1812, Ducoudray-Holstein briefly passed through New York and Philadelphia, where he met agents of the Republic of Texas who appointed him general de brigade in the republican army of Mexico. By the time he arrived to the Gulf Coast, the Republic of Texas was no more. He joined another short-lived project against Texas led by Spanish philosopher Juan Bautista Mariano Picornell and French veteran Jean-Joseph Amable Humbert, thus bringing the new government up to three members.[13] Ducoudray-Holstein soon crossed the Gulf to join the Republic of Cartagena as commander-in-chief of the forts of Boca Chica. He worked with French captain Louis-Michel Aury, Saint-Dominguan officer Sévère Courtois, and Spanish republican Manuel Cortés Campomanes.[14] After the fall of the Republic, Ducoudray-Holstein rallied behind Simón Bolívar and served as a general until 1820. He honed his talents as a publicist and wrote reports he sent to newspapers in the United States and Europe.[15] He then lived as a language and piano teacher on the Dutch island of Curacao before hatching a revolutionary plot against Puerto Rico and seeking support on the U.S. Atlantic seaboard.

In Philadelphia, Irvine was drawn to Ducoudray-Holstein's reputation and pedigree, and Ducoudray-Holstein was drawn to Irvine's list of contacts among politicians and paper editors. Irvine was the Irish American editor of the *New York Columbian* and a fierce supporter of Latin American independence. In addition to promoting this cause in his editorials, he also provided material assistance to the insurgents. He notably assisted Louis-Michel Aury's agent, Vicente Pazos, when he unsuccessfully attempted to obtain reparations from the U.S. government after the seizure of Aury's republican headquarters on Amelia Island in 1818.[16] Irvine even met Bolívar when he served briefly as a U.S. agent in Venezuela in 1819.[17]

Not only did Ducoudray and Irvine circulate in the same networks, but they also shared the same skills as publicists. Irvine described Ducoudray-Holstein in effusive terms: "Led by the spirit of his profession, and a love of liberty, he entered early into the French revolutionary army and fought under the tri-color for nearly twenty years." Irvine concluded, "It is thus that the French Revolution, by contributing experience and genius to the new world, accomplish its emancipation, compensates, in some measures, for the misfortune of its disasters in the new world."[18] For Irvine, Ducoudray-Holstein was avenging the honor of the French Revolution.

Love of liberty was one argument in favor of the expedition to liberate Puerto Rico. Economic opportunity was the other. Evidence of a thriving commerce with the Caribbean and Latin America populated the pages of newspapers in New York, Philadelphia, and Baltimore.[19] Ducoudray-Holstein published a manifesto inviting merchants and volunteers across the Atlantic seaboard to subsidize the expedition. Describing the Spanish colony as a fertile island where merchants could sell their products easily, Ducoudray-Holstein announced that the new independent republic would adopt free trade.[20] In order to drum up more support, Irvine published a book entitled *On the Commerce of South America* that detailed trading opportunities with the Southern Hemisphere.[21]

A second thread connected the Boricua expedition to the French Atlantic and the Greater Caribbean region through the figure of Georges Nicolas Jeannet-Oudin. He circulated within the same transregional networks of republican exiles and supporters as Ducoudray-Holstein and Irvine, but he did not share their gift with words. He was, however, the only one with administrative experience. A merchant from the Champagne region in northern France, Jeannet-Oudin switched careers after the French Revolution along with the rest of the family.[22] His uncle, Danton, became one of the main figures of the French Republic and posted Jeannet-Oudin to the colonies of Guyana and Guadeloupe, where he earned a reputation as a radical firebrand. After his fall from grace with Napoléon's government, Jeannet-Oudin moved to the Louisiana-Texas region in the United States and set

up a short-lived colony with other European exiles.²³ Jeannet-Oudin then
moved to various Caribbean islands and probably met Ducoudray-Holstein
while they were both in Curacao. Jeannet-Oudin recruited more supporters
in Guadeloupe and Saint Barthélemy before traveling to New York around
April 1822 to coordinate plans with Ducoudray-Holstein and Irvine.²⁴

Revolutions were not cheap. Publicizing the expedition served two purposes: the first was to obtain sponsors who could provide money, arms, and
ammunitions, and the second was to enlist soldiers who could make up expeditionary forces. Together, Ducoudray-Holstein, Irvine, and Jeannet-Oudin
raised almost $20,000, but the captain-general of Puerto Rico put this figure
at $35,000.²⁵ The revolutionaries obtained an advance of $1,200 from a Philadelphia merchant who also provided them with one hundred muskets, one
hundred and twenty sabers, thirty pairs of pistols, and fifty kegs of powder.
In addition, this merchant supplied sixty trumpets and fifty drums to enable
communication with the troops. Ducoudray-Holstein also bought printing
materials.²⁶ On August 1, he transferred the equipment—large quantities of
muskets, sabers, pistols, gunpowder, and uniforms—onto three vessels. The
first ship departed Philadelphia, declaring Haiti as the official destination.
Five days later, the second ship departed New York, officially setting sail for
Saint Barthélemy and Saint Thomas. The ships cleared customs easily. A third
ship also left New York but escaped surveillance.²⁷

The ships were on their way to the Swedish colony of Saint Barthélemy,
where the financiers of the expedition were waiting for them. A third thread
connected the Boricua expedition to the Lesser Antilles through the participation of the bold and dashing brothers Philippe "Titus" and Benjamin Bigard
and their collaborators St. Rose, Binet, Dubois, and Gauchier.²⁸ They were all
Afro-Caribbean men originally from the French colony of Guadeloupe.

The participation of Afro-Caribbean revolutionaries in the Boricua expedition exemplified the rich connections across the islands of the Lesser Antilles, particularly around Saint Barthélemy. France had traded the colony to
Sweden in 1784, but contacts with the French colonies remained tight. A free
port, Saint Barthélemy was a transregional meeting place for ships of various
flags.²⁹ On their way from the United States, the expedition against Puerto
Rico stopped there for over ten days, buying military supplies and recruiting personnel. They purchased another ship before leaving in mid-September.
However, the connections between the revolutionaries and Saint Barthélemy ran much deeper. The colony was a hub for smuggling and privateering. Fourchue, also called Five Islands, an islet lying about three miles from
the capital Gustavia, boasted a cove perfect for small, fast vessels. It became

a base of operations for Spanish American privateers. Louis-Michel Aury operated there for a few months after his expulsion from Amelia. British volunteers transited there on their way to the Spanish continent. One of them commented that it was "a place of general rendezvous for smugglers of every description."[30]

In addition to Saint Barthélemy's entanglement with transregional trade and American independence movements, migratory routes tightly connected the island to Guadeloupe. As part of his policy to restrict the rights of people of African descent in 1802, Napoléon decided to deport nearly a thousand Afro-Caribbean soldiers and officers. Many Guadeloupeans escaped and dispersed across neighboring islands: Puerto Rico, Saint Thomas, and especially Saint Barthélemy.[31] Some of these exiles had worked with Victor Hugues, the republic commissioner of Guadeloupe, who outfitted more than one hundred privateers against British ships and territories between 1794 and 1798—an era historian Robin Blackburn dubbed "a revolutionary emancipationist offence."[32] Some, like the Bigard brothers, had collaborated with Jeannet-Oudin when he briefly took over the governance of Guadeloupe in 1800.

Dispersed across the Lesser Antilles, a few men decided to resume their collaboration with Jeannet-Oudin and directed their attention toward Puerto Rico. Among them was Pierre Binet, a former shoemaker. Binet's connections reached across political and linguistic boundaries since his wife lived in the British colony of Antigua. A tall and elegant man, Binet worked with his brother-in-law, Pierre Dubois, and a fellow shoemaker, Joseph, also known as Albert or St. Rose. While Jeannet-Oudin involuntarily caught the eye of various onlookers because of his missing left hand, earning him the nickname "main pote" or lumpy hand, witnesses observed that his Afro-Caribbean collaborators deliberately dressed to impress. Their style was flamboyant: the forty-year-old Binet wore gold and green spectacles, gloves, boots, and a brown redingote with a velvet collar. The twenty-five- or thirty-year-old St. Rose liked to wear a blue redingote with a velvet collar. They made a point of traveling by horse to signal their privileged status or their former military status.[33]

The governor of Guadeloupe noted that Jeannet-Oudin had a "particular predilection" for conspiring with people of African descent.[34] Another native of Guadeloupe living in Saint Barthélemy, Georges Gauchier, was involved in the expedition against Puerto Rico. The Swedish colony expelled Gauchier after an altercation, or "an act of impertinence with a merchant," and he traveled with Jeannet-Oudin to New York to organize the Boricua expedition.[35] When Jeannet-Oudin and Gauchier returned to Saint Barthélemy a few months later, they reunited with the Bigard brothers and with Binet and recruited more participants. A U.S. observer described them "mostly black, and of the lowest class."[36] One of these sailors decided that the venture was too risky; when the ships arrived in Saint Barthélemy, he deserted, informed the authorities, and returned to Guadeloupe.[37] If Jeannet-Oudin was "the soul and the motor of the pernicious projects [against Puerto Rico]," the governor of Martinique wrote, the Bigard brothers in Saint Barthélemy were "the instruments that direct these intrigues."[38]

The activities of the Bigard brothers exposed a deep-seated conviction in racial equality and a resourceful financial savviness. At the time of the expedition, Titus was forty-five and fluent in several languages, while Benjamin, two years his junior, spoke French and English.[39] They owned a mercantile house in the capital of Gustavia.[40] They petitioned for the emancipation of nine of their enslaved personnel between 1819 and 1822.[41] Most of them were from Guadeloupe and had probably moved with the Bigard brothers. A few years after arriving in Saint Barthélemy, the Bigards and other free men of color petitioned the governor, complaining that the Swedish Empire had "introduced maxims of political disparity and unequal right" by establishing "disqualifications of Colour and Complexion." They called for the end of political disenfranchisement and made an argument based on class: property owners ought to receive equal voting rights and representation, regardless of the color of their skin. The crown turned down the request.[42] The brothers started to walk a tightrope. On one hand, they appealed, as many wealthy people of color had been doing since the late eighteenth century, to metropolitan authorities to obtain political rights, bypassing and antagonizing local authorities in the process. On the other hand, they actively schemed against the Spanish Empire, antagonizing colonial authorities across the Caribbean.

Thanks to their transregional trading networks, the Bigard brothers were valuable assets to the Boricua expedition. Not only did they provide financial support, but they also had access to a web of connections around the West Indies. In February 1822, after another petition from the Bigard brothers, the Swedish colonial department announced that free men of color could vote under severe restrictions. It was a humiliating victory: they needed to register early and prove residency, five years of property ownership, and loyalty to the crown.[43] Around the same time, Jeannet-Oudin and other conspirators of African descent met at the house of the Bigard brothers to hatch their revolutionary plans. The information made its way to the governor of Martinique, who sent a complaint to the governor of Saint Barthélemy, Nordeling, asking him to arrest the conspirators, seize their possessions, and deliver everyone and everything to the French admiral sent to collect them. Nordeling took offence at the implication that his administration was "so weak and incompetent" that he would let "vagabonds assemble here for the purpose of plotting" against an allied nation. When it came to the Bigard brothers, his hands were tied, he explained, since Swedish laws prevented him from searching a commercial house without evidence.[44] When a Stockholm gazette and Caribbean newspapers published the correspondence with the French administration, Nordeling's mortification became transatlantic.[45]

Tensions continued to rise. The Bigard brothers and their collaborators probably hoped to take advantage of economic opportunities should Puerto Rico break away from Spain and the Republic of Boricua adopt free trade. The republic was also predicated on ending racial and ethnic discriminations for all citizens—a principle dear to the Bigard brothers. In July 1822, Titus Bigard filed a complaint against the Swedish governor for whipping three men of color without a trial and sent it to the crown in secret. The Swedish colonial department followed the petitioner's instructions and reprimanded Governor Nordeling, reminding him of the importance of securing the loyalty of free people of color.[46] The game of chess continued. In August, the governor arrested Titus after he received news that a schooner and two brigs had arrived in Gustavia with provisions and munitions. Nordeling suspected that Titus was part of a larger network of political destabilization but, with no evidence, released him.[47] The arrest enraged the Bigard brothers even further.

Intricate webs connected the peripatetic revolutionaries who had long nurtured dreams of glory and adventure, whether it was the veteran Ducoudray-Holstein, the journalist Irvine, the administrator Jeannet-Oudin, or the merchants Bigards. Yet none of them had ties to Puerto Rico. Ducoudray-Holstein claimed that agents of the revolutionary party of Puerto Rico contacted him when he was living in Curacao. According to him, they assured him that "they placed entire confidence in [him], and in [him] alone." No documentation of this claim surfaced during the trials.[48] The revolutionaries probably chose Puerto Rico over Cuba because the Spanish government had shifted military and administrative resources to the latter after independence on the continent. Cuba now boasted a robust defense system. In addition, royalists had moved to Cuba after the independence of the Spanish American continent while Puerto Rico had experienced an influx of foreigners, particularly from the French Caribbean.[49] The revolutionaries counted on this foreign population to help them overthrow Spanish colonial rule.

Paper Republic

There was nothing clandestine about the Boricua expedition. The conspirators roamed the streets, merchant houses, and freemasonry lodges on the U.S. Atlantic seaboard and in the Lesser Antilles. They also etched their schemes on paper. The trove of documents laid bare how they constructed their legitimacy as liberators of a foreign country. The republic-to-be was to be named the Republic of Boricua, sometimes spelled Boriguen or Böuqua, the indigenous Taíno name of the island. Indigenous references were popular among revolutionaries in Haiti and Latin America. They provided a form of legitimization to overthrow imperial rule and create a sense of a distinctively American identity.[50] Irvine lamented the decision to have so many inculpating documents printed in advance: "to permit proclamations and papers to transpire was a folly."[51] The governor of the Danish West Indies agreed: these proclamations were "for the eyes of the whole world."[52]

As the revolutionaries eagerly broadcasted their dreams to the world, asking "friends of our cause, the journalists and merchants, reading the present appeal to assist us in propagating the same, by having it inserted in their papers, in the language of their country," the world was eager to listen.[53] The documents appeared in various newspapers, including the *New York Gazette* and the *Antigua Gazette*.[54] The Spanish vice consul in Philadelphia sent this information to the governor of Puerto Rico, who then alerted colonial authorities on all the other islands.[55] Far from seeing the expedition as the "zealous friends of independence" described by Ducoudray-Holstein, the captain-general of Puerto Rico lamented the sundry crew of foreigners plotting against his island. They were all "dishonorable men, adventurers," he told French authorities in Martinique. They "exhibit[ed] an appearance which indicated their evil Intentions, being people of all nations and all Colours," he told British authorities in Barbados.[56]

The Republic of Boricua was a sophisticated exercise in political bricolage. The highly mobile leaders were conversant in experiments ranging from the French revolutionary project of the 1790s to the constitutional republic of the United States, from the equality of the Mexican and Colombian republics to the free trade policy of the Swedish Empire. They selectively synthesized them in an eclectic blend. An example was their declaration of independence. The revolutionaries adopted the model for declaring independence pioneered by the United States in 1776 and reiterated by various groups across the Americas. Spanish American independents had adopted acts of independence, first after the Napoleonic invasion of the peninsula

(Tunja, Cartagena, and Venezuela in 1811, for example), then after the wars of independence (Chile in 1818 and Peru, Central America, and Mexico in 1821).[57] These documents functioned as birth certificates for the new countries whether their authors saw the demand for independence as a performative recognition of de facto independence or a message directed to the rest of the world. This genre of political writing was not part of every revolutionary movement. Some revolutionaries turned to constitutions and binational treaties to secure sovereignty. However, declarations of independence had become the prevalent mode of asserting secession by the time Ducoudray-Holstein, Jeannet-Oudin, and Irvine set sail for the Caribbean Sea. They therefore had a wide repertoire at their disposal.[58]

The leaders used the Boricua declaration of independence to indigenize their revolution. In an artful feat of ventriloquism, the declaration spoke in the voice of Puerto Ricans even if none of the revolutionaries had been born or raised in the colony. It listed grievances against the Spanish Empire that represented, the authors declared, "the most forcible proofs of its tyranny, its bad faith, and of its incapacity to protect and to govern us." The title of the Boricua document, *Solemn Act of the Declaration of Independence*, mimicked the *Solemn Act of Independence* that established the secessions of Venezuela in 1811 and Mexico in 1813, but the tone and content differed in many ways. While the declarations in Venezuela and Mexico drew their inspiration from Spanish intellectual and political traditions, arguing that the Napoleonic removal of the king of Spain had dissolved the social contract between the monarch and the people, the king had since regained his throne at the time of the expedition. This rationale for secession no longer applied.[59]

The Boricua declaration made three points; the first was to insist that the Spanish government had been incapable of governing Puerto Rico properly for three hundred years. This gesture referenced other Spanish American acts of independence (Mexico and Venezuela, for example), which often referred to this long Spanish "domination."[60] The second point acknowledged that Puerto Rico had remained faithful to the Spanish government from the moment Napoléon invaded the peninsula to the return of the Bourbons. Yet the declaration announced that Spain had been "deaf to our just and lawful remonstrance," namely, their demands for equality with the metropole. This rhetoric echoed the 1811 Venezuelan declaration: "Always deaf to the cries of justice on our part, the Governments of Spain have endeavored to discredit all our efforts, by declaring [us] criminal . . . [and] a flock of slaves." The declaration then moved to a third and final argument, turning to a universal language of natural rights. In a nod to the U.S. Declaration of Independence, it stated, "Fully impressed with these truths, we declare solemnly before the Almighty God, before the whole Universe, that we are resolved to suffer a similar tyranny no longer," and that only a free and independent government could provide "happiness, strength, and consistency." These last three principles echoed those in the Venezuelan declaration: preservation, security, and happiness.[61] While the format of the Boricua declaration resembled other American declarations of independence, notably Venezuela's, where Ducoudray-Holstein fought the Spanish Empire for six years, its tone and content were adapted to the specific conditions of Puerto Rico.

The declaration of independence was one of several documents produced to secure the legitimacy of the imagined Republic of Boricua. The revolutionaries embraced liberalism; they believed that constitutional governments ensured popular sovereignty and progress.[62] Constitutional articles laid the groundwork for the future republic. A founding principle of the republic was the "equality of rights, asylum, protection, and happiness," an adaptation on the inalienable rights promised by the U.S. declaration of 1776 (life, liberty, and the pursuit of happiness) and by the French Constitution of 1793 and 1795 (liberty, equality, safety, property). The decision to turn asylum into a constitutional right was idiosyncratic in the Atlantic world. The French Constitution of 1793 granted the right of asylum to foreigners banished from their homelands "in the name of liberty." Although this constitution was never implemented, Jeannet-Oudin was a member of the government at the time and was undoubtedly familiar with it. Many countries provided asylum to foreigners banished or persecuted because of their political beliefs, but only the southern republic of Haiti had incorporated the practice into its constitution in 1816.[63] In the case of Haiti, however, the right of "sacred and inviolable" asylum aimed at protecting enslaved fugitives. It recognized enslavement as a form of persecution that merited the granting of asylum.[64]

The promise of asylum in the Republic of Boricua shows that the revolutionaries intended to create a truly cosmopolitan country. In addition to the principle of asylum, equality was a cornerstone of the republic. All citizens would therefore obtain political or military positions, "according to their merit, their conduct, his experience, and abilities."[65] Distinctions between foreigners and creoles, between whites and blacks, would no longer exist. Many people of African ancestry from Guadeloupe, Saint-Domingue, Curacao, Venezuela, and Colombia resided in Puerto Rico. Some of them wished to escape revolutions and conflicts; some came because of an 1815 Cédula de Gracias that encouraged foreign immigration, particularly from allied Catholic countries.[66] When the authorities of Puerto Rico arrested

Pierre Dubois, a free man of color from Guadeloupe, they found several documents authored by Ducoudray-Holstein in his possession. These papers invited foreigners in Puerto Rico to join the revolution: the republic was going to offer the same rights to every citizen, "regardless of his color, his religion, and his place of birth."[67] The expansiveness of the principle of "equality" was a rhetorical strategy aimed at groups both within and outside Puerto Rico.

The Republic of Boricua rested on key liberal principles, including the freedoms of trade, religion, press, and expression; the separation of powers; and, above all, equality of citizens. Slavery, however, remained legal; the constitution explained, "otherwise, the country would be ruined, and the greatest disorders would take place."[68] The Boricua expedition targeted European colonial rule but could not escape the wars around freedom and slavery that engulfed the Atlantic world. Twenty years earlier, in 1793, enslaved crowds in Guyana had greeted Georges-Nicolas Jeannet-Oudin with a rousing rendition of the "Marseillaise" and praises: "Liberté! Liberté chérie!"[69] In return, he promised them, "Black citizens, you are newborns to Liberty, but equals to your elders, in the eyes of our *patrie*. . . . Liberty is not a gift that can be taken back."[70] But the gift was taken back by Napoléon a few years later. Like Jeannet-Oudin, Ducoudray-Holstein might have been personally opposed to slavery: he proudly remembered that his father was the first in the kingdom of Denmark to give "freedom and liberty" to his farmers, noting that "they were formerly slaves."[71] In his scathing biography of Bolívar, he reluctantly credited the Spanish American leader with keeping the promise he made Haitian president Pétion to abolish slavery in the new republics. He regretted, however, that emancipation was limited to those who fought in the insurgent armies or who purchased their own freedom.[72] Despite these previous emancipationist experiences, the Boricuan revolutionaries offered little place for enslaved populations. Despite the presence of Haiti and its free-soil policy a mere 400 miles from Puerto Rico, Ducoudray-Holstein and Jeannet-Oudin upheld slavery for its practicality and profitability.

Sophisticated exercises in political bricolage, the dreams of the Republic of Boricua were born out of disappointment and disillusionment with other political projects. Ducoudray-Holstein publicly complained about the xenophobia he faced in Colombia. "Creoles," he wrote, "are generally jealous of all foreigners and display their aversion to the leaders who do not belong to their province." The ingratitude of local leaders and populations extended, according to Ducoudray-Holstein, to foreigners of all colors, including troops from Guadeloupe and Haiti who helped secure independence.[73] He also lamented what he perceived as a betrayal of the principles of freedom of expression, freedom of religion, and racial equality that sparked the age of revolutions.[74] Disillusionment also marked Jeannet-Oudin's experience with the revolutionary Atlantic. When he arrived in Guyana in April 1793, he denounced the violence of slaveowners and, a year later, implemented the decree abolishing slavery.[75] Jeannet-Oudin attributed the failure of the radical project to white colonists' resistance, not emancipated citizens, who, he stressed, "behave[d] very well."[76] He was briefly posted in Guadeloupe in 1800 where he instigated a failed expedition against Curacao.[77] The Champ d'Asile colony of French refugees, which he joined in Texas in 1818, existed only for six months.[78] The Bigard brothers and their collaborators had also experienced failure and displacement. They had to leave their native Guadeloupe when Napoléon came into power, reintroduced racial discrimination, and threatened to deport the free men of color who had actively participated in the former republican government. All these acrimonious experiences fueled a desire to create a new republic—a republic that would reflect its founders learning from the mistakes and failings of other revolutions.[79]

Cross-Island Solidarity

Even if the documentation produced for the Republic of Boricua indicated that the leaders intended to maintain slavery, the expedition coincided with the discovery of a slave rebellion in the same location (Guayama) where the revolutionaries' ships had planned to dock. Authorities uncovered the plot at the end of September 1822. It remains unclear if the Boricua conspiracy and the slave revolt represented one coordinated plan of revolution or two separate plots. In his study of the trial records, historian Guillermo Baralt noted that the conspirators never disclosed whether the rebellion was linked to the expedition.[80] Local agents of the Boricua republic might have encouraged enslaved rebels, hoping that the uprising would facilitate the invasion of the island. Similarly, enslaved conspirators perhaps hoped to take advantage of the confusion triggered by the expedition and put their plans into action. Regardless of the absence of tangible evidence connecting the two events, contemporary observers considered them as part of the same movement. The coincidence of the Boricua expedition and the Guayama slave revolt is one of the very few occurrences in which a slave rebellion coincided with a project for political independence. As such, it spread waves of fear around the Atlantic world.

Authorities and officials scrambled to assemble, transcribe, and translate every piece of information so that they could retrace the expedition's support networks. They hoped to stifle future revolutionary attempts. When rumors of the expedition first started to spread across the Greater Caribbean, French officials suspected that Martinique or Guadeloupe was the ultimate goal. The implication of former governor Jeannet-Oudin as well as other French and French Caribbean participants set the colonies on high alert. The French consul in Philadelphia reassured the governors of Martinique and Guadeloupe that Puerto Rico was the intended target.[81] Yet French officials had little time to relax. In mid-October 1822, a month after the Boricua expedition stopped in Curacao and the Guayama conspiracy rocked Puerto Rico, between thirty and forty enslaved workers revolted while laboring on a canal in Carbet on the northwestern coast of Martinique. Military forces squashed the revolt. Officials arrested sixty-two people and sentenced twenty-one of them to death, ten to forced labor, and seventeen to whipping.[82]

In barely four months, between June and October 1822, an expedition to bring revolution to Puerto Rico had been thwarted fortuitously, two slave conspiracies had been discovered (the Denmark Vesey conspiracy in South Carolina and the Guayama conspiracy in Puerto Rico), and a full-fledged slave revolt had erupted in Martinique. World powers decided that this succession of anticolonial and antislavery events could not be coincidences and were part of a broader movement to disrupt the social and political order of the region. The governor of Barbados wrote his administration that the number of self-liberated runaways in the British colony was alarming and required coordinated defensive measures with the governors of Saint Lucia and Trinidad to prevent all "attempts of mischief" after the events in Puerto Rico and Martinique.[83]

In the minds of colonial officials, one person stood behind this grand plan to introduce chaos and insurrection to the entire region. These different events were part of a Haitian-orchestrated scheme, the governor of Martinique concluded. The Haitian president, Jean-Pierre Boyer, wished to create a new "Empire, or a Confederation of the West Indies."[84] Many feared Boyer's ambitions, especially after he invaded the Spanish colony of Santo Domingo and annexed it to Haiti in 1822.[85] Although the Boricua expedition was hatched in the United States, the captain-general of Puerto Rico, Miguel de la Torre, insisted that its instigator was actually Boyer, "a dangerous and enterprising Man, who aspires to the Subversion of all the neighboring islands . . . including the whole Archipelago of the Antilles." His objective was clear, de la Torre wrote British and French authorities: "The equality of

Colour throughout, and the modeling of these Governments similar to that of [his own]."[86] The governor of Martinique reached out to Spanish colonial authorities, remarking that the two nations were "old friends and allied by the blood of our kings."[87] They solicited the testimony of a free man of color from Saint Thomas who had heard that the expedition consisted of no fewer than "twenty-four vessels fitted out from the Haytian Government to make the Conquest of the Island of Portico [with] four thousand five hundred Haytian troops."[88] This was a far cry from the four vessels and 500 men of the actual expedition, but amid rumors and contradicting information, this testimony convinced colonial authorities that Haiti had nefarious ambitions in the region.

Tensions escalated between the Haitian government and French authorities in the Caribbean. The governor of Martinique implored his administration to renew a travel ban on people of color. The metropolitan government was surprised: they were unaware, or so they claimed, that the ties between Martinique, Guadeloupe, and Haiti were so intense.[89] The Bourbon monarchy hoped to negotiate with President Boyer and grant Haiti a special status in the French Empire. They had lifted a ban on relationships with Haiti; promoted the importation of coffee, cotton, and Campeche wood; and encouraged the return of members of the Saint-Domingue diaspora.[90] After all these efforts, they were reluctant to follow the suggestions of their governors in the Caribbean to return to a strict isolationist policy. However, the accusations of the governors of Martinique and Guadeloupe angered Boyer and prompted him into action. He prohibited all relationships between Haiti and the Leeward islands (including the French colonies of Guadeloupe and Saint Martin) in May 1823.[91] But Boyer's ban was more symbolic than effective: interactions between Haiti and the rest of the Caribbean continued as before.

The Boricua expedition created a movement of solidarity and cooperation among colonial powers. It also provoked an intense debate over the nature of diplomatic protection and jurisdictional limits in the Greater Caribbean. The multinational nature of the expedition against Puerto Rico posed a serious conundrum when the expedition stopped in Curacao. As the governor of Saint Thomas mused, these men had wished to create their own republic; therefore, he asked, "Who do [they] belong to?"[92] Not only did the nationalities of these subversive actors implicate various consuls and diplomatic agents, but the preparation of the expedition also traced back to U.S., French, and Swedish territories. Almost every power present in the Greater Caribbean claimed jurisdiction over the offending parties. As the country under attack, Spain wanted a fair punishment. Spanish and Dutch authorities went head to head. The captain-general of Puerto Rico argued that these men did "not belong to any recognized government, not even to those newly created; they belong to no state . . . to no nation."[93] Since Puerto Rico was their objective, he claimed that he had jurisdiction.[94]

The governor of Curacao, on the other hand, argued that the revolutionaries had to be tried where they were arrested according to the international legal principle of *ubi te invenio, ibi te judicabo*: the offense should be tried in the jurisdiction where it occurred. Articulated by various legal scholars since the seventeenth century, including Hugo Grotius and Emmer Vattel, this principle found its origin in the idea that states had a shared interest in the prosecution of certain crimes.[95] The governor of Curacao argued that these men were enemies of the public peace—they were "pirates," and any state had the right to prosecute them.[96]

Some of the conspirators had already left Saint Barthélemy for Puerto Rico ahead of the expedition. They had gone up and down the southeastern region of the island to circulate the republic's promises and recruit some support. A French planter betrayed the Guadeloupean Pierre Dubois and alerted local authorities. The planter's testimony and the pamphlets Dubois carried with him were damaging evidence.[97] After a quick trial in October 1822, Puerto Rican authorities executed Dubois for conspiring with foreigners against the government.[98] Binet managed to escape and became the target of a manhunt. He sought refuge in his home in Saint Thomas, so the governors of Puerto Rico and Martinique instructed Danish authorities to arrest him. When the police arrived at his residence, they found that he had already gotten a passport for Granada and left the colony.[99] In Puerto Rico, the government began to punish any form of dissent severely; they dissolved Masonic lodges and ended freedom of the press.[100]

Cross-island negotiations were under way when French authorities contacted the governor of Saint Barthélemy to investigate the Guadeloupeans in the colony. The Bigard brothers escaped persecution, but they retreated from engaging in further revolutionary activities. Smuggling was an unpredictable source of income, and they experienced financial difficulties after the Swedish crown signed an anti–slave trade treaty with Britain in 1824 and started to police their waters more carefully. This trade had been an important source of income for Saint Barthélemy until Sweden and France made it illegal in 1813 and 1815. Ships used to bring enslaved people tax free, and Swedish authorities made a profit by collecting an export tax when they shipped out.[101]

Despite the internationalization of the abolition of the slave trade, human trafficking continued.[102] The Bigard brothers outfitted slave ships.

Guadeloupean authorities, for example, captured the *Jaloux* carrying 107 enslaved Africans in 1824.[103] The Bigards listed one of their employees, a free man of color named Panilio, as shipowner so that the authorities could not prosecute them. Eventually, they bailed their employee and placed him on one of their boats for Saint Martin. Shortly after, Panilio got involved with another slaver in Saint Thomas and transported ninety enslaved Africans, selling ten of them in Guayama on Puerto Rico's southern coast, the intended landing site of the Boricua expedition.[104] The governor of Saint Barthélemy warned shipowners that they would be prosecuted should their vessels be used for carrying enslaved people.[105] The Bigard firm was liquidated shortly after.[106]

Free men of color took serious risks when copying, carrying, and distributing political propaganda. Unlike white revolutionaries, they received little to no diplomatic protection. Spanish authorities executed Pierre Dubois without outrage from Swedish or French officials. In Curacao, the white leaders of the Boricua expedition, Ducoudray-Holstein, Jeannet-Oudin, and Irvine, were sentenced to thirty years of labor in salt mines.[107] They sent three appeals to the Superior Court in The Hague.[108] Their defense case was as legally plural as was their prosecution, involving various legal systems and polities. They also attempted to convince the U.S. government to intercede in their favor. A former diplomatic agent, Irvine frequently appealed to Henry Clay, denying the legitimacy of the Curacao governor to prosecute them. He deemed him a "Dutch kidnapper" at the head of a colony run by "a gang of legalized freebooters."[109]

Balancing prosecution and protection, the U.S. consul in Curacao tried to rescue the U.S. Americans involved in the expedition, arguing that they were young and "of considerable respectability." He pressured Dutch authorities to retain jurisdiction, assuming that they would be more lenient than Spanish courts. He visited the prisoners often and obtained passports for thirteen of them, who, according to him, "have been shamefully deceived into an expedition which could bring on them nothing but disgrace and destruction."[110] Eager to clear the reputation of the United States where the expedition had been organized, he forwarded the documents of the expedition to the secretary of state, waiting for more instructions.[111] The captain of a U.S. warship entered Curacao and asked the Dutch governor to release Irvine. Irvine was no longer a U.S. citizen, the governor responded: the documents found aboard the ship identified him as secretary of state for the Republic of Borigua and had therefore transferred his allegiance.[112] The U.S. government was reluctant to intervene more forcefully.

The wretched revolutionaries launched an international campaign to save their skin. In addition to the appeals they sent to Dutch metropolitan authorities and to the U.S. government, they also sent letters to major newspapers across the Atlantic world. Irvine cited Vattel's *Law of Nations* on the legality of the war between Spain and its American colonies: "From the popular movement against despotism would result in *a civil war*," Irvine argued, "that would produce in the nation two independent parties who consider each other as enemies, and *acknowledge no common judge*."[113] They were not pirates, Irvine disputed; they were patriots helping a people to achieve the most fundamental rights of men across the world—to be free and independent.[114] After all, foreigners like Lafayette and Kosciuszko had espoused the cause of the U.S. revolution, and many "gallant foreigners" had recently flocked to liberate the Greeks from the Ottoman Empire. Surely, Irvine noted, these precedents counted in favor of his attempt to bring revolution to Puerto Rico.[115]

Many European and U.S. newspapers covered the Boricua affair. Ducoudray-Holstein quickly realized that charges of piracy tainted his character and endeavored to shift the tide of public opinion in his favor. He insisted that Curacao did not have jurisdiction since the expedition did not target this colony. The expedition targeted a Spanish colony, and since the revolutionaries were not Spanish subjects, he contended, they could not be prosecuted for a crime against a foreign sovereign. He accused Dutch officials of destroying evidence when they burned the expedition's "liberal and republican papers" in the public square at the Amsterdam fort in Curacao.[116] Although they were under the arrest, Ducoudray-Holstein and Irvine's rank and status shielded them and kept them out of jail. Ducoudray-Holstein lived with his wife in a house in Willemstad, receiving friends and going for walks. He even kept his pistols on hand.[117] The publicity campaigns paid off: Irvine and Ducoudray-Holstein's third appeal was successful, and the Curacao court suspended legal proceedings. They left the Dutch colony after nearly a year and a half of house arrest.[118]

The Dawn of U.S. Interventionism

The expedition against Puerto Rico marked one of the first extraterritorial interventions of the United States into the Caribbean. Until then, U.S. military operations had stopped at Florida—including the takeover of Amelia Island in 1817. With the exception of the so-called naval Quasi-War between the United States and France in 1798 to 1800 when several small warships fought French privateers in Caribbean waters, the United States was a relatively new participant in the geopolitics of the region.[119]

The ease with which the revolutionaries acquired weapons and volunteers in Philadelphia and New York exposed the lax enforcement of U.S. laws despite recent revisions of the legislation. A few years earlier, President James Monroe had asked Congress for stricter neutrality laws as complaints from the Spanish and Portuguese ministers intensified against Latin American privateers fitted in the United States. The U.S. government was taken to task for not policing its ports. In 1817, a proposed amendment to the existing Neutrality Laws of 1794 and 1797 stipulated that customs collectors could detain suspect vessels.[120] The amendment also required customs officers to detain vessels "manifestly built for warlike purposes," whose cargo consisted mostly of arms and whose crew contained a suspicious number of foreign men.[121] Congress codified the major provisions of the Neutrality Acts of 1794 and 1797, as well as the 1817 amendment into the Neutrality Act of 1818, reinforcing the power of the executive branch. The following year, Congress passed the Piracy Act, which made piracy a crime punishable by death for all "illegitimate" individuals. New provisions in 1820 defined slave trading as piracy. The Piracy Act of 1819, together with the 1820 provisions, granted the president power to use the U.S. navy to suppress piracy and allowed the navy to recapture U.S. citizens and vessels "unlawfully" taken upon the high seas.[122] Through a series of legislation, the administration of President James Monroe and Secretary of State John Quincy Adams removed the enforcement of U.S. neutrality from local customs officials' hands, reasserted federal authority, and sent the message that laws would now be enforced.[123]

Having adopted the Neutrality and the Piracy Acts, the U.S. government now had a more robust legal arsenal at its disposal to expand its jurisdiction on domestic and international waters.[124] The Boricua affair, however, exposed that U.S. state control was still inadequate at best, negligent at worst. The leaders of the expedition met no obstacle during their summer preparations. U.S. law required two-thirds of ship crews to be U.S. American. The revolutionaries suspected that the presence of French and Afro-Caribbean men could raise concern. They quickly found a solution: after clearing New York customs, one of the ships lingered for a few days around Staten Island to embark Jeannet-Oudin, two of his family members, and several Afro-Caribbean men.[125]

In October 1822, the failed expedition against Puerto Rico made the front pages of newspapers around the United States. The ineffectiveness of the government to enforce its own laws on its own soil became public. When

U.S. special envoy Joel Roberts Poinsett stopped at Puerto Rico, Spanish authorities expressed their discontent. Poinsett wrote his administration and recommended that U.S. authorities exercise more vigilant policing on their soil since these expeditions were "so dishonorable to our country."[126] Appalled that "something so disgraceful [happened] to our country," the press pressured the government to launch an inquest: "The piracies *abroad* give us trouble enough," the *Niles' Weekly Register* wrote. "Let us have no *domestic* expeditions that have any *resemblance* to piracy."[127] The press shamed the government. Allowing foreigners to organize such "wild, or worse than wild expedition" on U.S. soil constituted "illegal, unwarrantable practices," warned the *Niles' Weekly Register.*[128]

In December 1822, the secretary of state commissioned the U.S. district attorney for Philadelphia, Charles Jared Ingersoll, who concluded his inquest within two months. The lack of secrecy around the expedition meant that he easily gathered evidence, including insurance policies and ship manifestoes. He interviewed the collectors of Philadelphia and New York who pleaded ignorance.[129] In short, Ingersoll concluded, "Why and how this expedition so far eluded the notice of the public officers of the United States as to have met no obstruction" was a mystery.[130]

The word "pirate" inflamed the public's imagination. An observant Philadelphian kept count of "piratical acts" committed in the West Indies between 1815 and 1822; they numbered precisely 3,002.[131] The *East Florida Herald* published several stories on the pirates in their neighborhood, including a poem on piracy and degeneracy in Cuba. The island begged for U.S. intervention, "Ere the Eagle of Freedom on thy turret shall light."[132] Shipowners, as well as newspapers, demanded action. The Boricua expedition was on everyone's mind when, in November 1822, the U.S.S. *Alligator* attacked pirates off Matanzas in Cuba. Naval officer William H. Allen was mortally wounded, and his death sparked fury in U.S. public opinion.[133]

"Death to the pirates!" became a rallying cry. All eyes were now on the Caribbean. The government grew concerned about its reputation with foreign powers. Members of the government were keen to put the scandal behind them. They wanted to show both the world and their own citizens that the United States was a country of law and order. The United States decided to extend its power at sea. In December 1822, President Monroe asked Congress to dispatch a permanent squadron for the suppression of piracy in the West Indies and the Gulf of Mexico.[134] He noted that the situation was out of control: Spanish authorities were weak or incompetent, and the United States needed to intervene. "The public prints were full of complaints on the subject," Monroe insisted, and "inquiries were constantly made . . . why our force did not repress those evils."[135] In addition to the defense of law and order, humanitarian concerns were raised. The U.S. agent in Cuba sent Congress the testimony of a young U.S. sailor that pirates had hanged the captain of his ship from the yardarm.[136] Anxious to restore its international image as well as protect U.S. trade and populations, Congress voted a budget of over $100,000, or a tenth of the navy's annual budget. Forces cruising on the coast of Africa cost over $150,000 a year and the forces in the Mediterranean almost $300,000.[137] Congress also consolidated executive powers and made "permanent law" that the president could use public vessels to respond to piracy threats.[138] Under Commodore David Porter, the West Indies squadron sailed off in February 1823.[139]

As the first significant venture of the United States into Caribbean waters, the West Indies squadron experienced early setbacks. Sovereignty both on land and at sea presented a challenge that was perhaps more devastating than yellow fever. U.S. forces did not have the right to search vessels flying the flag of other countries. They could not detain anyone suspected of piracy captured in Spanish waters and had to turn them over to authorities in Cuba and Puerto Rico.[140] The same authorities prohibited U.S. forces from setting foot on their territories to pursue alleged pirates. A guard at the Moro fort in San Juan shot a U.S. officer in early 1823. The governor of Puerto Rico explained to the U.S. commodore that it was an unfortunate but predictable mistake since the recent Boricua expedition was on people's minds. Puerto Ricans were reluctant to let vessels flying the U.S. flag enter their ports.[141] The comparison of his squadron to Ducoudray-Holstein's "lawless invaders" outraged the commodore. Defending the honor of his country, he found it unjust to blame the United States. "Bad men escape, sometimes," he noted, "the vigilance of the most rigid authorities."[142] The same commodore, David Porter, was later court-martialed for breaching Puerto Rican territorial sovereignty by landing a party on Puerto Rican soil to intimidate local authorities.[143]

The West Indies squadron had more success buttressing the international reputation of the United States. "There has been a degree of publicity given to the expedition, and an interest felt in it, that have rarely been equaled," the commodore of the squadron remarked. "The whole of the civilized world was interested in its success."[144] In fact, the world did take notice. This new interventionist policy was a concern across the Atlantic. The French consul in Philadelphia forwarded news of Monroe's intentions to Paris and remarked, "The machinations, the discourses, and the intrigues that have preceded the invasion of Amelia Islands, and of Florida, are repeating themselves with striking similarity." He noted that the size of the U.S. force sent to the Caribbean "was too important to fight a few unfortunate pirates."[145] Piracy, the French authorities concluded, was merely an excuse to extend the U.S. presence in the region and enhance U.S. political, strategic, and commercial interests. In April 1823, a French army invaded Spain to end constitutional monarchy and restore the absolute power of the Bourbon king. This intervention revived fears of France's ambitions in the Americas.[146] Should a revolution disrupt Puerto Rico and Cuba, the governor of Martinique was instructed to assist Spanish colonial authorities without giving any reason to Britain or the United States to think that a French annexation was in the cards. The U.S. secretary of state warned the French government that the United States would intervene should it attempt to occupy Cuba or Puerto Rico.[147]

U.S. Congress considered moving its intervention from the sea to the islands themselves. Indiana representative John Test argued that the "shores of Cuba and Puerto Rico [had] been lent, literally lent, to a band of pirates" and that Spain was unable to protect its Caribbean colonies from the "pollutions of piracy." He concluded that piracy and the weakness of the Spanish to control it justified annexing the two colonies.[148] Secretary of War John Quincy Adams expressed an "ardent desire that the island of Cuba should become part of the United States."[149] New York representative Cadwallader D. Colden made a parallel between Aury's occupation of Amelia Island and Ducoudray-Holstein's attempted takeover of Puerto Rico. The United States should not tolerate any hostile expedition against Puerto Rico, he argued: "Our justification for [invading Amelia] was that it was a harbor for pirates or a place where expeditions were fitted out." The same should happen, he implied, with Puerto Rico or Cuba.[150]

The two Spanish colonies were also the objects of attention in South America. A joint Colombian-Mexican military alliance to liberate the Spanish colonies was short-lived. Bolívar feared that an independent Cuba or Puerto Rico would turn into another republic of Haiti and decided against direct intervention.[151] U.S. president John Quincy Adams shared this fear. A Colombian-Mexican expedition against Cuba would provoke the British into occupying the island. Even worst, Adams cautioned, an expedition might upend the status quo and unleash the racial horrors of another Haiti.[152] Various world powers, including the United States, France, Britain, and Gran Colombia, toyed with the idea of annexing Cuba and Puerto Rico. In the end, the fragile political equilibrium and the fear that political independence would inflame enslaved populations meant that Spanish control prevailed in the Caribbean.[153]

Bolívar and other Latin American leaders began to distance themselves from the Caribbean. They not only halted plans to liberate Cuba and Puerto Rico but also severed ties with Haiti. They grew concerned with alienating other governments. Bolívar, the recipient of Haitian president Alexandre Pétion's support, assistance, and shelter during the wars of independence, did not invite Haiti to the Pan-American Congress of Panama in 1826.[154] His racial prejudices and political strategizing led him to exclude "the North Americans and the Haitians," because, he argued, "they are foreigners and have a heterogeneous character for us."[155] Bolívar eventually reached out to the United States but remained firm and refused to invite Haiti. The exclusion of Haiti further isolated the black-led independent state. When France recognized the independence of its former colony in 1825, it imposed a heavy financial compensation, which crippled Haitian economic development.[156] Great Britain extended official recognition soon after France did. Britain recognized Latin American republics only in November 1825, and France refrained from following suit.[157]

Political independence in the Caribbean came to a halt. Haiti stood alone surrounded by islands—Cuba, Puerto Rico, Saint Barthélemy, Saint Thomas, Guadeloupe, and Jamaica—still under imperial rule. The contagion of revolution had been contained.

*   *   *

Defining who had a legitimate right to revolution had immediate practical implications. Should the revolutionaries have the rights of lawful combatants, or should they be prosecuted as criminals? Atlantic powers never fully decided on an answer. After the Boricua expedition, they did wish to send a message to other aspiring revolutionaries. Authorities in Curacao charged the leaders of the expedition first with piracy, then with treason.[158] They were "adventurers without a home, without a nation," the captain-general of Puerto Rico declared.[159] Governments and newspapers all around the Atlantic Ocean categorized them as pirates, adventurers, and vagabonds. Yet, despite these condemnations, the revolutionary leaders suffered no grave consequences.

The lack of existing treaties or conventions meant that consuls and diplomats were initially hesitant to extend diplomatic protection, but they eventually intervened on behalf of the prisoners. The men's pasts—Ducoudray-Holstein as an officer of the Napoleonic and Bolivarian armies, Jeannet-Oudin as a colonial administrator, and Irvine as a journalist—attracted public attention and protected them. Dutch authorities recognized them as political prisoners, letting them await their judgment in the comfort of boarding and private houses, not in the damp walls of a jail. The diplomatic maelstrom around their arrest showed the fluidity, or rather the confusion, around the legal framework governing jurisdictions and diplomatic protection in the early nineteenth century. The lack of clear international rules sometimes benefited the revolutionaries accused of piracy. It rarely benefited revolutionaries of African descent, as evidenced by Dubois's execution in Puerto Rico. In his case, the association between a revolutionary plot and a slave rebellion, combined with the color of his skin, proved fatal.

On his return to the United States, a pardoned but disgraced Ducoudray-Holstein was cruelly reminded of the contingency of heroism when President James Monroe invited the Marquis de Lafayette, the French hero of the U.S. revolution. Ducoudray-Holstein sensed an opportunity to clear his name and took pen to paper once again. In September 1824, as Lafayette embarked on a thirteen-month tour throughout the country, Ducoudray-Holstein published *Memoirs of Lafayette*: "From one extremity of the Union to the other, but one cry is heard, *Welcome La Fayette!*"[160] Critics were not enthralled (the *North American Review* found the book "not entitled to credit"), but the public was eager to read this laudatory biography, and 5,000 copies sold within a few months.[161] Although Ducoudray-Holstein failed to make history with the Boricua republic, he made a career of his proximity to more famous revolutionaries. He published *Memoirs of Bolivar* in 1829. Despite—or probably because of—his portrait of the Libertador as a despotic and lascivious character, the book was a success and swiftly appeared in London, Paris, and Hamburg. Ducoudray-Holstein then shifted his attention to another national hero and made a nice income writing stories about Napoléon.[162]

Defining who had a legitimate right to revolution also had wider political implications. The response to the Boricua expedition revealed how international cooperation could expand the regulatory reach of modern states. Governments across the Atlantic depicted the expedition as part of an uncontrollable wave of piracy and political subversion that needed to be stopped. When the Boricua expedition showed the inability of the U.S. government to exert control over its territory and enforce its own laws, the United States was provoked to demonstrate its respectability vis-à-vis other states as well as U.S. public opinion. The government turned to maritime intervention to promote the image of the United States as a serious geopolitical actor and demonstrate parity with European powers. In his presidential message to Congress in late

1823, President Monroe pointed with pride to the expansion of the U.S. navy protecting "public law and public interest" in the Caribbean.[163]

The 1820s was a decade of reconfiguration and recalibration during which European governments recognized the sovereignty of independent states in Latin America and Haiti formally. Financial capital in the form of loans and investments soon followed in the wake of this diplomatic recognition.[164] The governments of Mexico and Gran Colombia decided not to intervene in Cuba and Puerto Rico and suspended extraterritorial revolutionary plans for fear of provoking further havoc. Republics would not rise on the soils of the two islands in the nineteenth century.

CHAPTER 5

Crocodiles and Country Houses

Revolutionary Memories

Around 1835, Costante Ferrari redacted his memoirs while staying in his country house in northern Italy. His tale was of a life well lived. His decision to enlist in the French revolutionary army as a teenager had launched a tumultuous career that spanned two continents and multiple battlefields. His comrade-in-arms, Agustín Codazzi, had been by his side. Together, they traveled to the Caribbean and fought in the cosmopolitan forces of the French republican Louis-Michel Aury. They went back to Europe after a few years. The return journey had been perilous, Ferrari recounted. The intoxicated captain of their ship hit a sandbar near the coast of Cuba and immobilized the vessel. A small group, including Codazzi, grabbed a pirogue and paddled up a river full of crocodiles to get help. When they returned to the beach, a terrible storm broke out; Codazzi and his group became disoriented. A member of the small rescue party safely guided them back to the schooner.[1] The man who saved the day was Francesco, an African-born sailor who, along with another African named Mameluk, managed to get the ship off the sandbar. The four men resumed their journey together. The Italian revolutionaries headed for their region of origin, the northern Italian province of Emilia Romagna, and a happy reunion with friends and family, while their African companions entered foreign lands. The four of them purchased a country estate near Lugo—a quiet sanctuary from the world of adventures and crocodiles they had left behind. Ten years later, Ferrari sat in the house, alone with his memories.

This anecdote in Ferrari's memoirs illustrates the complicated forms of affiliation and historical memory in the revolutionary and postrevolutionary periods. Codazzi and Ferrari served across Europe in Napoléon's armies before crossing the Atlantic Ocean to seek new exciting opportunities.

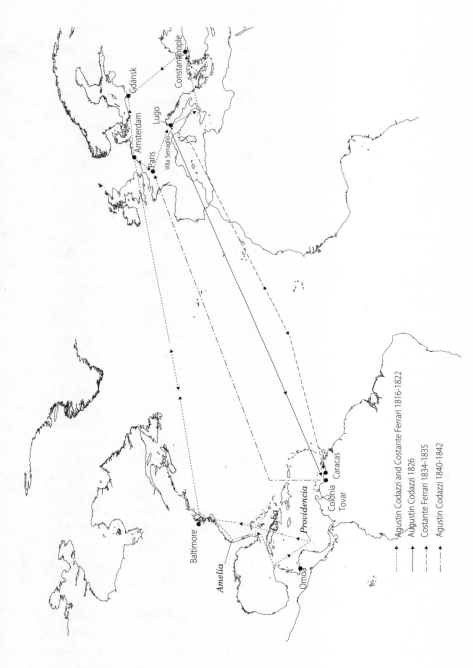

Map 6. The voyages of Agustin Codazzi and Costante Ferrari, 1815–1842.

Gdánsk
Constantinople
Lugo
Amsterdam
Paris
Villa Serraglio

Baltimore
Amelia
Cuba
Providencia
Colonia Tovar
Caracas
Omoa

Agustin Codazzi and Costante Ferrari 1816-1822
Agustin Codazzi 1826
Costante Ferrari 1834-1835
Agustin Codazzi 1840-1842

Mameluk and Francesco had first crossed the Atlantic Ocean on a Spanish slave ship. They became the property of Codazzi and Ferrari when the revolutionaries captured the ship and brought the enslaved crew to the Caribbean enclave of Providencia Island. The Africans gained their freedom but remained with the two Italians. All four men cultivated, lost, and regained personal, national, and supranational affiliations as they moved across space. Power rested at the heart of mobility. The Italian and the African revolutionaries experienced mobility differently: one pair was pursuing liberty and fortune, and the other was caught in the exploitative slave trade. When Ferrari recounted Francesco saving the day in Cuba, the African soldier knew what was at stake. Cuba had a thriving slavery-based economy, and the coast where the vessel hit a sandbar, the Jardines de la Reina, was infamous for slave ships smuggling their cargoes on isolated cays. While Codazzi and Ferrari feared losing their hard-earned money, Mameluk and Francesco feared losing their freedom.

Personal transformation often accompanied physical movement. The nineteenth century marked the high tide of historical writing: historians and intellectuals wrote national histories and founded museums, archives became depositories of a common past, and history turned into a scholarly discipline.[2] But educated elites were not the only ones popularizing history. Individuals across the Atlantic world were eager to explore their own pasts and make their voices heard thanks to changes in printing techniques, spread of literacy, and an emerging mass consumer culture.[3] War recollections and memoir writing notably flooded the literary scene in Western Europe after Napoléon's defeat in Waterloo.[4] Codazzi and Ferrari produced various vehicles of historical self-presentation throughout their lifetimes, whether written (memoirs) or visual (maps and drawings). They used retellings of the past to reinvent themselves.[5]

The trail of self-documentation exemplified the gradual nationalization of historical memory: the two men began their careers eschewing imperial and national spaces, borders, and identities until these spaces, borders, and identities gradually came to circumscribe them. Their first memoirs, produced after they bought an Italian country house in the mid-1820s, celebrated an unmoored, military, and cosmopolitan mode of affiliation. Moving from one war to the next, their uniform was their identity: the flag for which they fought had little importance. The appeal of a settled and peaceful life in the Italian countryside proved short-lived, however. Codazzi and Ferrari soon parted ways, with the former embarking on a career as a geographer in Gran Colombia and the latter fighting in Greece and in Italy. These travels between the mid-1820s and the 1850s coincided with centralizing states promoting national histories against local or cosmopolitan identities.[6] Codazzi and Ferrari began to fashion themselves into a Colombian and an Italian patriot, respectively. They linked their personal histories to nationally and territorially bounded histories to make claims to compensations, rights, and benefits that began to be attached to national citizenship. In doing so, they eventually participated in consolidating fragile nation-states.

For the Africans Mameluk and Francesco, the choice between a cosmopolitan fraternity and a citizenship confined to the bound space of a nation-state occurred in an environment of violence and insecurity. They risked reenslavement as well as political and legal disenfranchisement. Not only did the four men experience mobility and affiliation differently, the imbalance of sources documenting the lives of these men also reflected asymmetrical relations of power. Historical memories resulted from the violence embedded in the experience of place and mobility.[7] Storytellers with the "ability to exchange experiences," Codazzi and Ferrari were able to enter the historical records on their own terms.[8] In contrast, the two Africans did not leave introspective records revealing the ways they imagined their voyages or their understandings of affiliation in the Atlantic world.[9] The reconstruction of Mameluk and Francesco's lives remains fragmentary—their experiences filtered through the memories of their enslavers.[10]

The Excitement of Military Life

Both Codazzi and Ferrari's memoirs described restlessness early in their lifetimes: "I was craving since my youngest age, for travel and for a military career," Codazzi recalled, "a type of life that, would allow me to cross faraway seas, to see remote regions, and the various and prodigious natural wonders from one end to the world to the other."[11] This restlessness was hard to reconcile with ordinary life. The two men wrote their memoirs while staying in their Italian estate between two adventures. Codazzi drafted his account around 1825 after serving the republican cause in the Caribbean; Ferrari wrote his in 1835 after taking refuge in France to escape retaliations after participating in a liberal uprising in Italy. The transition to civilian life was difficult, and both felt restless. Ferrari described his melancholia becoming "invincible" during times of peace.[12] They hoped to counter these feelings by putting pen to paper and reminisced about their pasts. The two men were born about eighty miles apart, Ferrari in 1785, Codazzi in 1793, in the agricultural region of Emilia Romagna. At the time, Italy was a "geographical expression," as Europe's leading diplomat Count Metternich later called it. It was not a nation but a conglomeration of principalities occupying a space known as the Italian peninsula.[13] On the other side of the Alps, a revolutionary government executed Louis XVI in January 1793 and declared war on European monarchies. In July, Giovanni Battista Agostino Codazzi was held over the baptismal font of the church in Lugo, a small city of about 8,000 inhabitants, which belonged to the Papal States. Three years later, the quiet city erupted with the drums of the French Revolution.

French revolutionary troops advanced throughout northern Italy at a fast pace. In October 1797, Napoléon, the commander-in-chief of the Armée d'Italie, signed the Treaty of Campo Formio, placing Emilia Romagna within a newly created Cisalpine Republic, a sister- or client-republic of France. He imposed a constitution and stated that the French Republic had acquired northern Italy "by right of conquest," he continued, "and leaves the Republic free and independent."[14] The French government of the Directory and Bonaparte claimed to support the spread of republican principles in Europe, but most of these republics were occupied lands under a mix of French and local control.[15] The inhabitants of Lugo initially resisted but capitulated after a few hours of street altercations.

The upheaval of war changed the daily lives of many Italians. Costante Ferrari wrote that as soon as he could walk, he loved to play with wooden sabers.[16] The army received a warm welcome in Reggio a few weeks after they took over Lugo. A provisional government was set up, and volunteers pushed back an Austrian attack. Among them was the eleven-year-old fiery teenager Ferrari, who fought alongside his father. Familial and national prides were intertwined, and Ferrari moved to Milan to join the militia with one of his brothers. His beloved parents began to express their doubts: the pay was low, and they did not deem militia service respectable.[17] Meanwhile, Napoléon's ambitions continued to grow; he overthrew the Directory government and became first consul. Ferrari embraced the new regime and joined the ranks of the French army in 1802. In 1805, following his assumption of the title of Emperor of the French, Napoléon turned the Italian republic into a kingdom, with himself as sovereign and his stepson as viceroy. Napoléon waged war on other European powers, and the conflicts took Ferrari away from his native region. He went to France for training and then to Spain to control the anti-Napoleonic resistance, which he later remembered as "truly a cruel and terrible war."[18] The Spanish resistance also featured a politico-religiously inspired protest, fueling Ferrari's mistrust of Catholicism and religions in general.

Back in Lugo, Codazzi started to study philosophy but found the prospects of adventure and travel promised by military life more appealing:
"Neither domestic conditions, nor paternal advice, neither the inevitable
pain of leaving my dear family nor the dangers of the war that was tearing
up Europe, could temper my desires."[19] Indeed, in 1810, as soon as he turned
seventeen, Codazzi left school and trained in the horse artillery. He went
on to serve in the German and Russian campaigns. A series of defeats in
1814 weakened Napoléon, who went into exile. The Grande Armée was in
disarray.[20] Codazzi joined the Italo-British forces at Genoa when the commander of British troops, Lord Bentinck, attempted to overthrow the French
occupation by circulating liberal proclamations and plans for an independent Italy. Embarrassed, the British government recalled Bentinck. Codazzi
was demobilized.[21] So was Ferrari. When Ferdinand VII regained his throne
in Spain, Ferrari's battalion returned home. Unsure of what his future held,
Ferrari recalled that his only bright moment was when he reunited with his
father. The two men shared news about relatives and friends along with their
apprehensions about the situation. By then, Ferrari had been serving in the
army for almost half of his life.[22]

By 1815, Napoléon's attempted "liberation" of the European continent had
failed; Bentick's unauthorized liberation of Italy had suffered a similar fate.
But Codazzi and Ferrari's experiences with failed political and social schemes
had only just begun. Like thousands of demobilized soldiers and officers, the
two men needed employment. Codazzi picked up a mercantile career and
traveled to Constantinople. He became quickly bored; he was a soldier, not a
merchant. At a café, he met a group of destitute ex-Napoleonic officers who
were futilely looking for military opportunities in the Ottoman Empire. He
crossed paths with his compatriot Ferrari. Over a bottle a rum, the two men
discovered that they had much in common—notably a predilection for grand
projects. They briefly considered creating their own colony and set their
sights on an isle in the Princes' Islands—an archipelago near Constantinople.
However, the lack of enthusiasm shown by other veterans put a damper on
the plan.[23]

The veterans-turned-mercenaries-for-hire struck a lifelong friendship,
pledging "to be forever united, to defend each other, and to share one wallet and one will."[24] To be united and to defend each other was one thing; to
fill up a wallet was another. They heard that the Russian emperor Alexandre
I was hiring, and they traveled through the Balkans—then under Ottoman
rule—reaching Bucharest, Moldavia, and Ukraine. Meeting former veterans
on the way, they learned that demobilized Polish officers had saturated the

mercenary market in Russia. With their funds diminishing, they listened intently to tales of opportunities in the Americas. They received a recommendation from a former Napoleonic general in Gdańsk, and in January 1817, they embarked for Amsterdam. Shortly after, they boarded another ship, along with 250 other Europeans, in the direction of North America.[25]

Battlefields were supposed to forge heroes; they created instead an unemployed pool of officers and soldiers. Chance played a key role in the lives of the men scattered across Europe after the massive military mobilization of the revolutionary and Napoleonic wars. Codazzi and Ferrari may have well ended up in Russia or in the Ottoman Empire instead of revolutionary America. Redacting their life stories allowed the two men to create order out of this serendipity that transported them from one place to another. Memoirs were a way to immortalize their names by linking them to the Grande Armée. Furthermore, the public was eager to read firsthand recollections of recent history.

The military rhetoric of the Napoleonic wars had emphasized a political and emotional connection among officers and soldiers across vast geographic spaces. Napoléon's armies were fulcrums where thousands of men from Europe and North Africa met. They reached their maximum size of 600,000 men at the start of the invasion of Russia in 1812. The memoirs written by veterans celebrated this kind of intense military friendship that superseded all other affiliations. It then developed into a model of affection and camaraderie among nineteenth-century circles of radicals and romantics.[26] Ferrari devoted three-quarters of his memoirs to his adventures in the Napoleonic army, concluding on the "sadness and regret of all the officers" when they parted ways "after such a long time of common lives and common dangers."[27]

Imagined military affiliations created a vast network of veterans. When Codazzi and Ferrari traveled throughout Europe and the Ottoman Empire, they relied on this network for hospitality and information. Their memoirs foregrounded this insatiable need for both adventure and support. When Codazzi and Ferrari crossed the Atlantic Ocean and arrived in Baltimore in 1817, they stayed in an inn managed by a French immigrant. At least the food was good. After months of deprivation, Ferrari devoured his potato-based dishes. He was not so fond of the tea he drank, dejectedly reminiscing about "the excellent wines of our Italy." The potatoes and the tea came with opportunities: the innkeeper introduced them to a French ex-officer, Admiral Villaret.[28] He had worked as captain of a corsair in Guadeloupe under revolutionary civil commissioner Victor Hugues. He joined the Republic of Cartagena around 1812 when he befriended Louis-Michel Aury, following him to Haiti and Texas. When he met the two Italians in Baltimore, he was on a mission to recruit volunteers for the independence cause.[29]

After years of service in imperial armies, Codazzi and Ferrari were now ready to promote the cause of independence and republicanism. Villaret warned the two prospective revolutionaries, "Our war is bloody . . . the parties at war offer no quarter to one another: our troops sometimes live in abundance, and sometimes they lack the bare minimum." Although clothes and pay might be hard to come by, Villaret promised that there were "means to grow rich, and the [Venezuelan] Government is rather generous towards those who serve zealously and faithfully giving them lands, habitations, and advancement."[30] Codazzi and Ferrari did not hesitate. Ferrari abhorred the "ferocious" Spaniards, having fought them for five years in Europe; he was also eager to put his experience at the service of a people that was trying, he remembered, "to acquire the sacred rights of Independence."[31]

A brief stay in the United States also gave the two men a chance to enrich their political education. If Ferrari was as uninterested in U.S. politics as he was in their wines, Codazzi was more curious. A freemason, he admired that "the laws [were] dictated by a people truly sovereign, ruled by civil laws and not by religion like in Italy."[32] He believed that popular sovereignty, free education, and religious freedom were people's natural rights. Codazzi ruminated on these ideas as he and Ferrari boarded the Venezuelan ship *América Libre* and sailed to Norfolk, Philadelphia, and Charleston. At each port, they enlisted men until the ship boasted more than 200 French, Polish, Italian, American, Spanish, and African American volunteers.[33] The motley crew sailed to Amelia Island, where Louis-Michel Aury had set up the Republic of the Floridas. Their stay was brief. They left when the U.S. army occupied the island in January 1818. Codazzi and Ferrari followed Aury when he seized Providencia Island in July 1818. When Aury died three years later, the two friends assessed their options.

Ferrari and Codazzi decided that the itinerant and adventurous military life was over. They desired, Codazzi wrote in his memoirs, to have "a life less dangerous [than] the one that took [them] on the field of glory, or on the fragile ships in an unstable element."[34] They received two years' worth of pay, half in cash and half in merchandise (mostly indigo). Ferrari also had a good luck at gambling.[35] They met Aury's sister in Paris so that they could give her a share of her brother's inheritance before returning to Lugo. The two men shared the same dream: according to Ferrari, they pledged to finish their lives together, "settle down and have a family." The two men purchased a farm in the countryside of Massa Lombarda, near their native towns of Lugo and

Reggio, so that they could "live more freely," Ferrari claimed.[36] They reno-
vated the house in the neoclassical style with clear straight lines of pilasters
and picots. They named it Il Serraglio.

However, quiet settled life proved to be unsatisfying. Ferrari wrote that
he longed for his "garments of soldier."[37] An opportunity arose in 1824 when
hundreds of volunteers from Paris, Geneva, London, Philadelphia, and New
York flocked to Greece to assist rebels against the Ottoman Empire. This
international movement of solidarity felt familiar to Ferrari. For Italians,
volunteering with the Greeks was also a way to stand against the conservative and royalist legitimists who had imposed their policies on Italy at the
Congress of Vienna. They were the same legitimists who, at the Congress of
Laibach, officially branded the Greek revolt a product of the same anarchical
spirit that had produced revolts in Spain, Portugal, Piedmont, and Naples.[38]

The "cause of freedom" was enticing, and Ferrari yearned to hold a
weapon again. Although the number of volunteers who went to Greece was
relatively small (over a thousand, most of them English, French, and Italian),
the Greek war of independence was the revolution of the Romantic age. It
inspired painters, poets, and patriots the world over, including Lord Byron.
Unlike Byron, Ferrari made it back to Italy alive but broke. Codazzi convinced his friend to marry the daughter of a wealthy professor to keep the
Serraglio afloat. The young bride moved to the Serraglio in July 1825.[39]

The Serraglio exemplified a phenomenon that grew out of the intense
friendships formed during wartime: veterans depended on these bonds to
navigate political disfavor and material hardships in postwar Europe, and
they sometimes shared a retirement. The Restoration government in France
paid most veterans only half-pensions, often denying the claims of foreigners.
Codazzi and Ferrari relied on each other.[40] The two men created their own
mini-homeland on their estate in the Italian countryside. It was a small bit of
landed property where they could rule a domestic space together.

In their memoirs, Codazzi and Ferrari displayed a strong sense of regional
pride even as foreign powers occupied their homeland. In his memoirs,
Codazzi used the expression *la mia patria* (my country) to refer to Lugo, his
native town. Writing ten years later when the Italian liberation movement
was on the rise, Ferrari used the same expression to refer to "Italy." Although
Ferrari's memoirs briefly invoked the dream of a sovereign and united Italy,
his ultimate attachment was to the region where he was born.

Codazzi wrote his memoirs around the time Ferrari went to Greece. His
goal was to give his friends "a more circumstantial version of [his] adventures," but this "circumstantial version" reveals that Codazzi was an unreliable

narrator. He inserted himself into at least two adventures in Texas and in Argentina. According to his memoirs, he went to Texas to meet Aury and Xavier Mina to attack Mexico. However, Codazzi and Ferrari joined the revolutionary movement in September 1817; by then, Aury had left Galveston and Mina was already in Mexico.[41] Codazzi also described a trip Aury's squadron took to Rio de la Plata in spring 1818—a trip that never took place.

Codazzi's embellishments in his memoirs derived from his conversations with other members of Aury's forces. By associating himself with Xavier Mina, a Spanish hero who resisted Napoléon's invasion of the Iberian Peninsula and fought Ferdinand VII's absolute monarchy first in Spain and then in Mexico, Codazzi drew a parallel between his and Mina's career. Mina was a *cause célèbre* in liberal circles. Mina had come, Codazzi noted, "to erase the shame and the blood that still stain the places where Moctezuma used to walk."[42] Although Codazzi had fought in the same Napoleonic army that Mina had opposed, he saw no contradiction in comparing himself to Mina. Both men were international freedom fighters in his view. Similarly, the invented trip to Rio de la Plata legitimized Codazzi's actions retrospectively since it was there, according to his memoirs, that, in February 1818, the director of the United Provinces of Rio de la Plata officially granted Codazzi the title of artillery captain and Ferrari that of infantry sergeant major for the republics of Buenos Aires and Chile. The two men did receive these titles in February 1818 but from an unsanctioned agent of the South American republics.[43]

Codazzi's sojourn in the West Indies marked a turning point in the way he defined his affiliation. His memoirs included a reflection on postrevolutionary consolidation of power and praised the skills of Gran Colombian's vice president Santander: "if Bolívar liberated [the state of Gran Colombia], Santander was the one who turned it into a nation."[44] Santander was "the father of all," according to Codazzi, and he was the ideal political leader: fair, humble, rational, embracing Creoles and foreigners equally—as opposed to Bolívar. The Spanish American revolutions might have been the first time that Codazzi had to define his political loyalty and make decisions according to his own convictions. However, Codazzi's affiliations remained shaped by affection. He fought for Spanish American independence because it was the cause of his commanding officer, Louis-Michel Aury, who, Codazzi claimed, "had a tender heart and noble feelings," and he "loved his soldiers and was friends with his officers." In his memoirs, Codazzi insisted that he refused to join Gran Colombia's forces because Bolívar had unfairly treated foreigners and especially Aury, "a good general, a brave soldier, and a

committed republican."⁴⁵ As governments and chances for employment vac-
illated around Codazzi and Ferrari, personal connections and loyalties were
the driving forces behind their decisions.

Silenced Lives: Africans Across the Atlantic Ocean

At the Serraglio estate, two men planted white mulberry trees to feed a colony of silkworms: Mameluk and Francesco. They had settled in the Italian
countryside alongside Codazzi and Ferrari but as laborers rather than as land-
owners. For men who journeyed through so many regions of the world, from
Africa to the Caribbean and from Honduras to Italy, Mameluk and Francesco barely left any historical traces. They only briefly appeared in Codazzi
and Ferrari's memoirs. Codazzi summarized Mameluk and Francesco's existence in one sentence: they were "natives of the coast of Africa, whom we had
bought in Providencia and emancipated." He wrote, "but they wanted to follow us of their own free will and have remained with us, faithful companions
in various difficult situations, and it can be said that from 1819 until now they
have always been at our side."⁴⁶ Ferrari indicated simply that Mameluk and
Francesco were "our Moors" living at the Serraglio with them.⁴⁷

Mameluk and Francesco disrupt our understandings of affiliation for
Africans in the Atlantic world. Unlike many others, their story was not that
of a one-way journey from Africa to the Americas; it was one of multiple
passages, with each journey redefining their claim to full humanity. Within
ten years, the two men were torn from their native Africa, put in shackles on
a crowded Spanish ship, crossed an ocean, became soldiers on an island ruled
by an unrecognized government, crossed the Atlantic once more, traveled
to the bustling European capitals of Amsterdam and Paris, and moved to
the northern Italian countryside with their former enslavers.⁴⁸ The name
Mameluk hints at a possible connection with Napoléon since the French
imperial army included a special Mameluk corps. Many of them were formerly enslaved Arabs, Egyptians, or Turks. Codazzi and Ferrari might have
fought alongside this Mameluk corps in Russia or Spain and given him this
name. Other possibilities include Mameluk coming from northern Africa or
being Muslim.⁴⁹ The same mystery surrounds the name Francesco: Ferrari
might have chosen this name because it was his father's.

The stories of Mameluk and Francesco were rooted in the Atlantic commodification of African bodies. The two African men probably traveled on
the Spanish slave ship, the *Catalina*, seized by Louis-Michel Aury's privateer

vessels in 1819 and taken to Providencia.[50] The *Catalina* represented a new stage in the Atlantic slave trade. Starting in the 1810s, after Britain, which was the largest slave trader in the Atlantic world and the main importer of enslaved Africans to the Caribbean, outlawed the slave trade, Cuban colonists sent their own vessels directly to Africa.[51] Mameluk and Francesco were only two of over 40,000 enslaved men and women carried against their will by Spanish ships to the Caribbean between 1819 and 1822, the years when the two men lived in the republican establishment of Providencia. These were the years when large-scale sugar production in the Spanish colony of Cuba began to thrive and became the cornerstone of the island's economy. Cuba needed enslaved workers, preferably young men like Mameluk and Francesco. The number of slave ships sent from Cuba to Africa tripled between 1825 and 1835, the years when Mameluk and Francesco were in Italy.[52]

Shortly after the Congress of Vienna in 1815 condemned the slave trade as "irreconcilable with the principles of humanity and justice," Britain and Spain signed a bilateral treaty in agreement with this principle, but the Spanish government did little to enforce it. The trip the *Catalina* took was risky. The British Royal Navy patrolled the Atlantic Ocean. Between 1815 and 1825, over 100 slave ships left Cuba for Africa: the British arrested more than 30 of them and tried them at mixed commission courts in Sierra Leone.[53] Had the British navy arrested the *Catalina* near the coast of Africa, Mameluk and Francesco would have joined the so-called liberated Africans in Sierra Leone. They would have been baptized, received Christian names, and made to work for the British colony. Had British ships captured the *Catalina* close to American shores, they would have ended up in the Bahamian archipelago. There, although technically free, they would have been apprenticed for seven to fourteen years.[54] Had the *Catalina* made it to the Spanish colony, Mameluk and Francesco's life expectancy on a sugar plantation would have shrunk to eight years. The sugar harvest required backbreaking work, and enslaved laborers toiled long, hard hours clearing land and cutting cane.

Mameluk and Francesco's options broadened only slightly when they relocated from the hull of the *Catalina* to the beaches of Providencia. Codazzi and Ferrari never explained their reasons for emancipating Mameluk and Francesco, nor did they record how long they were enslaved. Both royalist and patriot armies during the wars needed enslaved soldiers, promising freedom in exchange for military service. The fact that Providencia was not an important plantation economy made Mameluk and Francesco more valuable as soldiers than as field hands. When Aury took over the island, he gathered the roughly 350 enslaved inhabitants and integrated them into his troops.

These enslaved soldiers, according to Ferrari, "were burning with liberalism" and embraced the new republic. When they turned eighteen, they received their freedom—which angered local planters. Yet Aury's decision proved to be providential. Shortly after his arrival, a terrible hurricane struck Providencia, and most of the troops fell ill. Provisions became scarce, and hunger drove the men mad. Insects turned into the stuff of nightmares. Sand fleas afflicted sailors and soldiers to the point that some lost their feet and legs. The formerly enslaved soldiers knew how to extract the fleas and calmed the wounds with tobacco ashes. They helped Aury keep control of the island against local planters and his own disgruntled troops until provisions, ammunitions, and money finally arrived from Jamaica.[55]

Codazzi's memoirs mentioned that Mameluk and Francesco joined the republican cause "of their own free will," which might indicate that they bargained for freedom in exchange for military service. However, the idea of "free will" obfuscated the mechanisms of domination that existed in the slavery-dominated world of the Caribbean. Mameluk and Francesco's relationships with the two Italian revolutionaries rested on an uneasy power imbalance that stood somewhere between Codazzi's egalitarian description of them as "faithful companions" and Ferrari's possessive descriptor "our Moors." The options of the two Africans were limited. Haiti would have been their only safe option in the region. The Haitian Constitution of 1816 reaffirmed the principle of free soil and declared that African and Afro-descendant refugees could enjoy the right of citizenship after one year of residence.[56] Mameluk and Francisco probably knew about these politics of free soil and black citizenship as Providencia frequently traded with Haiti, but they made no apparent attempt to settle there. They did not remain in Providencia when two ambitious free men of color from Saint-Domingue, Sévère Courtois and Jean-Baptiste Faiquère, came in power. Chances of being reenslaved were high. Europe, in the company of their former enslavers, probably appeared as a much safer alternative.

It is hard to imagine how the two Africans reacted to the hyperbolic declarations about "independence" and "liberty" made by the multinational, multiracial, and multilingual forces in Providencia. Mameluk and Francesco probably took part in a revolutionary expedition against the coast of Honduras in 1820. The resistance of local populations and their attachment to the Spanish Empire—including troops of African descent—certainly showed Mameluk and Francesco that political definitions of "free will" varied greatly. There were still 167 enslaved inhabitants in Providencia, most of them children, when Mameluk and Francesco left in 1822.[57] Providencia officially integrated the Republic of Colombia in June 1822. A year earlier, the Congress had passed the "free womb" law that stated that freeborn children of enslaved women had to work for their mother's masters until age eighteen as a form of compensation. The emancipation process did not conclude until 1851, when forty enslaved people still lived in Providencia.[58]

The two men were not the only enslaved Africans the Italians acquired. When the republican troops captured a Spanish slaver in 1818, each of the officers received a "prize." They chose enslaved women, except for Ferrari, who chose a young boy he named Souwarow. The rest of the enslaved prisoners were sold in Tortuga, off the northwest coast of Haiti, to be transported to various colonies. Souwarow was about twelve, and his age factored in Ferrari's decision to keep the young boy with him. As he explained in his memoirs, his intention was to "instruct him as I pleased."[59] The name Ferrari gave him, Souwarow, is intriguing—a possible reference to the famous Russian general Alexandre Suvorov, an impassioned counterrevolutionary who attempted to drive the French revolutionary forces out of northern Italy in 1799—the same forces in which Ferrari had enlisted as a teenager. The ambiguities around the young boy's name are an example of what Michel-Rolph Trouillot identified as "the interplay between inequalities in the historical process and inequalities in the historical narrative."[60] Whereas Suvorov, the Russian general who patrolled the European continent, entered posterity, Souwarow, the enslaved African who briefly lived on a small Caribbean island, only survived through the scant words written by his enslaver. Ferrari sold Souwarow when he left Providencia on the condition that he be freed after five years of service.[61]

Although Mameluk and Francesco were emancipated in Providencia, they constantly faced threats of reenslavement. When they embarked on a vessel alongside Codazzi and Ferrari and left Providencia, dodging crocodiles, pirates, and storms on the way, they viewed the schooner bound for Europe as their escape from these perils. Mameluk and Francesco adapted to their new lives at the Serraglio. The low-lying plains of Massa Lombarda bore little resemblance to the mountainous and wooded terrains of the Caribbean—although the marshes might have felt familiar. Francesco went with Codazzi to see his family, but the memoirs are silent on whether he was introduced as his "faithful companion" or as his servant. Did Mameluk and Francesco contribute to the purchase when Ferrari and Codazzi bought the Serraglio? Did they share the Italians' dream to live from the products of the land? The region was undergoing major transformations as subsistence farming dwindled and agriculture became more commercialized. We will never know if Mameluk and Francesco missed their lives in the Caribbean. Neither

Codazzi nor Ferrari could deal with this "life less dangerous" and rejoined military life in Colombia and in Greece. It is not known whether the Africans followed Codazzi and Ferrari in their adventures. Ferrari's memoirs last mentioned Francesco when the two men accompanied Codazzi to Bologna before he embarked for America in 1826.[62] Ferrari apparently returned to Lugo alone; Francesco might have stayed in Bologna or returned to America with Codazzi. Mameluk vanished from the records.

For Mameluk and Francesco, as for their enslavers Ferrari and Codazzi, personal connections might have been the determining factor in making decisions. They appeared more reliable than racial or community affiliations. In the case of Mameluk and Francesco, their affiliation with the Americas was tenuous, since they only spent three years in the Caribbean. The process of assimilation, acculturation, or resistance richly detailed for other Africans can only be surmised for Mameluk and Francisco.[63] Some scholars have shown that mobile individuals in the African diaspora articulated performative identifications and self-fashioning within each immediate location. As James Sweet argued, "A shift to a more thoroughly Atlantic approach can emphasize the multitude of overlapping cultural circuits and their influences on the individuals who moved through them."[64] The scant information contained in the few lines found in the memoirs of their enslavers or the inventory of their slave ship leaves the scholar struggling to fill in the gaps in their stories.

The voices of enslaved men were not the only ones that were silenced. Because they lived in societies ruled by the commodification of black bodies, sources on women of African descent are also fragmentary, especially when these women were involved in an economy of sexual labor.[65] Codazzi explained that many officers traveled to Jamaica and Haiti and "obtained" women who were brought back to Providencia.[66] These women provided essential services, cooking food, cleaning clothes, and building houses. In archives that ricocheted but never amplified their lives, they appeared as simultaneously oversexualized and domesticating figures.[67] "[Haitian] women, born in hot climates, possess a correspondingly hot temperament but," Codazzi noted, "they are faithful and behave with the care and affection that make good families."[68] In a Caribbean world with few white women, a white man's companionship with an Afro-Caribbean woman was but a pleasurable and temporary arrangement.[69]

The commodification of enslaved women was evident when the republican troops captured a Spanish slave ship in 1820. When Aury found a "gorgeous Negress" on board, he instructed Ferrari to take her to the fort on Providencia. Ferrari's description of the eighteen-year-old woman recalled the sentimental novels of the time. Praising her beauty, Ferrari insisted on her vivacity and intelligence. She was not an ordinary woman, Ferrari pointed out; she was the "fiancée" of one the enslaved Africans, whom Ferrari identified as a chief or a king. She was brokenhearted, but Ferrari's gentleness, or so he claimed, eventually consoled her. She remained a nameless entity, only described through the racial identity "Negress" assigned to her. Through this anecdote, Ferrari cast himself in the role of the gentle and caring slave trader, concerned about the woman's safety. The notion of "care" was crucial in the way race, gender, and republicanism intersected for revolutionaries like Codazzi and Ferrari. This notion gave them social and moral legitimacy as they portrayed themselves not only as men of arms but also as considerate gentlemen. By emphasizing how they cared for Africans—Souwarow, Mameluk, Francesco, the "gorgeous Negress"—in their memoirs, Codazzi and Ferrari framed themselves as benevolent patriarchs who looked after the powerless. In doing so, they concealed the ways they exploited them—and the contradictions of their egalitarian commitments.

Legal and Affective Affiliations

African-born Mameluk and Francesco never got a chance to write their own stories—or, if they did, these stories did not survive. These archival silences echoed political silencing. Countries across Europe and the Americas tentatively centralized their authority and developed more efficient, if still uneven, border controls and travel regulations. Bureaucracies began to use documentary evidence to parse citizens from noncitizens and trace boundaries of national communities. Most governments around the Atlantic basin did not recognize the full legal personhood of men of African descent: Napoleonic France, for example, enacted a series of repressive measures curtailing the rights of free people of color, including the right to travel freely. Authorities imprisoned and deported people of African descent found on French soil without permission.[70]

The participation of foreigners in the wars between Spain and its colonies reveals the tensions between the rights and the risks attached to national citizenship. Secretary of State John Quincy Adams deplored that "they [Latin-American independents] have countenanced and encouraged foreigners to enter their service, without always considering how far it might affect either the rights or the duties of the nations to which the foreigners belonged."[71] European and U.S. governments pursued a policy of neutrality, and the participation of their citizens could possibly force them to get involved. Furthermore, this participation showed the rest of the world that these governments were incapable of controlling their citizens.

The participation of foreigners in the Spanish-American wars occurred at a crucial moment as postrevolutionary countries such as the United States, France, and Haiti mobilized large numbers of men into national armies. In doing so, they fused patriotism and military service. The beginning of the nineteenth century marked the decline of mercenarism and the rise of the citizen-solider.[72] Soldiers deepened the meaning of national affiliation by making their sacrifice the ultimate gift citizens could offer to the homeland. Less honorable were those fighting for a country that was not theirs. Any act perceived as a transfer of allegiance, including bearing arms for another country, was punished. The United States passed three Neutrality Acts in 1794, 1797, and 1819 forbidding U.S. citizens at home and abroad from conspiring against states with which the United States was at peace. The 1819 act also forbade anyone within the United States from enlisting in a foreign military service.[73] Around that time, Secretary of State John Quincy Adams declared that the protection of the United States extended to citizens in foreign countries, but this declaration contradicted a proposed constitutional amendment in 1810 that would have sanctioned serving a foreign government with a loss of U.S. citizenship.[74] The French Civil Code was clearer: it denationalized those who entered the military service or the government of a foreign power without authorization.[75]

The foreigners serving under Spanish American flags presented unprecedented issues around the nature of national citizenship. To return to Secretary of State Adams, he instructed his agents to inform South American governments that "a Citizen of the United States cannot accept and act under such a commission, without at once violating the Laws of this country and forfeiting his rights and character as a citizen."[76] In Adams's view, citizenship was indivisible. However, what comprised these "rights and character as a citizen" was not clear. It was not even clear whether the U.S. government had the authority to denationalize or punish its citizens for actions taken abroad. The United States and France had come to a consensus: national affiliation was freely chosen and had to be exclusive. "One cannot have two homelands," the French Conseil d'Etat simply stated during the debates around the Civil Code in 1804.[77] Yet many felt that citizenship was an inalienable right, not a favor dependent on a government's whims.[78]

Despite states attempting to centralize and standardize the rights of citizens across and outside their territories, the meaning of national citizenship in the early nineteenth century remained fluid.[79] Enforcement was the key to this fluidity. Foreign military service might have been criminalized, but the application of these restrictions proved hazardous. Consular networks were small at the time: states such as France and the United States simply did not have the resources to control, police, and punish wayward nationals. These new definitions of patriotism and nationality as exclusive sometimes clashed with the ways individuals defined their affiliations. These affiliations often prevailed due to the weakness of central states.

The "statelessness" of Codazzi and Ferrari might have been a liberating status, an escape from the burdens of citizenship, and a gateway to cosmopolitanism, but it was also a status filled with vulnerability and precariousness. If countries punished their nationals, they also protected them. Codazzi and Ferrari might have been Italian patriots, but they were not Italian citizens. Italy became a unified state only in March 1861. There was no Italian consular network before that date. When U.S. troops took over Amelia, they preferred to negotiate. That was a stroke of luck for Codazzi and Ferrari: if the two men had no state authority to respect, they also had no state authority to protect them. When foreign volunteers from Britain, France, and the United States were captured, they turned to their consuls for help. Had U.S. or Spanish troops arrested Codazzi and Ferrari in America, no one would have come to their rescue.

Navigating the troubled waters of the Atlantic world, Codazzi and Ferrari's pledge "to be forever united, to defend each other, and to share one wallet and one will" was a chosen affiliation based on affection rather than a formal state-centered acceptance. In such an unstable world, the personal bond between the two men was their compass. This bond shattered when Codazzi returned to Gran Colombia in 1826. He was then a dashing thirty-four-year-old man, with a horseshoe-style mustache going down to his jawline. He exchanged a promise with Ferrari: he was to return within three years. Codazzi probably remembered Admiral Villaret's words ten years earlier when he first arrived in America: "the Venezuelan Government is rather generous towards those who serve zealously and faithfully giving out lands, habitations, and advancement."[80] Codazzi resumed his military career, this time under the official flag of Gran Colombia. His four-year stay in Europe probably helped him expunge his past association with the "pirate" Louis-Michel Aury. He led the artillery forces in the department of Zulia and defended the coast against Spanish naval forces from Cuba. This task turned into a new career as he launched a cartographic mission to map the department.[81]

During the 1820s, the place of foreigners in Colombian society became a matter of controversy. Many foreign veterans had to legitimize their presence in the country in order to secure their rights.[82] As noted in the Constitution of 1819, "those of the military, whether natives or foreigners, who fought for the liberty and independence of the *patria* in this war will enjoy the benefits of active citizenship."[83] A political consensus had emerged. The *Gaceta de Colombia* emphatically proclaimed that "thanks to the heroic triumphs won in bloody combats by our soldiers worthy of justice of our cause," the government promised the same rewards regardless of birthplace. This debate about the inclusion of foreigners in the new republics was part of a broader debate about defining national identities and reconstructing state infrastructures.[84] The 1821 Constitution, however, did not automatically give veterans full citizenship as promised in 1819: the offer of citizenship was hedged with property qualifications, a three-year residency, and marriage, thereby excluding many traveling soldiers. The foreigners who had connections among merchants, politicians, and administrators often had their claims rewarded, but others did not.[85] When military threats from Spain waned, military titles alone did not suffice. Marriage, not military service, became the principal criterion for integrating foreigners into the national family.[86] By marrying a woman from Cumanà in 1826, Codazzi secured his Colombian citizenship and his acceptance into the new state.

The image of foreigners alternated between potential threats and valuable additions to the republics. Creole elites in Spanish America gradually constructed a memory of the wars of independence that downplayed foreign heroes in favor of a reappropriation of the indigenous past.[87] Xenophobia targeted Spanish subjects. Rumors of Spanish invasions caused Mexico to expel Spaniards in 1827, 1829, and 1833 as part of what Claudio Lomnitz called an "excluding ideology (even a xenophobic ideology)."[88] In 1823, the Colombian government expelled Spaniards, excepting those who had served in the republican militia. Guatemala expelled Spaniards suspected of disloyalty in 1829.[89] Other foreigners were accepted and even welcome. Wars and epidemic diseases (particularly yellow fever and malaria) had ravaged the economy and the population. State officials viewed immigrants, particularly from Europe, as a way to offset the low rate of population increase. In addition, immigration formed part of a liberal ideology that emphasized the free movement of people and ideas but within a framework that reassured Creole elites of their political and economic control. An immigration law in this spirit was passed in 1824. The presence of foreigners, especially white and European, helped the Gran Colombian state to solidify its power and commitment to liberal reform.[90]

In 1831, Venezuela and Ecuador seceded and Gran Colombia collapsed. Codazzi acted swiftly. He sent the new Venezuelan government a map of three western provinces—Maracaibo, Merida, and Trujillo—and convinced Congress that a cartographic exploration was "an enterprise of the most importance for Venezuela."[91] Borders had to be drawn, roads had to be planned, and statistics had to be garnered. Civil conflicts regularly interrupted the commission's work, preventing an unstable and impoverished Venezuelan administration from exercising control over much of the territory it claimed.[92]

The geographic survey provided Codazzi with the opportunity to gain legitimacy and recognition by interpreting the geographical memory of the wars of independence. It may seem odd to analyze maps alongside memoirs. After all, memoirs are an inherently subjective and personal exercise while neat lines and clean-cut drawings lend maps an air of scientific objectivity. Memoirs foreground their authors while maps and atlases disguise them. The latter appear to reproduce and represent a geographical reality, adding a few lines and boundaries. They may be the product of political decisions and play a role in how the audiences imagine the space around them, but they are also vehicles through which their authors curate their own memories, feelings, and emotions.[93] Mapmaking is akin to memoir writing in the sense that both are acts of creation that reinvented their authors: Codazzi's *Atlas* is evidence of this process.

Codazzi traveled to Paris to oversee the publication of the *Physical and Political Atlas of Venezuela*. The *Atlas* was both a geographical and a historical work: "The most notable events of [Venezuela]'s history," Codazzi wrote in the prologue, "were intertwined with its geography."[94] He worked with Venezuelan army captain and writer Rafael María Baralt to publish a two-volume work, *Summary of the history of Venezuela*, to accompany the *Atlas*. A Parisian press published them in 1840. The wars of independence were central to both works: Baralt's second volume focused on the revolutionary and postrevolutionary years while Codazzi included four maps of the military campaigns. The works garnered honors from scientific societies in Europe and the United States.[95] The famous geographer and naturalist Alexander von Humboldt visited Codazzi and Baralt's workshop in Paris. These works "gave scientific form to the appropriation of territory," he noted approvingly, and "they affirmed the nascent republic and signified nationalist cohesion."[96]

Codazzi's *Atlas* and Baralt's *History* melded together revolutionary geographies and histories in order to legitimize the new republic in the eyes of the international community. Codazzi inserted himself in this narrative. Part of his effort to invent and disseminate an official genealogy of the Venezuelan state meant straightening out the messiness of his own past. Baralt's *History* only cursorily acknowledged the contribution of foreigners. European exiles joined the revolutions, but the motivations of these "pilgrims of liberty," as Baralt called them, were complex. Some were drawn by their "natural love for war, [some] obeyed their own revolutionary tendencies [while others] dreamed of fortune in the rich Hispano-American colonies."[97] There was no mention of Aury, Galveston, Florida, or Providencia in either work. Codazzi did not even include Providencia Island on the map that documented military campaigns against Spain. Only the island of San Andrés appeared at the very edge of the map. Codazzi successfully implanted himself in the Venezuelan national project by effacing his cosmopolitan past.

An earlier map reveals how Codazzi reinvented his past in fifteen years. Codazzi's first recorded mapping experiments took place when he wrote his memoirs in his Italian country house in the mid-1820s. He sketched three maps documenting his career in the Caribbean with Ferrari, Mameluk, and Francesco: the first was the Gulf of Mexico, the second was the Bay of Honduras where Aury's troops attacked twice, and the third was Providencia Island. The last one included a touch of color: using a red pencil, Codazzi added a road across Providencia. He used the same pencil to add five small and graceful houses to the town of Isabela, whose construction he detailed in his memoirs. Much the same way he constructed and reconstructed his participation to such major historical events as the Napoleonic wars and the Spanish-American wars of independence, Codazzi's cartographic archives reflect the plasticity with which he molded his past. While the Caribbean maps he sketched for his friends and family in 1825 foregrounded the revolutionary headquarters on Amelia and Providencia islands, the maps he produced for the 1840 national atlas of Venezuela did not acknowledge the existence of these two islands; he erased them from the national history of Venezuela.[98]

Territorial Borders and Identities

While Codazzi became the model naturalized citizen in Venezuela, reconstructing not only the geography but also the history of his new country, Ferrari transformed himself into the model patriot in his native land. Memoirs became narratives of self-reinvention. Ferrari's disillusionment with the Greek independence seekers convinced him that transnational collaboration was no longer a viable path of action. It was too precarious; he was paid, he recalled later, only with "ingratitude and bitter antipathy."[99] He focused his attention on turning his imagined homeland of Italy into a reality. In 1831, he offered his services to the liberal cause at home. As commander-in-chief at

Imola, some ten miles from his villa in Massa Lombarda, he declared that all "genuine Italians" desired national independence and unification.[100] The Austrian army sent troops to crush the insurrection. Ferrari escaped and joined the community of Italian political exiles in Marseille. Returning home after the general amnesty of 1833, Ferrari faced harassment from local authorities.[101]

Advancing in age, Ferrari had trouble managing the Serraglio estate on his own. He turned to his old friend Codazzi for help, having been without news for seven years. Ferrari made his way to Venezuela in 1834 and devoted over ten pages of his memoirs to this wild goose chase. The chase ended in sorrow. His old friend was married to a local woman and they expected a child. It finally dawned on Ferrari that Codazzi had forgotten about the Serraglio and their promise to live and die together. Dejected, Ferrari sailed back to Europe. It was at the time of his return that he wrote what he described as "Memoirs of my military life, my travels and the so many adventures I met." Carlo Ginzburg suggests that many writers use autobiography to tame the past.[102] Ferrari used writing to tame heartbreak. The collapse of the bond between the two men suffused the memoirs with melancholy. He declared his manuscript to be "a true confession so that my son can read and learn from the trials that tested his father, because it is what one can expect from the world, from men, and from fortune itself."[103] Ferrari was fifty and disenchanted. If personal affection was the only reliable bond in an unstable world, Ferrari took Codazzi's betrayal to heart. Now he felt utterly alone.

The former friendship between Codazzi and Ferrari turned sour. While editing his *Atlas* in Paris in 1840 and 1841, Codazzi wrote several letters to Ferrari about liquidating the farm and recuperating his original investment.[104] Ferrari ignored his demands. He donned his military garments again when the 1848 revolutions broke out. He commanded a troop of volunteers against the Austrians. Defeated, he retreated to the Serraglio only to learn that his son had died. When the newly elected Louis Napoléon sent French troops to defeat the republican government that had replaced the Papal States, Ferrari joined the protest in Rome in April 1849. Garibaldi and his forces were able to defend the city for two months, but the French ultimately restored the pope. Having experienced yet another failed political project, Ferrari returned to the Seragglio, where he died in 1851.[105]

While Ferrari was fighting the foreign occupation of northern Italy in the 1840s, Codazzi was scheming to bring foreigners to occupy what he described as empty lands in Venezuela. Following the publication of the *Atlas*, Codazzi set out to colonize the land not only representationally but also physically. According to his demographic and geographic survey, most of the population was rural and survived at subsistence level; about 80 percent of the population was illiterate.[106] Codazzi shared the Venezuelan elite's idea that the general population lacked the qualities of the ideal citizenry. The population was too small for such a vast country, the government argued, and impeded the development of natural resources. As a solution, Congress passed a law in 1831 promoting the immigration of Canary islanders. Immigrants received unclaimed public lands, citizenship rights, and an exemption from military service and from a direct assessment on their farms for ten years. In 1837, the government extended these concessions to all Europeans who wished to engage in agriculture or other useful enterprises.[107]

One remedy for labor shortages and unused lands was to sponsor contract immigration through governmental loans. While in Paris, Codazzi became the promoter of an ambitious project designed by the pro-immigration advocates the Conde de Tovar and his nephew Manuel Felipe Tovar to create the colony of Tovar in the Valley of Argua, near Caracas. Codazzi explained that he "naturally" turned to Germany, "where the United States have always drawn their largest immigrations."[108] Germans also had "little defined nationality," he argued, and could integrate easily.[109] In a way, he made the dream of his and Ferrari's younger selves come true. Back in 1816, they had dreamt of creating a colony for Napoleonic veterans near today's Istanbul. Now, his wish was to "open an immigration pathway serving as a model for many other populations."[110] Manuel Tovar received the largest governmental loan awarded to immigration projects, almost 100,000 pesos.[111]

Codazzi worked toward stabilizing and improving the country he had adopted and that had adopted him. In January 1843, the *Clemence* sailed for Venezuelan shores, transporting 389 migrants: over 200 of them were adults and two-thirds were men.[112] Despite schemes like these, immigration remained low. Between 1831 and 1857, over 12,000 foreigners arrived in Venezuela, not even 400 a year. Fifty-one Italians were naturalized between 1830 and 1851: thirty of them had been in the country since independence.[113] Foreign travelers noted that immigrants had a hard time in Venezuelan society.[114]

Codazzi successfully reinvented himself as a Venezuelan patriot, taking advantage of the new legal framework that promoted the immigration of white Europeans. He still experienced occasional bouts of xenophobia. When he became the conservative governor of Barinas, in western Venezuela, the liberal opposition questioned his patriotism and republicanism as a "foreigner who has made few sacrifices for the country." The liberal paper *El Barines* accused him of being "decorated with the Ribbons of the Legion of Honor (a horrible monarchical recognition)."[115] This hostility convinced

Codazzi to abandon Barinas and move to the Danish colony of Saint Thomas. There, he made plans to join a cartographic team in Colombia (New Granada at the time). In January 1849, he and his family crossed yet another border. The Colombian government charged Codazzi with the ambitious project of drawing a complete set of maps, using "chorography," a blend of narratives, images, and statistics.[116] Codazzi began fieldwork in January 1850, going on nine expeditions.[117]

The Chorographic Commission was a foundational moment in the formation of Colombia as a country.[118] The immediate goal was to help the new administration enforce laws and taxation. When Codazzi completed a chapter of his *Physical Geography*, he sent it to local authorities to centralize their governing practices. However, political and geographic landscapes were often mutating. In 1857, the twenty-four provinces combined into eight states, forcing Codazzi to redo many of the maps. These maps provided the new Latin American country with seemingly permanent boundaries, order, and legibility, belying the fragility of its claims over the territory and the complex societies depicted. "All maps have the power to contribute to the transformation of the spaces they represent," historian Jordana Dym and geographer Karl Offen noted. "Maps are not simply objects of factual record; they are part and parcel of the spaces they portray and help co-create."[119] Maps also had the power to transform their authors.

Codazzi might have reinvented himself time and again, but some elements of his personality never changed. Racial prejudice was one of them. Considering Codazzi's experience in the multiethnic forces of Amelia and Providencia, the way he utilized his geographic work to represent racial relations in Colombia in the 1850s deserves close attention. The survey of Chocó, a region on the Pacific coast with a large Afro-Colombian population, brought past and present together. In a report to the governor of the province of Chocó, Codazzi compared a visit he made in 1820 to the present situation (silencing the fact that he made this visit as an officer of the "pirate" Aury): "I have seen an increase in the African population that inhabits riverbanks that were once almost deserted, I have also noticed the regression of these people," Codazzi wrote.[120] He suggested that a racial crisis was under way.[121]

Codazzi's ambivalence regarding emancipation and racial equality traced back to the impressions of Haiti he recorded in his memoirs. "Because of the lack of education," he noted, "because they have just recently thrown off the yoke of slavery, ignorance is generally widespread." However, he noted, "I was surprised to find in [Haitians] a capacity to learn very quickly, unless pride and vanity lead them to despise education."[122] In other words, education was the way to prevent degeneration and chaos. The same patriarchal benevolence had governed Codazzi's treatment of the enslaved Mameluk and Francesco. His beliefs in the inherent laziness and ignorance of people of African descent had grown since his Caribbean sojourn thirty years earlier. Emancipation in Colombia had given "this rude and ignorant [people] the idea that they do not have to work for whites," Codazzi claimed.[123] He wished for roads or, better still, military roads to integrate these recently freed populations into the local economy and society.[124]

The two friends, Codazzi and Ferrari, drifted apart but died within four years of each other with an ocean between them. Ferrari died in Italy in 1851. Codazzi died of malaria in Colombia in 1859. The decades after their deaths saw the legalization of racial segregation in the United States and the rise of scientific racism and social Darwinism in Europe. In Latin America, liberals and elites equated the modernization of the nation with the whitening of the population and encouraged immigration from Europe.[125]

* * *

Understanding how restless border-crossers like Codazzi and Ferrari represented their relationships with their "home" land (Italy), their "host" country (Gran Colombia), and the ephemeral states they helped create (Amelia and Providencia) reveals that historical memories were unpredictable—be it the past of a soldier of fortune or that of a nation. Memoirs and other vehicles of historical self-presentation sutured severed histories and kaleidoscopic spaces. They disrupt the easy slippage between "homeland" as imagined by individuals and families and "homeland" as defined and made sacred by national ideologies. Codazzi and Ferrari's introspective narratives eventually perpetuated, if they did not create, national myths such as the French Grande Armée, South American independence, and the unification of Italy. The transition toward modern citizenship was risky. When Codazzi returned to Gran Colombia, he lived in a volatile country that soon divided into the successor states of Ecuador, Colombia, and Venezuela. Ferrari, his brother revolutionary, may have called himself an Italian patriot, but he was fighting for a country that would only formally come into existence ten years after his death.

Codazzi and Ferrari's efforts to document their lives guaranteed their fame long after their deaths. The Venezuelan state interned Codazzi's remains in the pantheon in 1942. The national institute of geography of Colombia adopted his name in 1957. In Italy, Ferrari's memory resurfaced in the 1890s when efforts to "modernize" Emilia Romagna intensified with

Figure 3. Agustín Codazzi and collaborators in the Yarumito camp,
Soto province, 1850. Biblioteca Nacional de Colombia.

railway constructions, new schools, and urban projects. A group of republicans and moderate conservatives, many veterans of the Italian war of independence, turned the Serraglio into a historic landmark and placed a plaque
on the wall. The plaque concisely reframed Ferrari's international career; he
was a "soldier of liberty" fighting for the republics of Spanish America, but
he was primarily "a soldier of patriotism." He died, the plaque reads, "with
the hope of a better tomorrow for his country."[126] Yet, traces of the two men's
cosmopolitan past never fully disappeared. In the 1990s to 2000s, a renova-
tion of the Villa Serraglio peeled off layers of paint and exposed strange lines
and shapes: Codazzi had painted a memory of his Caribbean adventures on
one of the walls.[127]

While national historiographies eventually made individuals such as
Codazzi and Ferrari valuable by excising some of their past, no historical
interest prompted anyone to reclaim the memories of their African companions and hostages, Mameluk and Francesco. Like many Africans in the
age of revolutions, the two men had a complicated relationship with space,
traversing landmasses and oceans and crossing imperial and national borders, most often unwillingly. For them, transnational geographic frames
were not necessarily liberating. Within the context of military camaraderie,
affection could safely express itself as a show of cosmopolitan patriotism,

but white European assumptions about racial and cultural differences never vanished.[128] The memoirs of Codazzi and Ferrari offered a few "facts" about two African lives without ever giving them a voice. Power, so intertwined with white supremacy, was the greatest determinant of which memories were celebrated and which ones fell into oblivion.

Monitoring the Contagion
of Revolution

Stories

Stories of revolutions, like revolutions themselves, are constantly made and remade, scripted and revised. Often these stories efface contingency in favor of historical determinism. Histories written after independence celebrated revolutions as foundational moments that brought different people together and delivered new nations to the world. Nation-states became the end points of colonial political transformations.[1] Writing stories of revolutions sorted legitimate from illegitimate endeavors and eliminated unsavory protagonists. In 1827, Minister of Interior José Manuel Restrepo published his master narrative of the independence wars, *History of the Revolution of the Republic of Colombia*. The *History* mentioned Louis-Michel Aury a few times, mostly in the context of the Spanish siege of Cartagena in 1815, where Restrepo noted his "ineptitude or disobedience." His activities in Providencia were the topic of a short paragraph. Aury had turned the archipelago into his "center of operations" for his privateer ships and "in such a way that his name became cursed in those seas, like the ancient filibusters."[2] Restrepo distanced Aury from the national history of the revolution.

More generally, Restrepo argued, the foreigners who came to America did more damage than good: "They wanted to act as they wished and refused to obey *established* governments."[3] The reference to established governments was a thinly veiled reference to the "rogue" revolutionaries that roved Caribbean waters. In his map of Gran Colombia that accompanied *History*, Restrepo distanced Providencia from the cosmopolitan revolutionary Caribbean tradition even more clearly—Providencia became a shadowy presence marked with dotted lines encircling an unnamed piece of land strewn with crosses.[4]

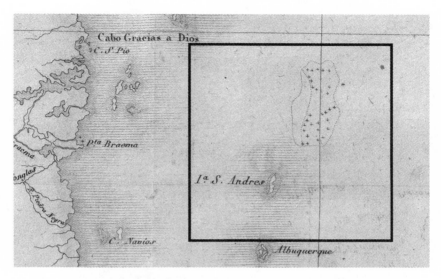

Figure 4. Detail from José Manuel Restrepo, *Carta de la República de Colombia*
(Paris: Libreria Americana, 1827). Courtesy of the David Rumsey
Historical Map Collection, Stanford University Library.

Foreigners were not the only group effaced from national histories. The
role of Africans and people of African ancestry also moved into the back-
ground. Restrepo's history of the revolution, for instance, silenced Haiti's role.
It portrayed Haiti solely as a place where patriots briefly took refuge after the
royalist takeover of Cartagena in 1815. Restrepo overlooked Pétion's financial
and material aid as well as Bolívar's promise to abolish slavery. The general of
African descent, José Padilla, was also missing from the narrative, as were the
Saint-Dominguans Sévère Courtois and Marcelin Guillot. Outside of history
books, race war scares justified the persecution of African-descended people,
and immigration policies became overtly racialized. However, the whitening and the nationalizing of histories and populations were never complete.
Stories about nonwhite revolutionary heroes continued to circulate around
the Caribbean through collective memories, songs, and performances.[5]

Aury's stories survived through circuitous routes. Vicente Perez Rosales
published his memoirs in the late nineteenth century. An itinerant soul,
Rosales lived through the early days of independence of Chile and Argentina,
witnessed the July revolution in Paris in 1830, became a miner in the California
Gold Rush in 1849, and then encouraged German immigration to Chile. Pin-
ing for the bygone era of international revolutionary solidarity when "Spanish

America was not a group of different nations, but a single state to be emanci-pated," Rosales celebrated the foreigners who brought "their precious and so badly needed contributions of blood" to the fight and turned Aury into a pan-American patriot. "Fellow countrymen!" Rosales quoted Aury, "The powerful United States of Buenos Aires and Chile, desirous of cooperating insofar as possible in the emancipation of their oppressed brethren, have charged me with carrying out this noble enterprise in New Granada."[6] Rosales's memoirs turned Aury into a romantic hero of the Western Hemisphere.

These tales of two Aurys represent the duality of the revolutionaries studied in this book who were alternatively discarded as opportunist pirates or, more rarely, celebrated as altruistic patriots. Their mobility, their cosmo-politanism, and their ephemeral states did not fit neatly in the national his-tories of revolutions. Silencing the ideologies of these men or turning them into picturesque egomaniacs and picaresque pirates allowed Americans to sort through the legitimacy of past revolutions and classify them as successes or failures. In doing so, they erased the contingency of some men's heroism and other men's piracy. On one side stood emergent countries slowly consol-idating and nationalizing their histories, their borders, and their people. On the other side, rogue revolutionaries appeared as ne'er-do-wells in a world that was growing uncomfortable with the lack of well-defined affiliations. They made their fortunes on the capture and sale of enslaved Africans when most countries officially turned their backs on the slave trade, but their pro-fessions of racial equality alienated them from white supremacy. These men quickly became obsolete in the new world they helped to create.

The stories of Aury and others teach us two lessons. The first is that legit-imacy was guaranteed ultimately by military and political power. The second is that states eventually became the sole repositories and arbiters of this power and, in the process, delegitimized competing claims. Diplomatic justi-fications, legal arguments, and military actions enabled certain postrevolu-tionary countries to gain a monopoly on legitimacy and on the use of force. It was a daunting task. Jurists in Europe or ship captains in the Caribbean Sea did not have an authoritative theory of sovereignty to justify secession from a metropolitan power.[7] State sovereignty included but did not always depend on foreign recognition. The projects conceived by revolutionaries of fortune remained unrecognized or contested states that, as political scientist Mikulas Fabry wrote, "have not had sovereign status internationally and have thus not been full and equal members of the society of states."[8] Yet, if only for a short time, these states exercised authority over territory, population, and government.

States already established in the international system struggled to separate legitimate from illegal entities since the international system itself was an inchoate creation, a dynamic web of relationships between and within several state entities, including empires, city-states, and nation-states. During this period of experimentation, sovereign nation-states established diplomatic recognition as the main instrument to slowly edge out their competitors.[9] Concurrent with this nineteenth-century development, Europeans and Americans adopted legal positivism, or modern international law. Until then, natural law, or the Law of Nations, theoretically applied to all people as individuals and to all states as sovereign nations. The Law of Nations, as described by Vattel, had strong universalist implications: "Every nation that governs itself, under what form soever, without dependence on any foreign power, is a sovereign state. Its rights are naturally the same as those of any other State. Such are the moral persons who live together in a natural society, subject to the law of nations. To give a nation a right to make an immediate figure in this grand society, it is sufficient that it be really sovereign and independent, that is, that it governs itself by its own authority and laws."[10]

Within this natural law tradition, actors such as the revolutionaries in this book, as well as the polities they created, could make legitimate claims to sovereignty. However, when mutual diplomatic recognition became the norm to prove and claim sovereignty after 1825, exclusion replaced inclusion. When U.S., British, and French policy makers recognized the secessions of Latin America and Haiti in the 1820s (with the caveat that the United States refused to recognize Haiti until 1862), they acknowledged that people had a natural right to live under the government of their choosing. This acknowledgment was not without tension and only applied to *certain* people. The stories of rogue revolutionaries illuminate the transformation of such concepts as revolution, sovereignty, and statehood in the Atlantic world. These men embodied and defended a universalist, cosmopolitan, and inclusionary understanding of these concepts. The stigmatization of these revolutionaries and their projects as failures reveals the triumph of exclusionary and nationalist understandings of these concepts.

As Europeans and free people of mixed European and African ancestry, these rogue revolutionaries were not immediately and deeply beyond the pale of an emergent international system. Although they did not have enough legitimacy to protect their territories from foreign intervention, their privateer ships from detention, or themselves from being branded pirates or outlaws, they were able to escape severe prosecution. When they were arrested, they were usually released and able to rejoin the revolutionary scramble. Insults, jail sentences, diplomatic isolation, and exclusion from national histories were certainly unpleasant, but they beat hanging from the gallows. American and European countries started to apply the same exclusionary principle to other entities and people. They drew a racialized line that restricted the polities they would recognize and with which they would cooperate. By the end of the nineteenth century, American and European powers had excluded most non-European societies and non-Euro-descendant people from both the international system and the protection of international law.[11]

Legacies

As alternatives to the seemingly ineluctable rise of nation-states disappeared, countries around the Caribbean successfully chipped away at rights of revolution and of state formation. The postindependence selection process saw states erecting formal mechanisms to legitimate some claims and invalidate others, to include some polities and exclude others. This incremental and piecemeal development is what historian Greg Grandin described as a "fight to define a set of nominally shared but actually contested ideas and political forms."[12] Included in this development was controlling the right of self-determination and the use of privateering commissions. In order to be internationally recognized as sovereign, states needed to assert their monopoly not only on the exercise of violence within their territory but also on the violence emanating from their territory that might affect the interests of other states.[13] President James Monroe passed a Neutrality Act in 1819 to control the former type of violence and a Piracy Act 1820 to control the latter.[14] Monroe viewed the West Indian naval squadron as a smashing success. Emboldened, he launched an international campaign against privateering. Secretary of State John Quincy Adams carried out this mission against what he called a "system of licensed robbery," which was nothing more than "the most atrocious character of piracy."[15] This campaign did not progress far, and negotiations with Britain, France, and Russia failed.[16] Monroe and Adams were not the only ones who equated privateering with piracy and plunder. The jurist James Kent in *Commentaries on American Law* (1826–1830) explained that "privateering, under all the restrictions which have been adopted, is very liable to abuse."[17] Nevertheless, many Americans wished to avoid a professional standing military and the U.S. navy remained small. Subsequent administrations were also reluctant to modify the Constitution, and privateering is still a right inscribed in the U.S. Constitution to this day.[18]

Sanctioning privateering despite its increasingly negative image, the United States followed the examples of Colombia, Venezuela, and Mexico. Privateering became a symbol of sovereignty for new countries around the Greater Caribbean. Latin American republics came under attack for their seemingly unregulated use of commissions during the wars against Spain, creating opportunities for men such as Aury to roam almost unchecked. These governments recognized the need to regulate privateering but defended their right to commission privateers and protect their territorial and maritime boundaries. Foreigners such as Aury had simply misused this right.[19] "The government of Colombia, from the first days of its existence, practiced this right, promoting privateering," asserted José Manuel Restrepo.[20]

Excesses were curbed. An ordinance in 1822 established a strict list of principles, duties, and obligations. Foreigners, for instance, needed to be inhabitants of Colombia and have their vessels nationalized. The process was centralized: agents abroad could no longer issue privateering commissions, and this power was strictly reserved to the commandant-general of the navy.[21] Privateering appeared in most Colombian and Venezuela constitutions in the first half of the nineteenth century.[22] Possessing a small navy, Mexico also remained attached to privateering and passed a decree authorizing commissions for both citizens and foreigners against the large number of Spanish forces remaining in San Juan de Ulúa, near Veracruz. Even after the two countries signed a peace treaty in 1836, Mexico remained the target of foreign invasions by France in 1838 and the United States in 1846.[23]

Attitudes to privateering differed greatly on the other side of the Atlantic Ocean where the development of national militaries made private citizens bearing arms or operating warships unnecessary.[24] An almost unprecedented period of peace in Europe after 1815 enabled British and French navies to extend control over oceanic spaces, especially after the arrival of steam navigation.[25] With the world's two largest navies, Britain and France had little use for privateering and pushed for its abolition in the Paris Declaration of 1856. Resisting European pressures, American powers argued that privateering was a legitimate practice of warfare as long as it remained the domain of recognized governments. Even if privateering was rarely, if ever, used, it had become a foundational right in the United States, Mexico, and Venezuela. These countries associated privateering with the continued defense of their sovereignty and declined to sign the Paris Declaration.[26]

The right of revolution also changed as the nineteenth century progressed. In the absence of international agreement as to how to ascertain legitimate popular will, many feared that the influence of rogue revolutionaries would lead the Americas into anarchy. Revolutions would continue to roil the continent. Newly independent countries were in the unprecedented position of defending and legitimizing their own revolutions while denying this right to others. Thomas Dew, a U.S. proslavery advocate and son of a revolutionary war soldier, asserted his belief that the "right of revolution" did not exist for "men, or set of men . . . attempting a revolution which *must certainly fail*; or if *successful*, must produce necessarily a *much worse* state of things than the pre-existent order." In particular, people of African ancestry were "totally unfit for freedom and self-government," according to him.[27]

These self-styled state entrepreneurs had raised the risk of unbridled revolutionary contagion. In response, established nations honed mechanisms of delegitimation. First, they carefully reined in the right to revolution by limiting the criteria for self-determination. This process was complicated, especially in the United States, where several state constitutions, the revolutionary-era Virginia Bill of Rights, and the Declaration of Independence included the right to rebel against arbitrary power and to "alter, reform, or abolish" governments. A few years later, this right was not included in the federal Constitution. The creation of judicial review, some legal scholars argue, served to domesticate the right to resist; people could turn to the courts but not the streets to redress their grievances toward the government.[28] In Mexico, article 4 of the Constitution of Apatzingán in 1814 asserted the "undeniable popular right to . . . establish . . . alter, modify, or completely abolish the government, whenever necessary for the people's happiness." This constitution was never ratified, however, and the right to revolution was absent from subsequent constitutions.

Second, American governments declared the right to secede as contextual, not absolute. In 1823, U.S. president James Monroe rejected the prospect of colonial projects by European powers in the Americas. Latin American countries quickly embraced this principle.[29] Legitimate revolution was limited to areas formerly ruled by European empires. Once these empires withdrew from the continent, the right to secede evaporated. Last, Latin American diplomats and jurists revitalized the Roman doctrine of *uti possidetis* in a series of postindependence treaties, conferences, and declarations. This doctrine provided that the borders of the newly formed states followed the colonial borders at the time of independence. The goal was to ensure territorial stability, to make borders theoretically immutable, and to ward off both foreign interventions and internal revolutions.[30]

Futures

The historical process of classifying state-sponsored actions as legitimate at sea (privateering) and on land (the right to revolution) was never complete. However, by the end of the nineteenth century, states had become more efficient in defining and policing their borders and their citizens while codifying international law, a set of rules by which recognized nation-states interacted with each other.[31] Nineteenth-century nations portrayed their conquests in the name of universal liberation, whether it was Manifest Destiny in the United States, global antislavery campaigns in Britain, or the imperial civilizing mission in France.[32] International law became a civilizational discourse that justified expansion and dispossession; it now intended to control "uncivilized" non-Western nations and enable "civilized" Western powers to use force to export the rule of law.

Yet individuals continued, as they do today, to contravene and reinterpret norms, laws, and principles in order to claim rights for themselves. Nonstate actors persisted in initiating unauthorized military endeavors against foreign territories and forming short-lived polities, most famously the filibustering movement in the United States in the 1840s to 1850s. William Walker led a series of expeditions against northern Mexico and Central America and created the short-lived republics of Sonora, Lower California, and Nicaragua, where he notably reestablished slavery. With varied motives, some filibusters sought to bring new territories into the United States while others tried to establish independent states under their own rule.[33] Outside the Americas, the infamous Voulet-Chanoine expedition in late nineteenth-century Chad/Mali saw French military officers violently try to establish their own independent state.[34]

The stories of rogue revolutionaries in the Greater Caribbean mirrored larger trends and global phenomena. Even though these alternatives ultimately washed away like sand castles, they show that seemingly self-evident norms of state sovereignty, racial identity, and national categories were fragile and historically produced. Full of twists and turns, collaboration and betrayals, friendships and loneliness, the stories of these men reflect this contingency of fate. While it may be tempting to focus on clear instances of world-changing moments, failed revolutions and evanescent states remind us that, in the words of the nineteenth-century French poet Charles Baudelaire, "modernity is the ephemeral, the fugitive, the contingent."

ABBREVIATIONS

ADMAE	Archives Diplomatiques du Ministère des Affaires Etrangères, France
AGI	Archivo General de las Indias, Spain
AGNC	Archivo General de la Nación, Colombia
AGNM	Archivo General de la Nación, Mexico
AGNM-Newberry	Archivo General de la Nación, Mexico, typescripts Newberry Library
AHN	Archivo Histórico Nacional, Spain
ANF	Archives Nationales de France
ASP	American State Papers
ANOM	Archives Nationales d'Outre-Mer, France
CAD	Centre des Archives Diplomatiques, France
DNA	Danish National Archives
LOC	Library of Congress, United States
NARA	National Archives and Records Administration, United States
NOPL	New Orleans Public Library, United States
TNA	The National Archives, United Kingdom

NOTES

Introduction

1. R. W. Meade to Secretary of State, December 17, 1822, Philadelphia, in "Expedition Against the Island of Porto Rico," 17th Cong., 2nd sess., no. 540, 1038.

2. Legitimacy is conformity to the law or to a rule but also more broadly to commonly known principles or established standards. Pierre Bourdieu, "Rethinking the State: On the Genesis and Structure of the Bureaucratic Field," *Sociological Theory* 2, no. 1 (1994): 15. Juan Linz defines legitimacy as "the belief that in spite of shortcomings and failures, the existing political institutions are better than others that may be established, and that they therefore can demand obedience." Linz, *The Breakdown of Democratic Regimes: Crisis, Breakdown, and Reequilibration* (Baltimore: Johns Hopkins University Press, 1978), 6. See also Alex Jeffrey, Fiona McConnell, and Alice Wilson, "Understanding Legitimacy: Perspectives from Anomalous Geopolitical Spaces," *Geoforum* 66 (2015): 177–183.

3. Following the 1815 Congress of Vienna, two frameworks of legitimacy emerged: the first revitalized the principle of dynastic legitimacy in Western Europe while the second championed de facto self-determination based on popular sovereignty in the Americas. Mikulas Fabry, *Recognizing States: International Society and the Establishment of New States Since 1776* (New York: Oxford University Press, 2010), 26–36.

4. The expression "state-entrepreneur" is inspired by Thomas W. Gallant's expression "military entrepreneurs" designating "armed predators . . . who operate in the interstice between legality and illegality. . . . They are entrepreneurs in the sense that they are purveyors of a commodity—violence." They may oppose and/or work for a state. Gallant, "Brigandage, Piracy, Capitalism, and State-Formation: Transnational Crime from a Historical World-Systems Perspective," in *States and Illegal Practices*, ed. Josiah McC. Heyman (New York: Berg, 1999), 25–61.

5. C. A. Bayly, *The Birth of the Modern World, 1780–1914: Global Connections and Comparisons* (Oxford: Blackwell, 2004), 86–120; David Armitage and Sanjay Subrahmanyam, eds., *The Age of Revolutions in Global Context, c. 1760–1840* (New York: Palgrave Macmillan, 2010).

6. Tom Ginsburg, Daniel Lansberg-Rodriguez, and Mila Versteeg, "When to Overthrow Your Government: The Right to Resist in the World's Constitutions," *UCLA Law Review* 60, no. 5 (2013): 1186–1260; Christian G. Fritz, *American Sovereigns: The People and America's Constitutional Tradition Before the Civil War* (New York: Cambridge University Press, 2008); Micah Alpaugh, "The Right of Resistance to Oppression: Protest and Authority in the French Revolutionary World," *French Historical Studies* 39, no. 3 (2016): 567–598.

7. Among others, Peter Onuf, "State-Making in Revolutionary America: Independent Vermont as a Case-Study," *Journal of American History* 67, no. 4 (1981): 789–815; Andrés Reséndez, *Changing National Identities: Texas and New Mexico, 1800–1850* (Cambridge: Cambridge

University Press, 2005); Jeremy Adelman, *Sovereignty and Revolution in the Iberian Atlantic* (Princeton, NJ: Princeton University Press, 2006); David Armitage, *The Declaration of Independence: A Global History* (Cambridge, MA: Harvard University Press, 2008); James Sanders, *The Vanguard of the Atlantic World: Creating Modernity, Nation, and Democracy in Nineteenth-Century Latin America* (Durham, NC: Duke University Press, 2014); Kathleen DuVal, *Independence Lost: Lives on the Edge of the American Revolution* (New York: Random House, 2015); Keith Michael Baker and Dan Edelstein, eds., *Scripting Revolution: A Historical Approach to the Comparative Study of Revolutions* (Stanford, CA: Stanford University Press, 2015).

8. Eliga H. Gould, *Among the Powers of the Earth: The American Revolution and the Making of a New World Empire* (Cambridge, MA: Harvard University Press, 2012); Daniel Gutiérrez Ardila, *El reconocimiento de Colombia: Diplomacia y propaganda en la coyuntura de las restauraciones 1819–1831* (Bogotá: Universidad Externado de Colombia, 2012); Julia Gaffield, *Haitian Connections in the Atlantic World: Recognition After Revolution* (Chapel Hill: University of North Carolina Press, 2015). For a broader comparative perspective, I used Prasenjit Duara, *Sovereignty and Authenticity: Manchukuo and the East Asian Modern* (Lanham, MD: Rowman & Littlefield, 2003) and Aleksandar Pavkovic and Peter Radan, *Creating New States: Theory and Practice of Secession* (Burlington, VT: Ashgate, 2007).

9. Jeremy Adelman, "An Age of Imperial Revolutions," *American Historical Review* 113, no. 2 (2008): 319–340; Marcela Echeverri, *Indian and Slave Royalists in the Age of Revolution: Reform, Revolution and Royalism in the Northern Andes, 1780–1825* (New York: Cambridge University Press, 2016).

10. Cynthia Weber, *Simulating Sovereignty: Intervention, the State and Symbolic Exchange* (Cambridge: Cambridge University Press, 1995); Saskia Sassen, *Territory, Authority, Rights: From Medieval to Global Assemblages* (Princeton, NJ: Princeton University Press, 2006), 3–4; Yarimar Bonilla, "Unsettling Sovereignty," *Cultural Anthropology* 32, no. 3 (2017): 330–339; Yarimar Bonilla and Max Hantel, "Visualizing Sovereignty: Cartographic Queries for the Digital Age," *sx archipelagos* 1 (2016), https://doi.org/10.7916/D8CV4HTJ.

11. Lara Putnam, "To Study the Fragments/Whole: Microhistory and the Atlantic World," *Journal of Social History* 39, no. 3 (2006): 615–630; David Hancock, *Citizens of the World: London Merchants and the Integration of the British Atlantic Community, 1735–1785* (New York: Cambridge University Press, 1995); Jill Lepore, "Historians Who Love Too Much: Reflections on Microhistory and Biography," *Journal of American History* 88, no. 1 (2001): 129–144; Miles Osborn, *Global Lives: Britain and the World, 1550–1800* (Cambridge: Cambridge University Press, 2008); Rebecca J. Scott and Jean M. Hébrard, *Freedom Papers: An Atlantic Odyssey in the Age of Emancipation* (Cambridge, MA: Harvard University Press, 2012); Francesca Trivellato, "Microstoria/Microhistoire/Microhistory," *French Politics, Culture and Society* 33, no. 1 (2015): 122–134.

12. These men performed what Lauren Benton calls "legal posturing." Benton, *A Search for Sovereignty: Law and Geography on European Empires, 1400–1900* (Cambridge: Cambridge University Press, 2010), especially 112–118, on the ways privateers used letters of marque to their advantage in the seventeenth and eighteenth centuries.

13. Marcus Rediker and Peter Linebaugh, *The Many-Headed Hydra: Sailors, Slaves, Commoners, and the Hidden History of the Revolutionary Atlantic* (Boston: Beacon, 2000); W. Jeffrey Bolster, *Black Jacks: African American Seamen in the Age of Sail* (Cambridge, MA: Harvard University Press, 1997); Joshua L. Reid, *The Sea Is My Country: The Maritime World of the Makahs, an Indigenous Borderlands People* (New Haven, CT: Yale University Press, 2015).

14. Anne Pérotin-Dumon, "Les Jacobins des Antilles ou l'esprit de liberté dans les Iles-du-Vent," *Revue D'histoire Moderne Et Contemporaine* 35, no. 2 (1988): 275–304; David Head, *Privateers of the Americas: Spanish American Privateering from the United States in the Early Republic* (Athens: University of Georgia Press, 2015); Tyson Reeder, "'Sovereign Lords' and 'Dependent Administrators': Artigan Privateers, Atlantic Borderwaters, and State Building in the Early Nineteenth Century," *Journal of American History* 103, no. 2 (2016): 323–346; Matthew McCarthy, *Privateering, Piracy and British Policy in Spanish America, 1810–1830* (Suffolk: Boydel, 2013); Edgardo Pérez Morales, *No Limits to Their Sway: Cartagena's Privateers and the Masterless Caribbean in the Age of Revolutions* (Nashville, TN: Vanderbilt University Press, 2018); William S. Cormack, *Patriots, Royalists, and Terrorists in the West Indies: The French Revolution in Martinique and Guadeloupe, 1789–1802* (Toronto: University of Toronto Press, 2019).

15. On the participation of foreigners in the Latin American independence movements, see Alfred Hasbrouck, *Foreign Legionaries in the Liberation of Spanish South America* (New York: Octagon, 1969); Sergio Elias Ortiz, *Franceses en la independencia de Gran Colombia* (Bogotá: Editorial ABC, 1971); Matthew Brown, *Adventuring Through Spanish Colonies: Simón Bolívar, Foreign Mercenaries and the Birth of New Nations* (Liverpool: Liverpool University Press, 2006); Moises Enrique Rodríguez, *Freedom's Mercenaries: British Volunteers in the Wars of Independence of Latin America* (Lanham, MD: Hamilton Books, University Press of America, 2006); Rafe Blaufarb, "The Western Question: The Geopolitics of Latin American Independence," *American Historical Review* 112, no. 3 (2007): 742–763.

16. Laurent Dubois, "An Atlantic Revolution," *French Historical Studies* 32, no. 4 (2009): 655–661; David A. Bell, "Questioning the Global Turn: The Case of the French Revolution," *French Historical Studies* 37, no. 1 (2014): 1–24.

17. Fred Halliday, *Revolution and World Politics: The Rise and Fall of the Sixth Great Power* (London: Macmillan, 1999).

18. David Bell argued that the concept of *patrie*, in the eighteenth century, had often a more political sense than the concept of nation, referring to a political unit to which a person felt ultimate loyalty. Bell, "The Unbearable Lightness of Being French: Law, Republicanism, and National Identity at the End of the Old Regime," *American Historical Review* 106, no. 4 (2001): 1219; Charles Minguet, "El concepto de nación, pueblo, estado, patria en las generaciones de la independencia," in *Recherches sur le Monde hispanique au dix-neuvième siècle*, ed. Jean-René Aymes (Lille: Presses Universitaires de Lille, 1973), 57–73.

19. Margaret Jacobs, *Strangers Nowhere in the World: The Rise of Cosmopolitanism in Early Modern Europe* (Philadelphia: University of Pennsylvania Press, 2006); Maurizio Isabella, *Risorgimento in Exile: Italian Émigrés and the Liberal International in the Post-Napoleonic Era* (Oxford: Oxford University Press, 2009); Philipp Ziesche, *Cosmopolitan Patriots: Americans in Paris in the Age of Revolution* (Charlottesville: University of Virginia Press, 2010); Janet Polasky, *Revolutions Without Borders: The Call to Liberty in the Atlantic World* (New Haven, CT: Yale University Press, 2015); Seema Alavi, *Muslim Cosmopolitanism in the Age of Empire* (Cambridge, MA: Harvard University Press, 2015). Most of the cosmopolitanism studied by Polasky and Alavi was anchored in publications and their circulation. While print culture is important, we also need to consider people's actions.

20. The expression "ephemeral states" comes from Jane Landers. Landers, *Atlantic Creoles in the Age of Revolutions* (Cambridge, MA: Harvard University Press, 2010), 102–106; R. R. Palmer, *The Age of Democratic Revolution: Political History of Europe and America, 1760–1800* (Princeton, NJ: Princeton University Press, 1959 and 1964); Lester Langley, *The Americas in the*

Age of Revolution, 1750–1850 (New Haven, CT: Yale University Press, 1996); Gordon Brown, *Latin American Rebels and the United States, 1806–1822* (Jefferson, NC: McFarland, 2015); Caitlin Fitz, *Our Sister Republics: The United States in an Age of American Revolutions* (New York: W. W. Norton, 2016).

21. Raúl Coronado call these alternatives "worlds not to come." Coronado, *A World Not to Come: A History of Latino Writing and Print Culture* (Cambridge: Cambridge University Press, 2013). Ernesto Bassi uses the expression "visions of potential futures." Bassi, *An Aqueous Territory: Sailors Geographies and New Granada's Transimperial Greater Caribbean World* (Durham, NC: Duke University Press, 2016), 4. Rachel St. John mentions "an array of schemes carried out by people within and around [U.S.] borders." St. John, "The Unpredictable America of William Gwin: Expansion, Secession, and the Unstable Borders of Nineteenth-Century North America," *Journal of the Civil War Era* 6, no. 1 (2016): 58. See also Manu Goswani, "Imaginary Futures and Colonial Internationalisms," *American Historical Review* 117, no. 5 (2012): 1461–1485.

22. Tozun Bahcheli, Barry Bartmann, and Henry Felix Srebrnik, eds., *De Facto States: The Quest for Sovereignty* (London: Routledge, 2004); Robert I. Rotberg, ed., *When States Fail: Causes and Consequences* (Princeton, NJ: Princeton University Press, 2004); Deon Geldenhuys, *Contested States in World Politics* (Basingstoke: Palgrave Macmillan, 2009); Nina Caspersen and Gareth Stansfield, *Unrecognized States in the International System* (Abingdon: Routledge, 2012).

23. Tanisha Fazal, *State Death: The Politics and Geography of Conquest, Occupation, and Annexation* (Princeton, NJ: Princeton University Press, 2007), 312–318; Miguel Centeno, *Blood and Debt: War and the Nation-State in Latin America* (University Park: Pennsylvania State University Press, 2002); Charles Tilly, "Reflections on the History of European State-Making," in *The Formation of National States in Western Europe*, ed. Charles Tilly (Princeton, NJ: Princeton University Press, 1975), 3–83.

24. Jonathan Hill, "Beyond the Other? A Postcolonial Critique of the Failed State Thesis," *African Identities* 3, no. 2 (2005): 139–154; Charles T. Call, "The Fallacy of the 'Failed State,'" *Third World Quarterly* 29, no. 8 (2008): 1491–1507; Errol A. Henderson, "Hidden in Plain Sight: Racism in International Relations Theory," *Cambridge Review of International Affairs*, 26, no. 1 (2013): 71–92; Arjun Chowdhury, *The Myth of International Order: Why Weak States Persist and Alternatives to the State Fade Away* (New York: Oxford University Press, 2017); Susan L. Woodward, *The Ideology of Failed States: Why Intervention Fails* (Cambridge: Cambridge University Press, 2017).

25. On discourses of Western modernity, see Stuart Hall, "The West and the Rest: Discourse and Power," in *Formations of Modernity*, ed. Stuart Hall and Bram Gieben (Oxford: Polity in association with Open University, 1992), 275–333. The polities studied in this book historicize German sociologist Max Weber's famous definition of a state in *Politics as a Vocation* (1918): "a state is a human community that (successfully) claims the monopoly of the *legitimate use of physical force* within a given territory." I am particularly interested in deconstructing the adverb "successfully" that Weber enclosed in parentheses as if it were an almost unnecessary qualifier of other fundamental characteristics of state building. Weber, *From Max Weber: Essays in Sociology* (New York: Oxford University Press, 1946), 4.

26. Exceptions are Gregory P. Downs, "The Mexicanization of American Politics: The United States' Transnational Path from Civil War to Stabilization," *American Historical Review* 117, no. 2 (2012): 387–409; Branwen Gruffydd Jones, "'Good Governance' and 'State Failure': Genealogies of Imperial Discourse," *Cambridge Review of International Affairs* 26, no. 1 (2013): 49–70.

27. Eric Selbin, "Stories of Revolution in the Periphery," in *Revolution in the Making of the Modern World: Social Identities, Globalization, and Modernity*, ed. John Foran, David Lane, and Andreja Zivkovic (London: Routledge, 2008), 130.

28. For instance, the Fragile States Index (formerly the Failed States Index), published annually by a U.S. think tank, listed 178 countries in 2019.

29. Nina Caspersen, *Unrecognized States: The Struggle for Sovereignty in the Modern International System* (Malden: Polity, 2012); Joshua Keating, *Invisible Countries: Journeys to the Edge of Nationhood* (New Haven, CT: Yale University Press, 2018).

Chapter 1

1. "Proclama," *Correo del Orinoco*, February 6, 1819. When the proclamation was reproduced in newspapers, some editors modified the original text. A version in the *American Mercury* (Connecticut) displays the slogan "Liberty! Independence! Or Death" at the end of Aury's proclamation.

2. Maurice Persat, *Mémoires du commandant Persat, 1806–1844* (Paris: Plon, 1910), 33.

3. Aury to Santander, July 3, 1820, in *Correspondencia dirigida al general Francisco de Paula Santander*, ed. Roberto Cortazar (Bogotá: Academia Colombiana de Historia, 1964–1970), 14: 282–283.

4. *Gaceta de Cartagena*, December 28, 1822.

5. On criteria for the recognition of new states, see James Crawford, *The Creation of States in International Law*, 2nd ed. (New York: Oxford University Press, 2006) and Daniel Philpott, "Sovereignty: An Introduction and Brief History," *Journal of International Affairs* 48, no. 2 (1995): 353–368.

6. Stanley Faye, "Commodore Aury," *Louisiana Historical Quarterly* 24 (1941): 611–630; Carlos A. Ferro, *Vida de Luis Aury, corsario de Buenos Aires en las luchas por la independencia de Venezuela, Colombia y Centroamérica* (Buenos Aires: Cuarto Poder, 1976), 611–697; Carlos Vidales, "Corsarios y piratas de la Revolución Francesa en las aguas de emancipación Hispanoamérica," *Caravelle* 54, no. 1 (1990): 247–262; Antonio Cacua Prada, *El corsario Luis Aury: Intimidades de la independencia* (Bogotá: Academia Colombiana de Historia, 2001); Robert C. Vogel, "Rebel Without a Cause: The Adventures of Louis Aury," *Lafitte Society Chronicles* 8, no. 1 (2002): 2–12.

7. Frank Lawrence Owsley Jr. and Gene A. Smith, *Filibusters and Expansionists: Jeffersonian Manifest Destiny, 1800–1821* (Tuscaloosa: University of Alabama Press, 1997), 7–31; William C. Davis, *The Pirates Laffite: The Treacherous World of the Corsairs of the Gulf* (Orlando, FL: Harcourt, 2005), 402–419; William Earl Weeks, *John Quincy Adams and American Global Empire* (Lexington: University Press of Kentucky, 2015), 62–69; Deborah A. Rosen, *Border Law: The First Seminole War and American Nationhood* (Cambridge, MA: Harvard University Press, 2015), 22–26.

8. Bartosz Stanislawski, "Para-States, Quasi-States, and Black Spots: Perhaps Not States, but Not 'Ungoverned Territories' Either," *International Studies Review* 10, no. 2 (2008): 366; Fabry, *Recognizing States*, 46–50; Sanjay Subrahmanyam and David Shulman, "The Men Who Would Be Kings? The Politics of Expansion in Early Seventeenth-Century Northern Tamilnado," *Modern Asian Studies* 24, no. 2 (1990): 225–248; Winston P. Nagan and Craig Hammer, "The Changing Character of Sovereignty in International Law and International Relations," *Columbia Journal of Transnational Law* 43, no. 1 (1992): 1–60.

9. John Dugard and David Raič, "The Role of Recognition in the Law and Practice of Secession," in *Secession: International Law Perspectives*, ed. Marcelo G. Kohen (Cambridge: Cambridge University Press, 2006), 94; James Ker-Lindsay, "Engagement Without Recognition: The Limits of Diplomatic Interaction with Contested States," *International Affairs* 91, no. 2 (2015): 1–16; Jens Bartelson, *A Genealogy of Sovereignty* (Cambridge: Cambridge University Press, 1995); Arjun Appadurai, "Sovereignty Without Territoriality: Notes for a Postnational Geography," in *The Geography of Identity*, ed. Patricia Yaeger (Ann Arbor: University of Michigan Press, 1996), 40–58; Hendrik Spruyt, *The Sovereign State and Its Competitors* (Princeton, NJ: Princeton University Press, 1994); Hent Kalmo and Quentin Skinner, *Sovereignty in Fragments: The Past, Present, and Future of a Contested Concept* (Cambridge: Cambridge University Press, 2014); Dieter Grim and Belinda Cooper, *Sovereignty: The Origin and Future of a Political and Legal Concept* (New York: Columbia University Press, 2015); Yarimar Bonilla, *Non-sovereign Futures: French Caribbean Politics in the Wake of Disenchantment* (Chicago: University of Chicago Press, 2015).

10. Aury to the Maignets, October 24, 1814, Library of Congress, Manuscripts Division, Luis Aury Papers (hereafter LOC/MD/LA), folder 6.

11. Aury to the Maignets, January 29, 1804, LOC/MD/LA, folder 5.

12. Aury to the Maignets, August 2, 1800, LOC/MD/LA, folder 3.

13. Aury to the Maignets, June 5, 1804, LOC/MD/LA, folder 3.

14. *Memorias de Agustin Codazzi*, trans. Andrés Soriano Lelras and Alberto Lee López (Bogotá: Publicaciones del Banco de la República, 1973), 291.

15. Correspondance à l'arrivée de la Guadeloupe an 10, ANOM, sous-série C7, A56–72.

16. Vattel, *Le droit des gens ou Principes de la loi naturelle appliqués à la conduite et aux affaires des nations et des souverains* (London, 1758), book 2, chap. 18, 346. Other jurists such as Bodin and Grotius also codified privateering. See Walter Rech, *Enemies of Mankind: Vattel's Theory of Collective Security* (Leiden: Martinus Nijhoff, 2013).

17. Aury to the Maignets, September 6, 1808, LOC/MD/LA, folder 6.

18. Aury to the Maignets, October 10, 1812, LOC/MD/LA, folder 4.

19. Louis Crispin's testimony, NOPL, Records of U.S. District Court for Eastern District of Louisiana, 1806–1814, M1082, reel 9, case 376.

20. Aury to Victoire Aury, December 10, 1812, LOC/MD/LA, folder 6.

21. Marixa Lasso, *Myths of Harmony: Race and Republicanism During the Age of Revolution, Colombia, 1795–1831* (Pittsburgh: University of Pittsburgh Press, 2007), 75–85; Aline Helg, *Liberty & Equality in the Caribbean Colombia, 1770–1835* (Chapel Hill: University of North Carolina Press, 2004), 121–139.

22. Caryn Cossé Bell, *Revolution, Romanticism and the Afro-Creole Protest Tradition in Louisiana 1718–1868* (Baton Rouge: Louisiana State University Press, 1997), 47; Anne Pérotin-Dumon, "Course et piraterie dans le Golfe du Mexique et la mer des Antilles," *Bulletin de la Société d'Histoire de la Guadeloupe* 53–54 (1982): 49–71; Johanna von Gafenstein, "Corso y piratería en el Golfo-Caribe durante las guerras de independencia hispano-americanas," in *La violence et la mer dans l'espace atlantique: XIIe–XIXe siècle*, ed. Mickaël Augeron and Mathias Tranchant (Rennes: Presses Universitaires de Rennes, 2004), 269–282; Alfonso Múnera, *El fracaso de la nación. Región, clase y raza en el Caribe colombiano, 1717–1821* (Bogotá: Banco de la República, 1998), 188–191; Pérez Morales, *No Limits to Their Sway*.

23. John Fairbanks Jr. to James Madison, April 26, 1813, in *The Papers of James Madison*, ed. Angela Kreider and J. C. A. Stagg (Charlottesville: University of Virginia Press, 2008), 6:

238–239. Fairbanks noted, "The country is rapidly increasing in population, in consequence of the arrival of strangers from various parts of the West Indies particularly Frenchmen."

24. Hoja de Servicio de Juan María Hernández, AGNC, República, t. 23, fol. 3–9.

25. Information regarding Joseph is in his file in the Service Historique de la Défense, Archives de l'Armée de Terre, and from "Joseph Courtois, sous-lieutenant," ANF, séries 2YE, file 943, F2C13; Dantes Bellegarde, *Histoire du peuple haïtien* (Port-au-Prince: Collection du Tricinquentenaire de l'Indépendance d'Haïti, 1953), 80–85.

26. Courtois to Santander, May 30, 1823, cited in Paul Verna, *Pétion y Bolívar: Cuarenta años (1790–1830) de relaciones haitiano venezolanas y su aporte a la emancipación Hispano-américa* (Caracas: Ediciones de la Presidencia, 1969), 295.

27. Petition to Andrew Jackson from Joseph Savary et al., March 16, 1815, in *Papers of Andrew Jackson* (Knoxville: University of Tennessee Press, 1991), 3: 315–316.

28. Lasso, *Myths of Harmony*, 189, n. 21.

29. *National Intelligencer*, February 10, 1818.

30. H. L. V. Ducoudray-Holstein, *Histoire de Bolívar, par le Général Ducoudray Holstein; continuée jusqu'à sa mort par Alphonse Viollet* (Paris: Imprimerie de Auguste Auffray, 1831), 1: 272.

31. Ibid., 1: 123–125.

32. Bassi, *Aqueous Territory*, 142–170; "Contestación de Simón Bolívar a las proposiciones de Luis Aury," March 1816, in *Simón Bolívar, Escritos del Libertador*, ed. Cristóbal Mendoza (Caracas: Sociedad Bolivariana de Venezuela, 1964), 9: 98–100.

33. Aury to Victoire Aury, March 15, 1816, LOC/MD/LA, folder 6.

34. Cienfuegos to Juan Ruiz de Apocada, September 1816, AGNM, Historia, Notas Diplomáticas, grupo 52, vol. 1, fol. 263.

35. Aury to the Maignets, an 10, LOC/MD/LA, folder 10.

36. Mimi Sheller, "Sword-Bearing Citizens: Militarism and Manhood in Nineteenth-Century Haiti," *Plantation Society in the Americas* 4, nos. 2–3 (1997): 233–278.

37. Landers, *Atlantic Creoles*; Nathaniel Millett, *The Maroons of Prospect Bluff and Their Quest for Freedom in the Atlantic World* (Gainesville: University Press of Florida, 2013).

38. *Morning Chronicle*, October 30, 1817.

39. *Orleans Gazette*, October 18, 1816, in Morphy to Cienfuegos, November 7, 1816, AGI, Cuba, leg. 1900.

40. Ducoudray-Holstein, *Histoire de Bolivar*, 1: 184.

41. *Diario del gobierno de la Havana*, October 16, 1816, AGNM, Historia, Notas Diplomáticas, grupo 52, vol. 1, fol. 254.

42. *Orleans Gazette*, October 18, 1816, in Morphy to Cienfuegos, November 7, 1816, AGI, Cuba, leg. 1900; "Representación de Rafael Diego Mérida en Providencia," May 10, 1821, AGNC, República, Historia, t. 9, fol. 777–780.

43. Aury to U.S. House of Representatives, December 12, 1816, *Niles' Weekly Register*, January 24, 1818.

44. Robinson, *Memoirs*, 60; Matilda Houston, *Texas and the Gulf of Mexico, or, Yachting in the New World* (London: John Murray, 1844), 1: 40. An article in the London *Morning Chronicle* dated from September 1816 reported that large quantities of goods were purchased in New Orleans to supply Aury's establishment.

45. Vicente Pazos, "Commissions and Employment of Don Luis Aury," January 7, 1818, in *Message from the President of the United States, transmitting, in pursuance of a resolution of the*

House of Representatives, of the 20th instant, information, not heretofore communicated, relating to the occupation of Amelia Island (Washington, DC: De Krafft, 1818), 37.

46. Louis Aury, governor of province of Texas, privateer commission given to Nicolas Aiguette, May 7, 1817, P. K. Yonge Library, University of Florida, Elizabeth Howard West collection, box 9.

47. Deposition of Juan Domingo Lozano, May 9, 1817, encl. in correspondence between Spanish consul at New Orleans and captain-general of Cuba, AGI, Cuba, leg. 1900.

48. According to Faye, Aury created a national currency with warehouse receipts. "Commodore Aury," 639. An observer in Galveston noted "[Aury's] bills are paid at sight." Extract of a letter from Natchitoches, state of Louisiana, dated February 4, 1817, in *Message from the President*, 7.

49. *Message from the President*, 11.

50. *National Intelligencer*, March 2, 1818.

51. Maxent to Cienfuegos, October 22, 1816, AGI, Cuba, leg. 1873.

52. Harris G. Warren, "Documents Relating to the Establishment of Privateers at Galveston, 1816–1817," *Louisiana Historical Quarterly* 21, no. 4 (1938): 1106.

53. Copia de declaración de Tiburcio López, June 6, 1817, AGI, Cuba, leg. 1900.

54. *Message from the President*, 36–37.

55. Persat, *Mémoires*, 33.

56. James Cusick, *The Other War of 1812: The Patriot War and the American Invasion of Spanish East Florida* (Gainesville: University of Florida Press, 2003), 38–55; Jane Landers, *Black Society in Spanish Florida* (Urbana: University of Illinois Press, 1999); Andrew McMichael, *Atlantic Loyalties: Americans in Spanish West Florida, 1785–1810* (Athens: University of Georgia Press, 2008).

57. Head, *Privateers of the Americas*, 105–107.

58. "To Assembly from Aury," December 12, 1817, in *Charleston Courier*, January 9, 1818.

59. *National Intelligencer*, October 17 and 24, 1817; Edmund Pendleton Gaines to Andrew Jackson, March 6, 1815, LOC, Manuscript/Mixed Material, https://www.loc.gov/item/maj005320/.

60. *The Weekly Recorder*, November 12, 1817; *National Intelligencer*, October 31, 1817, and March 2, 1818.

61. *National Intelligence*, October 24, 1817.

62. Costante Ferrari, *Memorie postume del Cav. Costante Ferrari* (Bologna: Editore Cappelli, 1855), 428.

63. Correspondence between Captain John Elton and Commodore Aury, November 3–12, 1817, in *Message from the President*, 40–44.

64. "Proclamation in Fernandina," November 5, 1817, P. K. Yonge Library, University of Florida, Miscellaneous Manuscripts (Fl).

65. Giorgio Agamben, *State of Exception*, trans. Kevin Attell (Chicago: University of Chicago Press, 2005), 1–30.

66. *Narrative of a Voyage to the Spanish Main: In the Ship "Two Friends"* (London: John Miller, 1819), 95–97.

67. Aury to Elton, November 4, 1817, in *Message from President*, 41.

68. *Charleston Courier*, November 28, 1817, and December 19, 1817.

69. *Report of the Committee Appointed to Frame the Plan of Provisional Government for the Republic of Floridas. P. Gual, V. Pazos, M. Murden. Fernandina: December 9, 1817, First of the Independence of Floridas*, in *La República de las Floridas: Texts and Documents*, ed. David Bushnell (México, D.F.: Pan American Institute of Geography and History, 1986), 62–64.

70. *The Examiner*, February 1819, and *Morning Chronicle*, December 5, 1817.

71. *Niles' Weekly Register*, October 4, 1817.

72. *Charleston Courier*, September 26, 1817, and November 11, 1817.

73. Correspondence between Attorney for Georgia and Secretary of State, March 24, 1820, July 27, 1820, September 4, 1820, NARA, Miscellaneous Letters to the Department of State, 179, roll 49.

74. *Niles' Weekly Register*, December 27, 1817; Richard Longeville Vowell, *Campaigns and Cruises in Venezuela and New Granada from 1817 to 1830* (London: Longman, 1831), 1: 14.

75. "Report of the Committee to Whom Was Referred So Much of the President's Message as Relates to the Introduction of Slaves from Amelia Island, January 10, 1818," U.S. Congress, 15th Cong., 1st sess.

76. Jeffrey Ostler and Nancy Shoemaker, "Settler Colonialism in Early American History: Introduction," *William and Mary Quarterly* 76, no. 3 (2019): 361–368. A history of the concept of settler colonialism is in Lorenzo Veracini, "'Settler Colonialism': Career of a Concept," *Journal of Imperial and Commonwealth History* 41, no. 2 (2013): 313–333.

77. "Message by John Quincy Adams," October 30, 1817, in *Memoirs of John Quincy Adams*, ed. Charles Francis Adas (Philadelphia: J. B. Lippincott, 1874–1877), 4: 15.

78. Paul A. Gilje, *To Swear Like a Sailor: Maritime Culture in America 1750–1850* (Cambridge: Cambridge University Press, 2016), 19.

79. Rosen, *Border Law*, 23.

80. McIntosh to Crawford, October 30, 1817, in *Message from the President*, 21.

81. Vicente Pazos, *Exposition, Remonstrance, and Protests of Don Vicente Pazos, Commissioner on Behalf of the Republican Agents Established at Amelia Island, in Florida, Under the Authority and in Behalf of the Independent States of South America* (Philadelphia: publisher not identified, 1818), 25.

82. Aury to Henley and Bankhead, December 22, 1817, in *Message from the President*, 8–9.

83. *Charleston Courier*, November 28, 1817.

84. Aury to Henley and Bankhead, December 22, 1817, in *Message from the President*, 8–9.

85. U.S. Congress, House committee report on the illicit introduction of slaves from Amelia Island, January 10, 1818, Annals of Congress, House, 15th Cong., 1st sess., 649–670.

86. Ronsen, *Border Law*, 215–216.

87. Ibid., 123–157.

88. In 1818, during the first Seminole War, General Andrew Jackson infamously executed two British subjects, leading to protests from the British and Spanish governments and a Congress investigation. See Deborah A. Rosen, "Wartime Prisoners and the Rule of Law: Andrew Jackson's Military Tribunals During the First Seminole War," *Journal of the Early Republic* 28, no. 4 (2008): 559–595. The U.S. administration probably wished to avoid another scandal against foreign nationals.

89. "Slaves Brought into the United States from Amelia Island, January 10, 1818," House of Representatives, 15th Cong., 1st sess., ASP: Foreign Relations, 38: 459.

90. *The Debates and Proceedings in the Congress of the United States: With an Appendix Containing Important State Papers and Public Documents, and All the Laws of a Public Nature; with a Copious Index; Compiled from Authentic Materials* (Washington, DC: Gales and Seaton, 1854), 646–648.

91. Charles H. Bowman, "Vicente Pazos and the Amelia Island Affair, 1817," *Florida Historical Quarterly* 53, no. 3 (1975): 273.

92. Pazos, *Exposition*, 7.

93. Ibid., 21.

94. Weeks, *John Quincy Adams*, 101.

95. Report of the Secretary of State—Department of State, Washington, January 28, 1819, in *Anales históricos de la revolución de la América Latina*, ed. Carlos Calvo (Bezançon: Jacquin, 1867), 5: 180.

96. *Message from the President*, 50.

97. Jennifer Heckart, "The Crossroads of Empire: The 1817 Liberation and Occupation of Amelia Island, East Florida" (PhD diss., University of Connecticut, 2006), 213–218.

98. Judith Ewell, *Venezuela and the United States: From Monroe's Hemisphere to Petroleum's Empire* (Athens: University of Georgia Press, 1996), 22; Maury Baker, "The Voyage of the U.S. Schooner *Nonsuch* up the Orinoco: Journal of the Perry Mission of 1819 to South America," *Hispanic American Historical Review* 30, no. 4 (1950): 487.

99. Charles O. Handy to John Quincy Adams, September 29, 1819, in *Diplomatic Correspondence of the United States Concerning the Independence of the Latin American Nations*, ed. William R. Manning (New York: Oxford University Press, 1925–1926), 2: 1178–1182.

100. "Sketch of Instructions for Agent for South America—Notes for the Department of State, March 24, 1819," in *Writings of James Monroe*, ed. S. M. Hamilton (New York: G. P. Putnam's Sons, 1898–1903), 6: 97.

101. *Correo del Orinoco*, March 27, 1819.

102. Albert Gallatin to John Quincy Adams, January 7, 1818, in Manning, *Diplomatic Correspondence*, 2: 1375.

103. Robert Kagan, *Dangerous Nation: America's Place in the World from Its Earliest Days to the Dawn of the Twentieth Century* (New York: Alfred A. Knopf, 2006), 97–99.

104. On the importance of courts in international diplomacy, see Gaffield, *Haitian Connections*, 147–148; Kevin Arlyck, "Plaintiffs v. Privateers: Litigation and Foreign Affairs in the Federal Courts, 1816–1822," *Law and History Review* 30, no. 1 (2012): 245–278; Lauren Benton, "Strange Sovereignty: The Provincia Oriental in the Atlantic World," *20/10: El Mundo Atlantico y la Modernidad Iberoamericana* 1 (2012): 89–107.

105. Edward G. White, "The Marshall Court and International Law: The Piracy Cases," *American Journal of International Law* 83, no. 4 (1989): 727–735.

106. Ferrari, *Memorie*, 430.

107. Commission from José Cortes Madariaga to Aury, June 3, 1818, AGNC, Secretario de Guerra y de Marina (hereafter SGM), 343, fol. 1024–1025.

108. José Cortes Madariaga to Juan Martin de Pueyrredón, August 25, 1818, in Ferro, *Vida*, 214–217.

109. Pedro Gual to Joaquín Mosquera, October 11, 1821, in Ferro, *Vida*, 291.

110. *Times*, June 26, 1819; Antonio García Reyes, *Memoria sobre la Primera Escuadra Nacional* (Santiago de Chile: Imprenta del Progreso, 1846).

111. James Parsons, *San Andrés and Providencia: English-Speaking Islands in the Western Caribbean* (Berkeley: University of California Press, 1956), 19. The 1803 Real Orden is the main source of conflict in the ongoing territorial conflict over the archipelago. See Bedoya Alvarado and Omar Alejandro, "El conflicto fronterizo entre Colombia y Nicaragua: Recuento histórico de una lucha por el territorio," *Historia Caribe* 9, no. 25 (2014): 241–271.

112. A detailed description of the island appears in C. F. Collett, "On the Island of Providencia," *Journal of the Royal Geography of London* 7 (1837): 203–210. On Providencia and the Mosquito Coast prior to Aury's arrival, see Frank Dawson, "The Evacuation of the Mosquito Shore and the English Who Stayed Behind, 1786–1800," *Americas* 55, no. 1 (1998): 63–89.

113. Jacob Dunham, *Journal of Voyages* (New York: published for the author, 1850), 39, 141; Parsons, *San Andrés*, 83.

114. Ferrari, *Memorie*, 435.

115. Louis Peru de Lacroix, "Relación presentada a Santander," December 1, 1822, AGNC, SGM, t. 343, fol. 1017–1018.

116. Courtois to Boyer, October 15, 1821, AGNC, SGM, t. 343, fol. 1030.

117. Memorial, 1820, Dolph Bricoe Center for American History, University of Texas at Austin, Louis Aury papers.

118. *Correo del Orinoco*, February 6, 1819, and *Censor of Maryland*, September 23, 1818.

119. Parsons, *San Andrés*, 20.

120. Aury to Santander, July 12, 1820, in Ferro, *Vida*, 258–259.

121. *Bermuda Gazette*, November 13, 1819.

122. *Alexandria Gazette*, October 28, 1819.

123. Aury to President of Venezuela, February 21, 1820, in Ferro, *Vida*, 223.

124. Aury to Santander, "Copia de la nota enviada por el general en jefe de las fuerzas de mar y tierra," July 8, 1820, AGNC, Colonia, Miscelánea, t. 132, fol. 654.

125. Codazzi, *Memorias*, 397.

126. Ferrari, *Memorie*, 446.

127. "El General Aury intima la rendición de la Plaza de Omoa," April 18, 1820, in Ferro, *Vida*, 237–238.

128. John Niles listed the population of Honduras at 382,845 in 1791 and 736,337 in 1820. Niles, *A View of South America and Mexico . . . by a Citizen of the United States* (New York: H. Huntington, 1825).

129. Robert S. Smith, "Indigo Production and Trade in Colonial Guatemala," *Hispanic American Historical Review* 39, no. 2 (1959): 181–211.

130. Lieut. Colonel Arthur to Foreign Office, June 22, 1819, TNA, CO 123/28, fol. 12.

131. Lacroix to Montilla, December 2, 1822, AGNC, SGM, t. 343, fol. 1026–1027; Medardo Mejia, *Historia de Honduras* (Tegucigalpa: Editorial Universitaria, 1983), 441–445.

132. Arthur to Foreign Office, May 29, 1819, TNA, CO 123/28, fol. 9 and 10; Arthur to Foreign Office, February 13, 1820, TNA, CO 123/29, fol. 24. A local merchant convinced a U.S. captain from Baltimore to take sixty-four kegs of gunpowder and deliver them to Aury's squadron. Arthur to Foreign Office, June 23, 1819, TNA, CO 123/28, fol. 13.

133. Aury, *Relation ou Détail de mes opérations militaires sur la province de Guatemala et des motifs qui les ont déterminés*, LOC/MD, South American independence: manuscript book, MMC, fol. 8–10.

134. José María Palomar, "Noticia de la invasión de Truxillo el 22 abril de 1820 verificada por las fuerzas de la Escuadrilla del Pirata Aury; y de los resultados que publica la Capitanía General para satisfacción de todos los habitantes de este fiel reyno," May 1, 1820, John Carter Brown Library.

135. April 28, 1820, in Ferro, *Vida*, 237–238.

136. Account of Omoa in Aury, *Détail Guatemala*, and Aury to Captain General of Guatemala, May 18, 1820, in Ferro, *Vida*, 241–242.

137. Aury, *Détail Guatemala*, 15.

138. For millenarist rhetoric in other revolutions, Claudio Saunt, *A New Order of Things: Property, Power, and the Transformation of the Creek Indians, 1733–1816* (Cambridge: Cambridge University Press, 1999); Eric Van Young, *The Other Rebellion: Popular Violence, Ideology, and the Struggle for Mexican Independence, 1810–1821* (Stanford, CA: Stanford University Press, 2001).

139. Aury, *Détail Guatemala*, 7.

140. Lacroix to Santander, November 11, 1822, AGNC, SGM, t. 343, fol. 1013–1016.

141. Luis Brión to Mariano Montilla, December 6, 1820, in Jaime Duarte French, *Tres Luises del Caribe ¿corsarios o libertadores?* (Bogotà: El Ancora Ediciones, 1988), 256.

142. Bolívar to Aury, January 18, 1821, in *Nuestros próceres navales*, ed. Francisco Alejandro Vargas (Caracas: Editorial Grafolit, 1964), 278.

143. *Gaceta de Cartagena*, July 10, 1824, no. 152.

144. François Dalencour, *Alexandre Pétion devant l'humanité* (François Dalencour: Port au Prince, 1928), 47.

145. Aury, *Détail Guatemala*, 8.

146. Aury changed his will in October 1820, and Eliza did not get anything. His nephew Adrien died before the will was changed. It is not known whether his share went to Aury's sister or was divided among his forces, LOC/MD/LA, folder 9. Codazzi and Ferrari traveled to Paris to meet Victoire Aury and give her money. A formerly enslaved Francesco was with them, who could be the one mentioned in Aury's will. Codazzi, *Memorias*, 476.

147. *Mémoires de la Société d'Histoire de Paris et de l'Ile de France* (Paris: H. Champion, 1893), 20: 148.

148. "Inventaire après décès de Victoire-Angélique Aury, épouse de Charles-Honoré Dupuis, rue Saint-Denis, n° 173, le 4 avril 1839," Archives Nationales de France, Minutes et répertoires du notaire Émile Louis Baudelocque, MC/RE/LXX/24.

149. Lacroix, "Relación reservada del Coronel L. Peru de Lacroix," January 20, 1822, AGNC, SGM, t. 343, fol. 1018.

150. "Proclama," *Gaceta de Cartagena*, December 21, 1822.

151. Courtois to Courtois, October 15, 1821, AGNC, SGM, t. 343, fol. 1030–1034; Courtois to Boyer, October 15, 1821, AGNC, SGM, t. 343, fol. 1030.

152. Lacroix, "Relación," fol. 1020.

153. Ibid., fol. 1046–1047.

154. *Gaceta de Cartagena*, January 4, 1823. Laws regarding freedom of the press had just been passed: *Cuerpo de leyes de la Republica de Colombia. Comprende la constitución y leyes sancionadas por el primer congreso general en las sesiones que celebro desde el 6 de mayo hasta el 14 de octubre de 1821* (Bogotá: Bruno Espinosa, 1822), 1: 96–108. Andrés Londoño, "Juicios de imprenta en Colombia (1821–1851). El jurado popular y el control de los libelos inflamatorios," *Anuario Colombiano de Historia Social y de la Cultura* 40, no. 1 (2013): 75–112.

155. Deposition of Jean-Louis Dutrieu aboard the *Amazon*, August 9, 1822, AGNC, SGM, t. 343, fol. 1041.

156. Sibylle Fischer, "Specters of the Republic: The Case of Manuel Piar," *Journal of Latin American Cultural Studies* 27, no. 3 (2018): 295–311.

157. "Boletín del Gobierno de Colombia sobre usurpaciones en la costa de Mosquitos e islas de San Andrés y Providencia, Bogotá, febrero de 1823," in Ferro, *Vida*, 254.

158. "Boletín del Gobierno de Colombia," in Ferro, *Vida*, 254; *Gaceta de Colombia*, February 2, 1823.

159. "Consejo ordinario de gobierno del martes 25 de febrero de 1823," in *Acuerdos del consejo de Gobierno de la Republica de Colombia 1821–1827*, ed. Enrique Ortega Ricaurte (Bogotá: Biblioteca de la Presidencia de la República, 1988), 1: 112.

160. Courtois to Santander, n.d., in Cortazar, *Correspondencia a Santander*, 5: 220–221; Departamento de Zuma 1823, *Gaceta de Colombia*, December 5, 1824.

161. *Acusación documentada que hizo al tribunal de censura el día 26 abril 1823, Severo Courtois del artículo firmado El Censor* (Cartagena: Imprenta del gobierno, 1823), John Carter Brown Library, Archivo Histórico Restrepo, fondo II, vol. 51, fol. 106–107.

162. Courtois's four ships, *Intrepido, Muerte, Minerva,* and *Cazador,* went to Maracaibo. Courtois to Santander, November 15, 1823, in Cortazar, *Correspondencia a Santander,* 5: 217; To Santander from Montilla, December 9, 1822, *Archivo Santander,* 9: 137–138; "Comanderia general de la escuadra de operaciones," *Gaceta de Colombia,* December 8, 1822.

163. Maria Elena Capriles, "Bolívar y la actuación de Venezuela en el Caribe a través de sus corsarios: Santo Domingo, Puerto Rico, Cuba y México," *Boletín de la Academia Nacional de Historia* 89, no. 355 (2006): 149–163.

164. "Instrucciones del Gobierno de Colombia," October 10–11, 1821, in *Documentos sobre el congreso anfictiónico de Panamá,* ed. German de la Reza (Caracas: Fundaciòn Biblioteca Ayacucho, 2010), 10.

165. Pedro Gual to Joaquín Mosquera, October 11, 1821, in Calvo, *Anales diplomáticos de Colombia,* 294.

166. *Times,* June 26, 1819.

167. A 2005 interview with Juan Ramirez Dawkins shows that the memory of Aury in Providencia lived on. His great-grandfather was a schooner captain whose parents worked with Aury. Ramirez Dawkins pointed out in the interview, "As you know, Aury played an important role in the history of our islands, and even in this country since he was Bolívar's collaborator." *Creole Raizales del archipiélago de San Andrés, Providencia y Santa Catalina que habitan la ciudad de Bogotá,* ed. Corporación Latinoamérica Misión Rural (Bogotá: Luar Comunica, 2008), 103.

168. Vives to Ministro de la Gobernación de Ultramar, September 28, 1823, in *Documentos para la historia de Venezuela en el Archivo Nacional de Cuba,* ed. José Franco (Havana: Archivo Nacional de Cuba, 1960), 95.

169. Clément Lanier, "Cuba et la conspiration d'Aponte en 1812," *Revue de la Société haïtienne d'histoire, de géographie et de géologie* 23, no. 86 (1952): 29; Philip Foner, *A History of Cuba and Its Relations with the United States* (New York: International Publishers, 1962), 112–120; Roque E. Garrigo, *Historia documentada de la conspiración de los soles y rayos de Bolívar* (Havana: Academia de la Historia de Cuba, 1929), 151–165.

170. Nicola Miller, "Reading Rousseau in Spanish America During the Wars of Independence (1808–1826)," in *Engaging with Rousseau: Reaction and Interpretation from the Eighteenth Century to the Present,* ed. Avi Lifscitz (Cambridge: Cambridge University Press, 2016), 114–135.

171. *Chilian loan. A report of the trial of Yrisarri v. Clement in the Court of Common Pleas, 19th December 1825* (London: E. G. Triquet, 1826).

172. "Message of the President," James Monroe to Congress, January 13, 1818, in *Niles' Weekly Register,* January 17, 1818.

173. Zea to Bolívar, June 8, 1819, in *Archivo Santander,* 2: 158.

174. *Jamaican Courant,* July 28, 1819.

175. "Proclamation in Fernandina," November 5, 1817, P. K. Yonge Library, University of Florida, Miscellaneous Manuscripts (Fl).

Chapter 2

1. The correspondence between Juan Bautista Mariano Picornell and Manuel Cortés Campomanes is in the U.S. and Spanish archives. See, for example, Picornell to Toledo, December 13, 1813, NARA, Correspondence Relating to the Filibustering Expedition Against the Spanish

Government of Mexico, 1811–1816, record group 59, microcopy T 286, and "Copia de una carta del coronel español Manuel Cortés Campomanes a don Juan Mariano Picornell," June 21, 1814, AGI, Indiferente General, fol. 1568.

2. In his study of revolutionary-era Texas, Raúl Coronado argued that the social relationship to writing underwent a radical change: in the late eighteenth and early nineteenth centuries and with the Latin American wars of independence. Coronado, *World Not to Come*, 51–55.

3. Andrew Pettegree, *The Invention of News: How the World Came to Know About Itself* (New Haven, CT: Yale University Press, 2014); Brendan Dooley, ed., *The Dissemination of News and the Emergence of Contemporaneity on Early Modern Europe* (Aldershot: Ashgate, 2010); Robert Darnton, "An Early Information Society: News and the Media in Eighteenth Century Paris," *American Historical Review* 105, no. 1 (2000): 1–35; Elizabeth Eisenstein, *The Printing Press as an Agent of Change: Communications and Transformations in Early Modern Europe* (Cambridge: Cambridge University Press, 1979). See also the ensuing discussion forum in *American Historical Review* 107, no. 1 (2002): 106–115.

4. For Venezuela, see Cristina Soriano, *Tides of Revolution: Information, Insurgencies, and the Crisis of Colonial Rule in Venezuela* (Albuquerque: University of New Mexico Press, 2018). For Peru, see Cecilia Méndez, *The Plebeian Republic: The Huanta Rebellion and the Making of the Peruvian State, 1820–1850* (Durham, NC: Duke University Press, 2005); Rebecca Earle, "The Role of Print in the Spanish American Wars of Independence," in *The Political Power of the Word: Press and Oratory in Nineteenth Century Latin America*, ed. Yvàn Jaksic (London: Institute of Latin American Studies, University of London, 2002), 9–33.

5. Polasky divides revolutionary print into different genres of documents in order to recover an alternative political sphere of revolutionary idealism. Polasky, *Revolutions*, 11–14.

6. Christopher Hill, *The World Turned Upside Down: Radical Ideas During the English Revolution* (New York: Viking, 1972), 30.

7. Bernard Bailyn, *Pamphlets of the American Revolution, 1750–1776* (Cambridge, MA: Harvard University Press, 1965), 8.

8. From John Adams to Hezekiah Niles, February 13, 1818, Founders Online, National Archives, http://founders.archives.gov/documents/Adams/99-02-02-6854; Bernard Bailyn, *The Ideological Origins of the American Revolution* (Cambridge, MA.: Harvard University Press, 1967), 160.

9. Benedict Anderson, *Imagined Communities: Reflections on the Origin and Spread of Nationalism* (London: Verso, 1991). On the public sphere in Latin America, see Víctor Uribe-Urán, "The Birth of a Public Sphere in Latin America During the Age of Revolution," *Comparative Studies in Society and History* 42, no. 2 (2000): 425–457; José Elías Palti, "Recent Studies on the Emergence of a Public Sphere in Latin America," *Latin America Research Review* 36, no. 2 (2001): 255–266. There is a vast literature on nationalism in the Americas. A good summary is Don H. Doyle and Eric Van Young, "Independence and Nationalism in the Americas," in *The Oxford Handbook of the History of Nationalism*, ed. John Breuilly (Oxford: Oxford University Press, 2013), 97–125.

10. José David Saldívar, *Border Matters: Remapping American Cultural Studies* (Berkeley: University of California Press, 1997); Kristen Silva Gruez, *Ambassadors of Culture: The Transamerican Origins of Latino Writing* (Princeton, NJ: Princeton University Press, 2002); Andy Doolen, *Territories of Empire: U.S. Writing from the Louisiana Purchase to Mexican Independence* (Oxford: Oxford University Press, 2014).

11. Roderick Cave, "Early Printing and the Book Trade in the West Indies," *Library Quarterly: Information, Community, Policy* 48, no. 2 (1978): 176.

12. Harold E. Sterne, *A Catalogue of Nineteenth Century Printing Presses* (New Castle, DE: Oak Knoll Press, 2001), 2; Elizabeth M. Harris, *Printing Presses in the Graphic Arts Collection, National Museum of American History* (Washington, DC: Smithsonian Institution, 1996).

13. Several scholars have made this point. Coronado argues against the idea that the arrival of the printing press shaped a different society and examines instead the meaning of the printing press in relation to existing forms of communication. Coronado, *World Not to Come*, 269; Soriano, *Tides of Revolution*.

14. Caracas—Sublevación—1797: Contiene la obrado prohibiendo la introducción y lectura del Libro titulado, *Derechos del Hombre, y del Ciudadano*, y cualesquiera papel sedicioso, AGI, Caracas 432, fol. 927.

15. Pedro Grases and Caracciolo Parra Pérez, eds., '*El Colombiano' de Francisco de Miranda, y dos documentos americanistas* (Caracas: Instituto Nacional de Hipódromos, 1966), 17.

16. "Declaracion de Patricio Ronàn," August 18, 1797, AGI, Caracas 427, fol. 75–81.

17. "Diary and Letters of Henry Ingersoll, Prisoner at Cartaghena, 1806–1809," *American Historical Review* 3, no. 4 (1898): 674; James Biggs, *The History of Don Francisco de Miranda's Attempt to Effect a Revolution in South America: In a Series of Letters*, 2nd ed. (Boston: Edward Oliver, 1812), 23.

18. Karen Racine, *Francisco De Miranda: A Transatlantic Life in the Age of Revolution* (Wilmington, DE: SR Books, 2003), 160–163.

19. Apodaca to Bardaxi, May 15, 1810, Archivo General de Simancas, Estado, fol. 8173. Karen Racine, "Newsprint Nations: Spanish American Publishing in London, 1808–1827," in *The Foreign Political Press in Nineteenth-Century London: Politics from a Distance*, ed. Constance Bantman and Ana Cláudia Suriani da Silva (London: Bloomsbury Academic, 2018), 15–32.

20. The full text of the newspaper is in Grases and Parra Pérez, *El Colombiano*.

21. William Spence Robertson, *The Life of Miranda* (Chapel Hill: University of North Carolina Press, 1929), 2: 60.

22. *Times*, August 12, 1810.

23. On the Hispanophone print culture in Philadelphia, see Anna Brickhouse, *Transamerican Literary Relations and the Nineteenth-Century Public Sphere* (Cambridge: Cambridge University Press, 2005); Nicolas Kanellos, "José Alvarez de Toledo y Dubois and the Origins of Hispanic Publishing in the Early American Republic," *Early American Literature* 43, no. 1 (2008): 83–100; Nancy Vogeley, "Spanish-Language Masonic Books Printed in the Early United States," *Early American Literature* 43, no. 2 (2008): 337–360.

24. Onis to Captain General of Cuba, March 4, 1813, in AGI, Cuba, leg. 1837.

25. Salcedo to Viceroy of New Spain, June 2, 1812, AGNM-Newberry, Historia, Operaciones de Guerra.

26. Only one issue of the *Gaceta* was printed. Kathryn Garrett, "The First Newspaper of Texas: *Gaceta de Texas*," *Southwestern Historical Quarterly* 40, no. 3 (1937): 200–215.

27. Morphy to Captain-General of Cuba, December 27, 1815, AGI, Cuba, leg. 1815; Sedella to Captain-General of Cuba, January 18, 1816, reproduced in Harris Gaylord Warren, "Documents Relating to Pierre Laffite's Entrance into the Service of Spain," *Southwestern Historical Quarterly* 44, no. 1 (1940): 82.

28. William Robinson, *Memoirs of the Mexican Revolution; Including a Narrative of the Expedition of General Xavier Mina* (London: Lackington, Hughes, Harding, Mavor, & Lepard, 1821), 58.

29. Fatio to Captain-General, December 4, 1817, AGNM-Newberry, Notas Diplomaticas, vol. 2, fol. 88.

30. Ibid., 83. Further evidence of the keen European—particularly British—interest in the Spanish American revolutions is the review of Robinson's *Memoirs* in the periodical *Gentleman's Magazine and Historical Chronicle* 91 (London: A. Dodd and A. Smith, 1821), 426–430.

31. "Boletín I de la División Auxiliar de la República Mexicana," AGI, Cuba, leg. 1900. No original copy survives, but a reprint can be found in Carlos María Bustamante's *Cuadro histórico de la revolución de la America Mexicana* (México, D.F: Imprenta del águila, 1843), 46; Manuel Ortuno Martinez, *Xavier Mina: Fronteras De Libertad* (Migallón: Porrúa, 2003).

32. "Boletín I."

33. *Morning Chronicle*, August 11, 1817.

34. Joaquín Infante, *Solucion á la cuestion de derecho sobre la emancipacion de la América* (Cádiz: Imprenta de Roquero, 1820); Carlos Trélles, *Apuntes biográficos del Dr. Joaquín Infante* (Havana: Academia de la historia de Cuba, 1928).

35. Lota M. Spell, "Samuel Bangs: The First Printer in Texas," *Southwestern Historical Quarterly* 35, no. 4 (1932): 267–278.

36. Coronado shows that revolutionaries in Texas drew from different philosophical traditions of conceptualizing sovereignty articulated during the colonial era, a mixture of neoscholastic natural law philosophy, Spanish humanism, medieval Castilian legal tradition (especially the Siete Partidas), indigenous philosophies, and the Hapsburgs' "quasi-federalist approach to ruling." This discourse coexisted with the Bourbons' "Enlightened absolutism," on one hand, and North Atlantic tradition of Lockean liberalism and individualism, on the other. Coronado, *World Not to Come*, 5.

37. George Bastin, "Traduction et révolution à l'époque de l'indépendance hispano-américaine," *Meta* 49, no. 3 (2004): 562–575.

38. "Últimas noticias sobre los reos de alta traición," July 31, 1800, AGI, Caracas 96, fol. 235.

39. *Gazette of the United States*, March 7, 1801. Mention of the French privateer *Carmagnole* in *Naval Warfare: An International Encyclopedia*, ed. Spencer Tucker (Santa Barbara: ABC-CLIO, 2002), 23.

40. AGI, Caracas 432, fol. 780–786.

41. Ibid., fol. 927.

42. Ibid., fol. 909.

43. Pedro Grases, *La conspiración de Gual y España y el ideario de la independencia* (Caracas: Instituto Panamericano de Geografía e Historia, 1949), 157–161.

44. *Actas del Congreso Constituyente de Venezuela en 1811*, in Grases, *Conspiración*, 165, n. 1.

45. Carlos Restrepo, *Primeras constituciones de Colombia y Venezuela, 1811–1830* (Bogotá: Universidad Externado de Colombia, 1993).

46. Toledo to Lancelle, November 25, 1813, NARA, RG 59, T 286.

47. Picornell to Toledo, December 13, 1813, NARA, RG 59, T 286.

48. Humbert to president of junta of Caracas, May 26, 1814, and Humbert to president of Cartagena, May 26, 1814, in *Documentos para la Historia de México existentes en el Archivo Nacional de Cuba*, ed. José Franco (Havana: Archivo Nacional de Cuba, 1961), 42.

49. Mona Ozouf, *L'Homme régénéré. Essais sur la Révolution française* (Paris: Gallimard, 2013).

50. "The Provisional Government of the Internal Province of Mexico to the Freemen of All Nations," December 5, 1813, Boston Public Library, Texas as province and republic 1795–1845, reel 17, no. 1051.

51. The 1798 proclamation is in John Jones, *An Impartial Narrative of the Most Important Engagements: Which Took Place Between His Majesty's Forces and the Rebels, During the Irish*

Rebellion, 1798 (Dublin: John Jones, 1799), 2: 205. The 1814 proclamation is enclosed in Morphy to Apocada, June 10, 1814, in Franco, *Documentos Mexico*, 42.

52. Enclosed in Sedella to Morphy, July 10, 1814, AHN, estado, leg. 5558, exp. 12.

53. Picornell to Onis, November 24, 1815, AGI, Cuba, leg. 1815.

54. Hyde de Neuville to Minister of Foreign Affairs, February 16, 1820, ADMAE, Correspondance Politique, Etats-Unis, vol. 77, fol. 28; Case 1590, Jean-Joseph Amable Humbert: Accessory to Piracy, 1820, NOPL, District Court at New Orleans, National Archives Southwest Region microfilm 7RA-119.

55. Guillemin to Ministry of Foreign Affairs, September 14, 1820, ADMAE, Correspondance Consulaire: New Orleans, vol. 2, fol. 307.

56. Humbert's obituary in *Louisiana Gazette*, April 1, 1823.

57. Robert Darnton and Daniel Roche, eds., *Revolution in Print: The Press in France, 1775–1800* (Berkeley: University of California Press, 1989); Jeremy Popkin, *Revolutionary News: The Press in France, 1789–1799* (Durham, NC: Duke University Press, 1990); Eric Slauter, "Reading and Radicalization: Print, Politics, and the American Revolution," *Early American Studies* 8, no. 1 (2010): 5–40; Rafael Rojas, *La escritura de la Independencia. El surgimiento de la opinión pública en México* (México D.F.: Taurus/Cide, 2003); Christopher Conwat, "Letras combinetes: relectura de la *Gaceta de Caracas*, 1808–1822," *Revista Iberoamericana* 214 (2006): 77–92.

58. Mary Louise Pratt, *Imperial Eyes: Travel Writing and Transculturation* (London: Routledge, 1992), 15.

59. Monica Henry, "Les États-Unis et la reconnaissance des indépendances des républiques hispano-américaines, 1817–1822," in *Les États-Unis face aux révolutions: De la Révolution française à la victoire de Mao en Chine*, ed. Pierre Mélandri and Serge Ricard (Paris: L'Harmattan, 2006), 83–95; Fitz, *Sister Republics*.

60. Jessica Harland-Jacobs, *Builders of Empire: Freemasons and British Imperialism, 1717–1927* (Chapel Hill: University of North Carolina Press, 2007) and "Worlds of Brothers," *Journal for Research into Freemasonry and Fraternalism* 2, no. 1 (2011): 10–37; Julius S. Scott, *The Common Wind: Afro-American Currents in the Age of the Haitian Revolution* (London: Verso, 2018); Steven C. Bullock, *Revolutionary Brotherhood: Freemasonry and the Transformation of the American Social Order, 1730–1840* (Chapel Hill: University of Carolina Press, 1996); Pierre-Yves Beaurepaire, *La République universelle des francs-maçons: De Newton à Metternich* (Rennes: Editions Ouest-France, 1999); Eric Saunier, "L'espace caribéen: Un enjeu de pouvoir pour la franc-maçonnerie française," *Revista de Estudios Históricos de la Masonería Latinoamericana y Caribeña* 1, no. 1 (2009): 42–56; R. William Weisberger, Wallace McLeod, and S. Brent Morris, eds., *Freemasonry on Both Sides of the Atlantic: Essays Concerning the Craft in the British Isles, Europe, the United States, and Mexico* (New York: Columbia University Press, 2002); Jossiana Arroyo, *Writing Secrecy in Caribbean Freemasonry* (New York: Palgrave-Macmillan, 2013); special issue "The Fraternal Atlantic, 1770–1930," *Atlantic Studies* 15, no. 3 (2018): 283–422.

61. Victor Marcías-González, "Masculine Friendships, Sentiment, and Homoerotics in Nineteenth-Century Mexico: The Correspondence of José María Calderón y Tapia, 1820s–1850s," *Journal of the History of Sexuality* 16, no. 3 (2007): 416–435; Jacob, *Strangers Nowhere in the World*, 95–121. On the role of freemasonry in early national Haiti, see Sheller, "Sword-Bearing Citizens," 252–254.

62. George L. Mosse, "Friendship and Nationhood: About the Promise and Failure of German Nationalism," *Journal of Contemporary History* 17 (1982): 351–367; Graham M. Smith,

"Friendship, State, and Nation," in *Friendship and International Relations*, ed. S. Koschut and A. Oelsner (London: Palgrave Macmillan, 2014), 35–50.

63. AGI Caracas 434, no. 85.

64. Casto Fulgencio López, *Juan Bautista Picornell y la conspiración de Gual y España* (Madrid: Ediciones Nueva Càdiz, 1955), 149.

65. Bassi, *Aqueous Territory*, 55–81; Maria Cristina Soriano, "A True Vassal of the King: Pardo Literacy and Political Identity in Venezuela During the Age of Revolutions," *Atlantic Studies, Global Currents* 14, no. 3 (2017): 275–295.

66. Mission de Mr Chasseriau à St. Thomas, 1827–1831, ANOM, séries géographiques/ Amer 34: Possessions Danoises.

67. Racine, "Newsprint Nations," 24.

68. "Real Orden del 24 de septiembre de 1789," AHN, Reales Ordenes, vol. 10, fol. 140.

69. Luis de Onís to Viceroy of New Spain, June 20, 1810, AGNM-Newberry, Historia, vol. 161.

70. Onís to Viceroy of New Spain, May 1, 1815, P. K. Yonge Library, University of Florida, Joseph Byrne Lockey Documents Related to the History of Florida.

71. Vidal to Onís, September 1, 1809, AGNM, Historia, vol. 161, fol. 60–75.

72. *España ensangrentada por el horrendo corzo, tirano de la Europa, auxiliado de su inicuo agente el vilísimo Godoy (alias el Choricero)* (New Orleans, LA: Press of Juan Mowry, 1808).

73. Vidal to Onís, September 1, 1809, AGNM, Historia, vol. 161, fol. 60–75.

74. Conde de Villanueva to Capt. General, April 14, 1829, Archivo Nacional de Cuba, reel 5, Asuntos Políticos, leg. 34, exp. 3, copy at the Historic New Orleans Collection, Archivo Nacional de Cuba—Louisiana, reel 5.

75. Petition of Juan Mariano Picornell, February 12, 1814, encl. in Sedella to Apocada, February 23, 1814, AGI, Cuba, leg. 1814.

76. Jaime O. Rodriguez, "Equality! The Sacred Right of Equality: Representation Under Constitution of 1812," *Revista de Indias* 67, no. 242 (2008): 97–122; José M. Portillo Valdès, *Crisis Atlántica. Autonomía e Independencia en la crisis de la monarquía hispana* (Madrid: Marcial Pons-Fundación Carolina, 2006).

77. J. J. Dauxion-Lavaysse, *Voyage aux îles de Trinidad, de Tobago, de la Marguerite, et dans diverses parties de Venezuela, dans l'Amérique Méridionale* (Paris: F. Schoëll, 1813), 119. The papal bulls mentioned by Dauxion were probably Pie VI's. In 1790, this pope informed the king of France that he opposed the project of civil constitution for the clergy and that he excommunicated the French nation.

78. Pekka Hämäläinen and Samuel Truett, "On Borderlands," *Journal of American History* 98, no. 2 (2011): 338–361.

79. Zea to Bolívar, June 8, 1819, in *Archivo Santander*, ed. Ernesto Restrepo Tirado and Diego Mendo (Bogotá: Aguila Negra Editorial, 1914), 2: 15; Donzelot to Ministry of Navy and Colonies, December 29, 1819, ANOM, SG/Amer53.

80. Cortés Campomanes to Bello, April 24, 1824, in *Andrés Bello: Obras Completas. Epistolario I* (Caracas: La Casa de Bello, 1984), 25: 184. Bello and Cortés Campomanes met through the Spanish American exile community in London in 1809–1810.

81. Cortés Campomanes to Bello, March 26, 1826, *Andrés Bello*, 25: 177.

82. Picornell's wife was Maria Celeste Villaso y Andry. This was Picornell's second marriage: when he was exiled from Spain, he left behind a wife and a three-year-old son. When he remarried twenty years later, his bride was thirty years younger than he was. Harris Gaylord

Warren, "The Southern Career of Juan Mariano Picornell," *Journal of Southern History* 8, no. 3 (1942): 322–323.

83. P. F. Thomas, *Essai sur la fièvreJaune d'Amérique . . . précédé de considérations hygiéniques sur la Nouvelle Orléans, par J.M. Picornell, membre de la Société Médicale de Paris* (New Orleans, LA: Baillière, 1823), 7.

84. *Jackson's Oxford Journal*, August 23, 1817.

Chapter 3

1. Gustavus Hippisley, *A Narrative of the Expedition to the Rivers Orinoco and Apuré, in South America; Which Sailed from England in November 1817, and Joined the Patriotic Forces in Venezuela and Caracas* (London: John Murray, 1819), 252.

2. For the North American war of independence, see George P. Clark, "The Role of the Haitian Volunteers at Savannah in 1779: An Attempt at an Objective View," *Phylon* 41, no. 4 (1980): 356–366 and John D. Garrigus, *Before Haiti: Race and Citizenship in French Saint-Domingue* (New York: Palgrave Macmillan, 2006), 207–224. For Latin America, see Verna, *Petión y Bolívar*, and William F. Lewis, "Simón Bolívar and Xavier Mina: A Rendezvous in Haiti," *Journal of Inter-American Studies* 11, no. 3 (1969): 458–465.

3. Matthew J. Clavin, *Toussaint Louverture and the American Civil War: The Promise and Peril of a Second Haitian Revolution* (Philadelphia: University of Pennsylvania Press, 2010), 11–12; Gregory Pierrot, *The Black Avenger in Atlantic Culture* (Athens: University of Georgia Press, 2019). On the specter of a race war in the United States, see Kay Wright Lewis, *A Curse upon the Nation: Race, Freedom, and Extermination in America and the Atlantic World* (Athens: University of Georgia Press, 2017).

4. Peter Blanchard, *Under the Flags of Freedom: Slave Soldiers and the Wars of Independence in Spanish South America* (Pittsburgh: University of Pittsburgh Press, 2008); Anne Pérotin-Dumon, "Free Colored and Slaves in Revolutionary Guadeloupe: Politics and Political Consciousness," in *The Lesser Antilles in the Age of European Expansion*, ed. Robert L. Paquette and Stanley L. Engerman (Gainesville: University Press of Florida, 1996), 25–79; Matt D. Childs, *The 1812 Aponte Rebellion in Cuba and the Struggle Against Atlantic Slavery* (Chapel Hill: University of North Carolina Press, 2006).

5. The best studies of Savary are Caryn Cossé Bell, *Revolution*, 62–70, and Sara E. Johnson, *The Fear of French Negroes: Transcolonial Collaboration in the Revolutionary Americas* (Berkeley: University of California Press, 2012), 91–120. While Cossé Bell places Savary in what she calls an "Afro-Creole protest tradition" and a strain of radical republicanism (64), Johnson moves away from territorial affiliations and nationalist frameworks to understand what she calls "intra-black class conflict," arguing that Savary was born free to a class of free people of color in Saint-Domingue who often owned, sold, and bought enslaved people (93).

6. Andrew Lambert, "Creating Cultural Difference: The Military, Political and Cultural Legacy of the Anglo-American War of 1812–1815," in *War, Demobilization and Memory: The Legacy of War in the Era of Atlantic Revolutions*, ed. Alan Forrest, Karen Hagemann, and Michael Rowe (Basingstoke: Palgrave Macmillan, 2016), 303–319; Flora Barboza, *El Lago De Maracaibo en la historia nacional* (Maracaibo: Acervo Histórico del Estado Zulia, 2003); "24 de julio: Hoy es el Día de la Armada Nacional Bolivariana," *Correo del Orinoco*, July 24, 2019.

7. Ben Vinson III, *Bearing Arms for His Majesty: The Free-Colored Militia in Colonial Mexico* (Stanford, CA: Stanford University Press, 2010); Jane Landers, "Transforming Bondmen into Vassals: Arming Slaves in Colonial Spanish America," and Laurent Dubois, "Citizen

Soldiers: Emancipation and Military Service in the Revolutionary French Caribbean," in *Arming Slaves: From Classical Times to the Modern Age*, ed. Christopher Leslie Brown and Philip D. Morgan (New Haven, CT: Yale University Press, 2006), 120–145, 233–254; Evelyn P. Jennings, "Paths to Freedom: Imperial Defense and Manumission in Havana, 1762–1800," in *Paths to Freedom: Manumission in the Atlantic World*, ed. Rosemary Brana-Shute and Randy J. Sparks (Columbia: University of South Carolina Press, 2009), 121–141; Michele Reid Vazquez, *The Year of the Lash: Free People of Color in Cuba and the Nineteenth-Century Atlantic World* (Athens: University of Georgia Press, 2011).

8. On the differences among free people of color between the "military leadership class" in the North and the reluctance to serve in the South, especially after the 1779 Savannah expedition, see Stewart R. King, *Blue Coat or Powdered Wig: Free People of Color in Pre-Revolutionary Saint Domingue* (Athens: University of Georgia Press, 2001), 226–265, and John D. Garrigus, *Before Haiti: Race and Citizenship in French Saint-Domingue* (New York: Palgrave Macmillan, 2006), 109–140, 195–225.

9. Cited in Garrigus, *Before Haiti*, 205.

10. Etat civil, Saint Marc, 1787, ANOM; Marcelino Guillot, AGNC, República, Hojas de Servicio, t. 19, fol. 1019.

11. John D. Garrigus, "Opportunist or Patriot? Julien Raimond (1744–1801) and the Haitian Revolution," *Slavery & Abolition* 28, no. 1 (2007): 1–21.

12. Nathalie Dessens, *From Saint-Domingue to New Orleans: Migration and Influences* (Gainesville: University of Florida Press, 2007); Susan Branson and Leslie Patrick, "Etrangers dans un Pays Etrange: Saint-Dominguan Refugees of Color in Philadelphia," in *The Impact of the Haitian Revolution*, ed. David Geggus (Columbia: University of South Carolina Press, 2001), 93–208; Ashli White, *Encountering Revolution: Haiti and the Making of the Early Republic* (Baltimore: Johns Hopkins University Press, 2010); Patrick Bryan, "Conflict and Reconciliation: The French Émigrés in Nineteenth Century Jamaica," *Jamaica Journal* 7 (1972): 13–19; Gabriel Debien and Philip Wright, "Les colons de Saint-Domingue passés à la Jamaïque (1792–1835)," *Bulletin de la Société d'Histoire de la Guadeloupe* no. 26 (1975): 3–216.

13. Paul F. Lachance, "The 1809 Immigration of Saint-Domingue Refugees to New Orleans: Reception, Integration and Impact," *Louisiana History* 29, no. 2 (1988): 109–141.

14. Cossé Bell, *Revolution*, 42–56.

15. Kimberly Hanger, *Bounded Lives, Bounded Places: Free Black Society in Colonial New Orleans, 1769–1803* (Durham, NC: Duke University Press, 1997), 110–136.

16. Claiborne to Maurice Rogers, August 9, 1809, in *Official Letter Books of W. C. C. Claiborne, 1801–1816*, ed. Dunbar Rowland (Jackson, MS: State Department of Archives and History, 1917), 4: 402.

17. Claiborne to Major Dubourg, January 14, 1811, *Official Letter Books*, 5: 100.

18. Louis Crispin's testimony, NOPL, Records of U.S. District Court for Eastern District of Louisiana, 1806–1814, M1082, Louisiana Division, reel 9, case 376.

19. Tousard to Serurier, November 8, 1813, ADMAE, Correspondance Politique, Etats-Unis, Supplément, no. 33, fol. 223.

20. Picornell to Onís, November 24, 1813, AGI, Cuba, leg. 1815.

21. David Narrett, "José Bernardo Gutiérrez de Lara: Caudillo of the Mexican Republic in Texas," *Southwestern Historical Quarterly* 105, no. 2 (2002): 194–228; Julia Garrett, "The First Constitution of Texas, April 17, 1813," *Southwestern Historical Quarterly* 40, no. 4 (1937): 290–308.

22. "Proclamation to the Free Colored Inhabitants of Louisiana," September 21, 1814, *Niles' Weekly Register*, December 3, 1814.

23. Service records of volunteer soldiers who served during the War of 1812 in the state of Louisiana, 2 Batt'n [D'Aquin's] Militia, USNA, War of 1812 service records, roll boxes 47 and 87. Roland McConnell, *Negro Troops of Antebellum Louisiana, a History of the Battalion of Free Men of Color* (Baton Rouge: Louisiana State University Press, 1968), 70; Rosemarie Fay Loomis, *Negro Soldiers: Free Men of Color in the Battle of New Orleans, War of 1812* (New Orleans: Aux quatre vents Limited, 1991).

24. McCausland to Jackson, February 24, 1815, in *Papers of Andrew Jackson*, 3: 287.

25. McConnell, *Negro Troops*, 98.

26. Joseph Savary et al. to Andrew Jackson, March 16, 1815, *Papers of Andrew Jackson*, 3: 315.

27. Joseph P. Sanchez, "African Freedmen and the Fuero Militar: A Historical Overview of Pardo and Moreno Militias in the Late Spanish Empire," *Colonial Latin American Historical Review* 3, no. 2 (1994): 165–184.

28. Depositions concerning slaves liberated by British forces after the Battle of New Orleans, ca. 1821–ca. 1825, Williams Research Center, Historic New Orleans Collection, mss. 199. Many fled to Trinidad, which British abolitionists had established as a refuge for free people of color. See Robert Kent Richardson, *Moral Imperium: Afro-Caribbeans and the Transformation of British Rule, 1776–1838* (New York: Greenwood, 1987); John McNish Weiss, *Free Black American Settlers in Trinidad, 1815–1816* (London: John Weiss, 1995).

29. Henry J. Richardson, "Mitchell Lecture, October 27, 2010," *Buffalo Human Rights Law Review* 17, no. 1 (2011): 2–25.

30. Douglas Bradburn, *The Citizenship Revolution: Politics and the Creation of the American Union, 1774–1804* (Charlottesville: University of Virginia Press, 2009), 103–104, 235–271.

31. The prohibition of interracial marriages is in the *Louisiana Civil Code* (1808), title IV, section 8, and the law regulating black-white interactions, *Acts Passed at the First Session of the First Legislature of the Territory of Orleans* (New Orleans, LA: Bradford & Anderson, 1807), sec. 40, 188–190. The prohibition of free black migration is in "A Supplementary to an Act Concerning the Introduction of Certain Slaves from Any of the States . . . January 29, 1817," in *Acts Passed by the Sixth Session of the Louisiana State Legislature* (New Orleans, LA: John Gibson, 1818). On the reenslavement of refugees from Haiti in Cuba and Louisiana, see Rebecca J. Scott, "Paper Thin: Freedom and Re-Enslavement in the Diaspora of the Haitian Revolution," *Law & History Review* 29, no. 4 (2011): 1061–1087.

32. Cienfuegos to Juan Ruíz de Apocada, September 1816, AGNM, Historia, Notas Diplomáticas, grupo 52, vol. 1, fol. 263.

33. "Captive at Galveston," May 14, 1817, in Warren, "Documents Relating to the Establishment of Privateers," 1098; Deposition by Captain Juan Domingo Lozano, May 1817, in Franco, *Documentos Mexico*, 1092. A Marcelin "Gilop" is listed among the commanders and captains of ships in Galveston in a declaration from April 26, 1817, in *Message from the President*, 45.

34. Ciénfuegos to Apodaca, May 14, 1817, AGNM, Historia, Notas Diplomáticas, grupo 52, vol. 2, fol. 80.

35. Ernesto Bassi, "Turning South Before Swinging East: Geopolitics and Geopolitical Imagination in the Southwestern Caribbean After the American Revolution," *Itinerario* 36, no. 3 (2013): 107–132. British and Spanish Honduras are studied separately. See O. Nigel Bolland, *Formation of a Colonial Society and Colonialism and Resistance in Belize* (Baltimore: Johns Hopkins

University Press, 1977); Mavis C. Campbell, *Becoming Belize: A History of an Outpost of Empire Searching for Identity, 1528–1823* (Kingston: University of the West Indies Press, 2011); Odile Hoffman, *British Honduras: The Invention of a Colonial Territory: Mapping and Spatial Knowledge in the 19th Century* (Belize: Cubola Productions, 2014); Robert A. Naylor, *Penny Ante Imperialism: The Mosquito Shore and the Bay of Honduras, 1600–1914* (Rutherford, NJ: Dickinson University Press, 1989); Nicholas Rogers, "Caribbean Borderland: Empire, Ethnicity, and the Exotic on the Mosquito Coast," *Eighteenth-Century Life* 26, no. 3 (2002): 117–138.

36. On how ideas about monarchism in West and Central Africa might have influenced political philosophy in the Americas, see John K. Thornton, "'I Am the Subject of the King of Congo': African Political Ideology and the Haitian Revolution," *Journal of World History* 4, no. 2 (1993): 181–214; David H. Brown, *Santeria Enthroned: Art, Ritual, and Innovation in an Afro-Cuban Religion* (Chicago: University of Chicago Press, 2003); Manuel Barcia, *West African Warfare in Bahia and Cuba: Soldier Slaves in the Atlantic World, 1807–1844* (Oxford: Oxford University Press, 2014).

37. David Geggus, *Haitian Revolutionary Studies* (Bloomington: Indiana University Press, 2002), 197–200; Nicolas Rey, *Quand la révolution aux Amériques, était nègre: Caraïbes noirs, negros franceses et autres oubliés de l'histoire* (Paris: Karthala, 2005); Rina Caceras, "On the Frontiers of the African Diaspora in Central America: The African Origins of San Fernando de Omoa," in *Trans-Atlantic Dimensions of Ethnicity in the African Diaspora*, ed. Paul E. Lovejoy and David Vincent Trotman (London: Continuum, 2003); Doug Thompson, "Between Slavery and Freedom on the Atlantic Coast of Honduras," *Slavery and Abolition* 33, no. 3 (2001): 403–416.

38. Log of HMS *Experiment*, TNA, ADM 51/1226 and ADM 1/1515; "Compañía de caribes de Roatán" 1797, Archivo General de Centro América, leg. 194, exp. 2025, section A3.16 (4).

39. Nancie L. Solien González, *Sojourners of the Caribbean: Ethnogenesis and Ethnohistory of the Garifuna* (Urbana: University of Illinois Press, 1988), 26.

40. "Visita hecha a los pueblos de Honduras, por el Gobernador Intendente Ramón de Anguiano. Año 1804," in *Boletín del Archivo General del Gobierno* 11, nos. 1–2 (1946): 119–120, 122–124; Jacques Houdaille, "Negros franceses en América Central a fines del siglo XVIII," *Antropología e Historia de Guatemala* 6, no. 1 (1954): 65–67; Jorge Victoria, "Los negros auxiliares de España en Centroamérica," *Boletín AFEHC* 21 (2006): 10.

41. *Honduras Gazette* 2 (84), October 17, 1827.

42. George Arthur to Foreign Office, February 2, 1819, April 8, 1819, TNA, CO 123/28, fol. 1–4.

43. Elizet Payne, "Presentación del Padrón de Truxillo de 1821," *Boletín AFEHC* 38 (2008).

44. "Noticia de la invasión de Truxillo el 22 abril de 1820 verificada por las fuerzas de la Escuadrilla del Pirata Aury; y de los resultados que publica la Capitanía General para satisfacción de todos los habitantes de este fiel reyno," May 1, 1820, John Carter Brown Library; Ruy Galvado de Andrade Coelho, *Los Negros Caribes de Honduras*, 2nd ed. (Tegucigalpa: Editorial Guaymuras, 1995), 46.

45. "Oficio del Comandante de Trujillo al Gobernador del Reino, Don Carlos Urrutia, dando cuenta del rechazo de la invasión de catorce naves que atacaron la plaza el 21, 22 y 23 de Abril de 1820," May 1, 1820, in Ferro, *Vida*, 231–236.

46. "Repuesta del Comandante de Omoa a la intimación del General Aury," April 28, 1820, in Ferro, *Vida*, 239; Aury, *Détail Guatemala*, 17.

47. Aury, *Détail Guatemala*, 17.

48. Echeverri, *Indian and Slave Royalists*; Maya Jasanoff, "Revolutionary Exiles: The American Loyalists and French Émigré Diasporas," in *The Age of Revolutions in Global Context, c. 1760–1840*, ed. David Armitage and Sanjay Subrahmanyam (New York: Palgrave Macmillan, 2010), 37–58; David Sartorius, *Ever Faithful: Race, Loyalty, and the Ends of Empire in Spanish Cuba* (Durham, NC: Duke University Press, 2013); Cassandra Pybus, *Epic Journeys of Freedom: Runaway Slaves of the American Revolution and Their Global Quest for Liberty* (Boston: Beacon, 2006); Ikuko Asaka, *Tropical Freedom: Climate, Settler Colonialism, and Black Exclusion in the Age of Emancipation* (Durham, NC: Duke University Press, 2017).

49. Aury, *Détail Guatemala*, 19.

50. Scott Eastman and Natalia Sobrevilla Perea, eds., *The Rise of Constitutional Government in the Iberian Atlantic World: The Impact of the Cádiz Constitution of 1812* (Tuscaloosa: University of Alabama Press, 2015); M. C. Mirow, *Latin America Constitutionalism: The Constitution of Cádiz and Its Legacy* (New York: Cambridge University Press, 2015).

51. Sartorius, *Ever Faithful*, 83–85; José Campos Garcia Melchor, *Republicanismos emergentes: continuidades y rupturas en Yucatán y Puebla, 1786–1869* (Mérida: Universidad Autónoma de Yucatán, 2010).

52. Jordana Dym, *From Sovereign Villages to National States: City, State, and Federation in Central America, 1759–1839* (Albuquerque: University of New Mexico Press, 2006).

53. Cited in Doug Tompson, "'Useful Laborers' and 'Savage Hordes': Hispanic Central American Views of Afro-Indigenous People in the Nineteenth Century," *Transforming Anthropology* 12, nos. 1–2 (2004): 23.

54. Ibid.

55. Ligny to Governor of Guadeloupe, July 24, 1826, ANOM, SG/Amer34, dossier "Mission de Mr Ligny à St Thomas."

56. Historians have debated the extent to which the Haitian Revolution influenced antislavery, slave emancipation, and racial thinking in the nineteenth-century world. Some have explored whether the revolution served as an example of resistance for enslaved and freed people. Other have assessed the revolution's impact of European and American abolitionism and development of scientific racism. The debate is summarized in David P. Geggus, ed., *The Impact of the Haitian Revolution in the Atlantic World* (Columbia: University of South Carolina Press, 2010) and David P. Geggus, "The Caribbean in the Age of Revolution," in *The Age of Revolutions in Global Context, c. 1760–1840*, ed. David Armitage and Sanjay Subrahmanyam (New York: Palgrave Macmillan, 2010), 83–100.

57. Gaffield, *Haitian Connections*, 5–6.

58. Morphy to Apocada, July 9, 1816, AGI, Cuba, leg. 1900.

59. St Gême family papers, Historic New Orleans Collection, mss. 100, fol. 146.

60. Letters from Secretary of State, Shipping Returns St Thomas 1813–1814, TNA, CO 259/1.

61. Sybille Fisher, "Bolívar in Haiti: Republicanism in the Revolutionary Atlantic," in *Haiti and the Americas*, ed. Carla Calarge (Jackson: University Press of Mississippi, 2013), 25.

62. Verna, *Pétion y Bolívar*, 181–197; Ferrer, "Haiti," 50–63; Bassi, *Aqueous Territory*, 159–166.

63. Morphy to Apocada, July 9, 1816, AGI, Cuba, leg. 1900.

64. Copy of Cienfuegos to Apocada, June 28, 1816, AGNM, Historia, Notas Diplomáticas, grupo 52, vol. 1, fol. 263.

65. Affidavit by Andrew Whiteman, October 6, 1813, NARA, entry 949, folder 4.

66. After the defeat of Hidalgo and his successor Morelos, Mexican insurgent leader Iturbide issued a proclamation freeing enslaved soldiers who fought with the republicans. Several

states abolished slavery in the mid-1820s until federal legislation was passed in October 1829. Robin Blackburn, *The Overthrow of Colonial Slavery, 1776–1848* (London: Verso, 1988), 367–372.

67. Morris to Crowninshield, June 10, 1817, in *Message from the President*, 22.

68. Additional testimony October 7, 1817, in *Message from the President*, 17–18.

69. Chew to Crawford, August 1, 1817, in *Message from the President*, 9.

70. Settlement of Estate 1821, LOC/MD/LA, folder 9.

71. Relación reservada del Coronel Luis Peru de Lacroix, January 20, 1822, AGNC, SGM, t. 343, fol. 1019–1022.

72. John Lynch, *Simón Bolívar: A Life* (New Haven, CT: Yale University Press, 2006), 213; Aline Helg, "Simón Bolívar and the Specter of Pardocracia: José Padilla in Post-Independence Cartagena," *Journal of Latin American Studies* 35 (2003): 447–471.

73. *Gaceta de Colombia*, December 9, 1822.

74. John Lynch, "Bolívar and the Caudillos," *Hispanic American Historical Review* 63 (1983): 30–31.

75. Lasso, *Myths of Harmony*, 117–128.

76. Padilla to Santander, August 30, 1824, cited in Helg, "Specter of Pardocracia," 452.

77. Padilla, *Al respetable público de Cartagena*, 1824, AGNC, República, Archivo Restrepo, fondo 12, caja 88, vol. 170, fol. 125–126.

78. Bolívar to Santander, April 7, 1825, in *Cartas Santander-Bolívar* (Caracas: Fundación Francisco de Paula Santander, 1990), 4: 344; *Gaceta de Colombia*, May 1, 1828.

79. Aline Helg, "Simón Bolívar's Republic: A Bulwark Against the 'Tyranny' of the Majority," *Revista de Sociologia e Política* 20, no. 42 (2012): 21–37.

80. Leonardo Reales, "The Contribution of Afro-Descendant Soldiers to the Independence of the Bolivarian Countries (1810–1826)," *Revista de Relaciones Internacionales* 2, no. 2 (2007): 11–31; Jason McGraw, *The Work of Recognition: Caribbean Colombia and the Post Emancipation Struggle for Citizenship* (Chapel Hill: University of North Carolina Press, 2014); Eduardo Restrepo, "Ethnicization of Blackness in Colombia," *Cultural Studies* 18, no. 5 (2004): 698–753; Martha Isabel Rosas Guevara, "De esclavos a ciudadanos y malentretenidos. Representaciones del negro en el discurso jurídico colombiano del siglo XIX," *HiSTOReLo. Revista de Historia Regional y Local* 6, no. 12 (2014): 271–302.

81. Manuel Restrepo, *Diario político y militar: Memorias sobre los sucesos importantes de la época para servir a la historia de la revolución de Colombia y de la Nueva Granada desde 1819 para adelante* (Bogotá: Imprenta Nacional, 1954), 1: 222; Lynch, *Simón Bolívar*, 108; Helg, "Simón Bolívar's Republic," 447–471.

82. Melanie J. Newton, *Children of Africa in the Colonies: Free People of Color in Barbados in the Age of Emancipation* (Baton Rouge: Louisiana State University Press, 2008), 65–67; Neville A. T. Hall, *Slave Society in the Danish West Indies* (Mona: University of the West Indies Press, 1992), 169–174; Gad Heuman, *Between Black and White: Race, Politics, and the Free Coloured in Jamaica* (Westport, CT: Greenwood, 1981), 21–41; Rebecca Schloss Hartkopf, *Sweet Liberty: The Final Days of Slavery in Martinique* (Philadelphia: University of Pennsylvania Press, 2009), 90.

83. Brown, *Adventuring*, 160–165.

84. *Gaceta de Colombia*, May 30, 1824.

85. Helg, "Símon Bolívar," 458.

86. AGNC, República, Hojas de Servicio, t. 21, fol. 572.

87. *Gaceta de Colombia*, February 2, 1823.

88. Lasso, *Myths of Harmony*, 130.

89. "Consejo ordinario de gobernio del 20 de enero de 1823," in *Acuerdos del consejo de gobierno de la república de Colombia* (Reprint, Bogotá: Edición de la Fundación para la Conmemoración del Bicentenario del Natalicio y el Sesquicentenario de la Muerte del General Francisco de Paula Santander, 1988).

90. *Gaceta de la Nueva Granada*, November 18, 1833.

91. AGNC, República, Hojas de Servicio, t. 19, fol. 1019 and vol. 62, fol. 572–576.

92. *El Correo de la Costa*, February 27, 1850; "Declaración del señor Marcelino Guillot," March 30, 1855, in *El libro de la justicia* (Bogotá: A. Cualla, 1858), 135.

93. House of Representatives, "An Act to Grant a Pension to Joseph Savary of the Regiment of Men of Colour," February 1819, in *Actes passés à la session de la législature de l'état de la Louisiane* (New Orleans, LA: State Printer, 1819), 10–11.

94. Fatio to Viceroy of New Spain, July 16, 1819, AGNM-Newberry, Historia, vol. 162, fol. 79.

95. Indenture of Antoine Grenoble with Joseph Savary, July 26, 1822, NOPL, Louisiana Division/City Archives, Office of the Mayor, Indentures, 1809–1843, vol. 3, no. 288; Mandat de paiement, June 13, 1821, Louisiana Research Collection, Tulane University, John Minor Wisdom Collection, box 23.

96. Indenture of Alfred Audige with Cherubin and Dessource, June 6, 1823, NOPL, Louisiana Division/City Archives, Office of the Mayor, Indentures, 1809–1843, vol. 4, no. 24.

97. No occupation listed. 1822 New Orleans City Directory: http://files.usgwarchives.net /la/orleans/history/directory/1822nocd.txt.

98. Savary, Historic New Orleans Collection, St Gême family papers, mss. 100, fol. 198.

99. Ibid. On the novelty of publicly funded marriage-based entitlements in the early nineteenth century for large classes of widows of veterans regardless of rank, see Kristin A. Collins, "Petitions Without Number: Widows' Petitions and the Early Nineteenth-Century Origins of Public Marriage-Based Entitlements," *Law and History Review* 31, no. 1 (2013): 1–60. Between 1830 and 1850, aging soldiers or their widows applied for pensions; former officers generally received $8 per month. Gene Allen Smith, *The Slaves' Gamble: Choosing Sides in the War of 1812* (New York: Palgrave Macmillan, 2013), 206.

100. On slave ownership by women of African descent, see Susan Socolow, "Economic Roles of the Free Women of Color of Cap Français," in *More Than Chattel: Black Women and Slavery in the America*, ed. David Barry Gaspar and Darlene Clark Hine (Bloomington: Indiana University Press, 1996), 286; Kimberly S. Hanger, "Landlords, Shopkeepers, Farmers, and Slave-Owners: Free Black Female Property-Holders in Colonial New Orleans," in *Beyond Bondage: Free Women of Color in the Americas*, ed. David Barry Gaspar and Darlene Clark Hine (Urbana: University of Illinois, 2004): 219–36; Kit Candlin and Cassandra Pybus, *Enterprising Women: Gender, Race, and Power in the Revolutionary Atlantic* (Athens: University of Georgia Press, 2015); Danielle Terrazas Williams, "'My Conscience Is Free and Clear': African-Descended Women, Status, and Slave Owning in Mid-Colonial Mexico," *Americas* 75, no. 3 (2018): 525–554; Erin Trahey, "Among Her Kinswomen: Legacies of Free Women of Color in Jamaica," *William and Mary Quarterly* 76, no. 2 (2019): 257–288.

101. Petitions for the emancipation of slaves, 1813–1843, NOPL, Louisiana Division/City Archives & Special Collections, no. 163, 1829, VCP 320, reel 98–5. An 1807 Louisiana law required slaves to have exhibited "honest conduct" for four years and to have reached the age of thirty before manumission. Sanite fulfilled these two requirements. Judith Schaffer counted thirty-eight individuals emancipated by the legislative process, eleven of them from free women

of color, usually their mothers. Schaffer, *Becoming Free, Remaining Free: Manumission and Enslavement in New Orleans, 1846–1862* (Baton Rouge: Louisiana State University Press, 2003), 5; Rebecca J. Scott, "'She . . . Refuses to Deliver Up Herself as the Slave of Your Petitioner': Emigres, Enslavement, and the 1808 Louisiana Digest of the Civil Laws," *Tulane European and Civil Law Forum* 24 (2009): 115–136.

102. Shaffer, *Becoming Free*, 6.

103. Scott and Hébrad, *Freedom Papers*, 76.

104. The influential 1810 *Adèle v. Beauregard* case held that people of color were competent witnesses against white people in Louisiana. Judith K. Schafer, *Slavery, the Civil Law and the Supreme Court of Louisiana* (Baton Rouge: Louisiana State University, 1994), 14–15; Sue Peabody, "'Free Upon Higher Ground': Saint-Domingue Slaves' Suits for Freedom in U.S. courts, 1790–1830," in *The World of the Haitian Revolution*, ed. David Geggus and Norman Fiering (Bloomington: Indiana University Press, 2009), 261–283; Kenneth R. Alakson, *Making Race in the Courtroom: The Legal Construction of Three Races in Early New Orleans* (New York: New York University Press, 2014); Laura Edwards, Ariela Gross, Hendrik Hartog, and Dylan Penningroth, "Black Litigiousness and White Accountability: Free Blacks and the Rhetoric of Reputation in the Antebellum Natchez District," *Journal of the Civil War Era* 5, no. 3 (2015): 372–398; Jessica Marie Johnson, "Death Rites as Birthrights in Atlantic New Orleans: Kinship and Race in the Case of María Teresa v. Perine Dauphine," *Slavery & Abolition* 36, no. 2 (2015): 233–256.

105. *Tachaud v. Richardson*, May 24, 1822, First District Court of New Orleans, no. 469 (Lexis-Nexis microfilm of original in NOPL).

106. Martha S. Jones, *Birthright Citizens: A History of Race and Rights in Antebellum America* (New York: Cambridge University Press, 2018).

107. *Berard v. Berard Louisiana 1833–1836*, First District Court of New Orleans, May 24, 1822 (Lexis-Nexis microfilm of original in NOPL).

108. Loren Schweninger, *Black Property Owners in the South, 1790–1915* (Urbana: University of Illinois Press, 1997), 81.

109. Victor M. Uribe-Uran, *Honorable Lives: Lawyers, Family, and Politics in Colombia, 1780–1850* (Pittsburgh: University of Pittsburgh Press, 2000), 90; Aline Helg, "Silencing African Descent: Caribbean Colombia and Early Nation Building, 1810–1828," in *Political Cultures in the Andes, 1750–1950*, ed. Cristóbal Aljovín de Losada and Nils Jacobsen (Durham, NC: Duke University Press, 2005), 184–205.

110. Sheller, "Sword-Bearing Citizens," 257–259.

111. "Free Negroes Leaving New Orleans for Haiti," *New Orleans Commercial Bulletin*, May 4, 1859; "Emigration Haïtienne," *Abeille de la Nouvelle-Orléans*, June 21, 1859; "Arrivage de Port-au-Prince," *Abeille de la Nouvelle-Orléans*, June 30, 1859; "Important Departure," *New Orleans Daily Picayune*, January 20, 1860; "Haytien Emigrants," *Abeille de la Nouvelle Orleans*, January 16, 1860.

112. "Souvenirs," *L'Opinion Nationale*, December 27, 1862; Jean-Marc Allard Duplantier, "Creole Louisiana's Haitian Exile(s)," *Southern Quarterly* 44, no. 3 (2007): 68–84; Rodolphe L. Desdunes, *Nos hommes et notre histoire* (Montréal: Arbour et Dupont, 1911), 111.

Chapter 4

1. Georges Jacques Danton, *La patrie en danger* (Paris: L. Boulanger, 1893), 7.

2. Proclamation, "Expedition Against the Island of Porto Rico," 1034.

3. Ursula Acosta, "Ducoudray Holstein: Hombre al margen de la historia," *Revista de Historia* 1, no. 2 (1985): 63–89; Guillermo A. Baralt, *Esclavos rebeldes: Conspiraciones y sublevaciones*

de esclavos en Puerto Rico, 1795–1873 (Río Piedras: Ediciones Huracán, 1985), 47–49; Federico Alzamora, *Mayagüez capital de la Republica Boricua* (Mayagüez: Oficina de Publicaciones Históricas, 2010).

4. Proclamation, "Expedition Against the Island of Porto Rico," 1035.

5. Anonymous communication attached to Tillotson to Secretary of State, January 23, 1823, "Expedition Against the Island of Porto Rico," 1032–1033; Baptis Irvine, *Traits of Colonial Jurisprudence or a Peep at the Trading Inquisition of Curacao* (Baltimore: Printed for the author, 1824), 7.

6. Ducoudray-Holstein, *Histoire de Bolivar*, 2: 298.

7. Miguel de la Torre and Francisco Gonzalez de Linares to Governor of Barbados, October 14, 1822, TNA, CO 28/91, fol. 120.

8. Proclamation, October 18, 1822, attached to October 27, 1822, ADMAE, Affaires Diverses Politiques: Etats-Unis (hereafter ADP/EU), vol. 2, dossier 9.

9. Monroe's address to Congress, March 8, 1822, ASP: Foreign Relations, 4: 819. William Spence Robertson, "The Recognition of the Hispanic American Nations by the United States," *Hispanic American Historical Review* 1, no. 3 (1918): 239–269.

10. Lauren Benton and Jeppe Mulich, "The Space Between Empires: Coastal and Insular Microregions in the Early Nineteenth-Century World," in *The Uses of Space in Early Modern History*, ed. Paul Stock (New York: Palgrave Macmillan, 2015), 153; Eliga H. Gould, "Entangled Histories, Entangled Worlds: The English-Speaking Atlantic as a Spanish Periphery," *American Historical Review* 112, no. 3 (2007): 764–786.

11. David Geggus, "Slavery, War, and Revolution in the Greater Caribbean," in *A Turbulent Time: The French Revolution and the Greater Caribbean*, ed. David Garry Gaspar and David Patrick Geggus (Bloomington: Indiana University Press, 1997), 20–21.

12. Anonymous communication attached to Tillotson to Secretary of State, January 23, 1823, "Expedition Against the Island of Porto Rico," 1033.

13. Ducoudray-Holstein to Champigny-Aubin, December 17, 1813, *Nouvelle Revue Rétrospective* (1896): 140–143.

14. Ducoudray-Holstein, *Histoire de Bolivar*, 1: 195.

15. *Baltimore Patriot*, July 27, 1816.

16. Weeks, *John Quincy Adams*, 100.

17. Despatches from Special Agent Baptis Irvine of the Department of State, 1818–19, NARA, RG 59, T 586, vol. 8.

18. *New York Columbian*, July 17, 1816.

19. *Boston Commercial Gazette*, March 18, 1822. On an earlier period, see Manuel Covo, "Baltimore and the French Atlantic: Empires, Commerce, and Identity in a Revolutionary Age, 1783–1798," in *The Caribbean and the Atlantic World Economy*, ed. A. B. Leonard and Daniel Pretel (London: Palgrave Macmillan, 2015), 87–107.

20. Ultramar, 1822, AHN, leg. 5568, exp. 15, no. 4.

21. Baptist Irvine, *On the Commerce of South America* (Philadelphia: T.T.H., 1822).

22. Alexandre Guenin, *Notice historique et biographique sur le département de l'Aube, 1789–1848* (Troyes: Imprimerie de Sainton, 1855), 310.

23. A letter by the French minister in Washington mentioned that Jeannet's wife might have died in Louisiana in 1820, in attachment March 17, 1823, CAD, Consulat de Nouvelle Orleans, series A, vol. 186.

24. Delorest to French Consul in the United States, March 17, 1823, CAD, Consulat de Nouvelle Orleans, series A, vol. 186.

25. Miguel de Torre and Francisco Gonzales de Linares, October 14, 1822, TNA, CO 28–91, fol. 119–122.

26. List of articles for General Ducoudray Holstein, August 1, 1822, "Expedition Against the Island of Porto Rico," 1029.

27. Collector's Office of Custom-House New York, December 24, 1822, "Expedition Against the Island of Porto Rico," 1039.

28. Lardenoy to Consul of New York, n.d., ADMAE, ADP/EU, vol. 2, dossier 9.

29. Francine Mayer and Carolyn Fick, "Before and After Emancipation: Slaves and Free Colored of Saint Barthélemy in the 19th Century," *Scandinavian Journal of History* 18, no. 4 (1993): 251–274; Francois Nault and Francine Mayer, "L'abolition de l'esclavage à Saint-Barthélemy à travers l'étude de quatre listes nominatives de sa population rurale de 1840 à 1854," *Revue francaise d'outre mer* 79, no. 296 (1992): 305–340.

30. James Hackett, *Narrative of the Expedition Which Sailed from England in 1817, to Join the South American Patriots* (London: J. Murray, 1818), 23.

31. Leo Elisabeth, "Déportés de petites Antilles françaises, 1801–1803," in *Rétablissement de l'esclavage dans les colonies francaises*, ed. Yves Bénot and Marcel Dorigny (Paris: Maisonneuve et Larose, 2003), 6–94; Ernouf to Minister, 20 prairial an 12 (1805), ANOM, C7/A61, no. 117.

32. Blackburn, *Overthrow of Colonial Slavery*, 262; Pérotin-Dumon, "Les Jacobins des Antilles."

33. Vatable to Lardenoy, April 19, 1822, and encl. to a March 17, 1823, letter, CAD, Consulat de Nouvelle Orleans, series A, vol. 186.

34. Lardenoy to New York consul, n.d., ADMAE, ADP/EU, vol. 2, dossier 9.

35. *St Christopher Gazette*, November 1, 1822.

36. Aaron Burns to Thomas Wattson, September 26, 1822, "Expedition Against the Island of Porto Rico," 1031.

37. Declaration of Jean Martin, October 17, 1822, ADMAE, ADP/EU, vol. 2, dossier 9.

38. Donzelot to Nordeling, May 4, 1822, ADMAE, ADP/EU, vol. 2, dossier 9.

39. Ibid.

40. Naturalization application of Carl Carlsson, October 14, 1812, ANOM, Fonds Suédois de Saint-Barthélemy (hereafter FSSB), vol. 277; Governor of Saint Barthélemy to Lacrosse, October 20, 1802, sous-série C7/A56.

41. Demande d'affranchissement by Balthazar Bigard, March 16, 1819; September 10, 1819; March 28, 1820; April 3, 1820; July 3, 1820 and by Philippe Bigard, January 15, 1822, ANOM, FSSB, série ES, vol. 286.

42. Ale Pålsson, "Our Side of the Water: Political Culture in the Swedish Colony of St Barthélemy 1800–1825" (PhD diss., Stockholm University, 2016), 156–157.

43. Proclamation by Johan Norderling, February, 20 1822, ANOM: FSB, vol. 135, fol. 223.

44. Nordeling to Donzelot, May 10, 1822, ADMAE, ADP/EU, vol. 2, dossier 9.

45. *St Christopher Gazette*, November 1, 1822; Ernest Ekman, "A Swedish Career in the Tropics: Johan Nordeling (1760–1828)," *Swedish Pioneer* 15, no. 1 (1964): 3–32.

46. Pålsson, "Our Side," 157.

47. Ibid., 159–160.

48. Baralt, *Esclavos rebeldes*, 47; Ducoudray-Holstein, *Histoire de Bolivar*, 2: 193; Baptist Irvine, "Expedition to Porto Rico," January 12, 1823, *Charleston City Gazette*, March 4, 1823.

49. Francisco A. Scarano, *Sugar and Slavery in Puerto Rico: The Plantation Economy of Ponce, 1800–1850* (Madison: University of Wisconsin Press, 1984), 18–25; Jorge I. Dominguez,

Insurrection or Loyalty: The Breakdown of the Spanish American Empire (Cambridge, MA: Harvard University Press, 1980), 214–220; Dale Tomich, "The Wealth of Empire: Francisco Arango y Parreno, Political Economy, and the Second Slavery in Cuba," *Comparative Studies on Society and History* 45, no. 1 (2003): 4–28.

50. Haitian state makers adopted the Arawak name Haiti or Ayiti in 1804. David Geggus, "The Naming of Haiti," *NWIG: New West Indian Guide/Nieuwe West-Indische Gids* 71, nos. 1–2 (1997): 43–68; Javier Ocampo López, *El proceso ideológico de la emancipación: Las ideas de genesis, independencia, futuro e integración en los origenes de Colombia* (Tunja: Universidad Pedagogica y Tecnologica de Colombia, Fondo Especial de Publicaciones, 1974); Rebecca Earle, "Creole Patriotism and the Myth of the 'Loyal Indian,'" *Past & Present* 172, no. 1 (2001): 125–145.

51. *Charleston City Gazette*, March 4, 1823.

52. Governor-General to King of Denmark, November 27, 1823, DNA, Government-General: copybooks of letters sent to the king 1816–1826, fol. 12.

53. Appeal of the general-in-chief, provisional president of the Republic of Bouqua, to foreigners of all nations, September 1822, "Expedition Against the Island of Porto Rico," 1037.

54. This issue of the *New York Gazette* was then collected by the French consul and sent to the French ambassador in Washington, DC, who then forwarded it to authorities in Guadeloupe and Martinique and in France. ADMAE, Correspondance Consulaire: Philadelphie, vol. 12, fol. 225.

55. Maria Cadilla de Martínes, *Rememorando el pasado heróico* (Arecibo: Author, 1946), 302–303.

56. De la Torre to Donzelot, October 14, 1822, ADMAE, ADP/EU, vol. 2, dossier 9; Miguel de la Torre and Francisco Gonzalez de Linares to Governor of Barbados, October 14, 1822, TNA, CO 28/91, fol. 120.

57. Alfredo Avila, Jordana Dym, and Erika Pani, eds., *Las declaraciones de independencia: Los textos fundamentales de las independencias americanas* (México, D.F.: El Colegio de México/ Universidad Nacional Autónoma de México, 2013).

58. Crawford, *Creation of States*, 97–99.

59. Josefina Zoraida Vasquez, "The Mexican Declaration of Independence," *Journal of American History* 85, no. 4 (1999): 1362–1369; Jaime E. Rodriguez, "Sobre la supuesta influencia de la independencia de los Estados Unidos en las independencias hispanoamericanas," *Revista de Indias* LXX, no. 250 (2010): 691–714.

60. Brading, *The First America*, 447–463, 467–491.

61. Solemn Act of the Declaration of Independence, "Expedition Against the Island of Puerto Rico," 1035.

62. John Johnson, *A Hemisphere Apart: The Foundations of United States Policy Toward Latin America* (Baltimore: Johns Hopkins University Press, 1990), 93; Glen Dealy, "Prolegomena on the Spanish American Political Tradition," *Hispanic American Historical Review*, 48, no. 1 (1968): 37–58.

63. Gérard Noiriel, *La tyrannie du national, le droit d'asile en Europe, 1793–1993* (Paris: Calmann-Lévy, 1991); Greg Burgess, *Refuge in the Land of Liberty: France and Its Refugees, from the Revolution to the End of Asylum, 1787–1939* (New York: Palgrave Macmillan, 2008).

64. Ferrer, "Haiti," 49–54.

65. Attached to a proclamation by the captain-general of Puerto Rico, n.d., ADMAE, ADP/ EU, vol. 2, dossier 9.

66. *Real Cedula* (St. Thomas: Jonas Englund, 1815), NARA, Reales Ordenes y Decretos, Governors of Puerto Rico RG 184, T 1122; Kathryn R. Dungy, "Live and Let Live: Native and Immigrant Free People of Color in Early Nineteenth Century Puerto Rico," *Caribbean Studies* 33, no. 1 (2005): 79–111.

67. Attached to a proclamation by the captain-general of Puerto Rico, n.d., ADMAE, ADP/EU, vol. 2, dossier 9.

68. Proclamation, "Expedition Against the Island of Puerto Rico," 1034.

69. Jeannet-Oudin to Minister of Navy, April 15, 1793, ANOM, C14/71, fol. 20.

70. "Compte-rendu de la gestion, Nicolas Georges Jeannet, commissaire civil délégué à Cayenne par la Convention Nationale, 28 brumaire an 3," ADMAE, Mémoires et Documents, Amérique, vol. 19, fol. 151.

71. Ducoudray-Holstein, "Memoirs of My Life. By an Old Soldier," *Zodiac*, November 1836.

72. Ducoudray-Holstein, *Histoire de Bolivar*, 1: 22; *Congreso de Cúcuta*, Acta 84, Sesión del día 19 de julio 1821. Slavery remained legal in Colombia until 1852.

73. Ducoudray-Holstein, *Histoire de Bolivar*, 1: lxiij and 2: 3–5, 113.

74. Ibid., 2: 3.

75. Jeannet-Oudin, Proclamation, July 11, 1797, ANOM, C/14/75, fol. 36; Yves Bénot, *La Guyane sous la Révolution, ou l'impasse de la révolution pacifique* (Kourou: Ibis rouge Éditions, 1997).

76. Jeannet-Oudin, Rapport du 30 messidor VI (July 18, 1798), ANOM, C14/76, fol. 10.

77. Han Jordaan, "Patriots, Privateers and International Politics: The Myth of the Conspiracy of Jean Baptiste Tierce Cadet," in *Curacao in the Age of Revolutions, 1795–1800*, ed. Wim Klooster and Geert Oostinide (Leiden: Brill, 2011), 147.

78. Rafe Blaufarb, *Bonapartists in the Borderlands: French Exiles and Refugees on the Gulf Coast, 1815–1835* (Tuscaloosa: University of Alabama Press, 2005).

79. In her study of Haitian constitutions, Sybille Fisher called them "expressions of aspirations and desires that went beyond any given political and social reality." Fisher, *Modernity Disavowed: Haiti and the Cultures of Slavery in the Age of Revolution* (Durham, NC: Duke University Press, 2004), 229.

80. De la Torre to Governor of Barbados, October 14, 1822, TNA, CO 28/91, fol. 121; Baralt, *Esclavos rebeldes*, 55–56.

81. Résumé attached to consular minutes of November 1822, ADMAE, ADP/EU, vol. 2, dossier 9.

82. The governor of Martinique noted that the *hivernage* season, when storms and hurricanes are the most frequent, or roughly August to November in the French West Indies, was plotting season. Sicknesses such as yellow fever decimated Europeans and particularly weakened troops and military forces. Cited in Françoise Thesée, "La révolte des esclaves du Carbet à la Martinique (octobre–novembre 1822)," *Outre-Mers* 301 (1993): 560; Hartkopf Schloss, *Sweet Liberty*, 93–94.

83. Warde to Sir Henry, October 23, 1823, TNA, CO 28/91, fol. 106.

84. "Rapport sur l'expedition."

85. Anne Eller, *We Dream Together: Dominican Independence, Haiti, and the Fight for Caribbean Freedom* (Durham, NC: Duke University Press, 2016), 5–10.

86. Miguel de la Torre and Francisco Gonzalez de Linares to Governor of Barbados, October 14, 1822, TNA, CO 28/91, fol. 120.

87. Donzelot to de la Torre, November 29, 1822, ADMAE, ADP/EU, vol. 2, dossier 9.

88. Abraham Balborda's testimony, September 15, 1822, ADMAE, ADP/EU, vol. 2, dossier 9.

89. Léo Elisabeth, "Les relations entre les Petites Antilles françaises et Haïti, de la politique du refoulement à la résignation, 1804–1825," *Outre-mers* 90, no. 340 (2003): 202.

90. Jean-Francois Brière, *Haiti et la France 1804–1848* (Paris: Karthala, 2008); Yun Kyoung Kwon, "When Parisian Liberals Spoke for Haiti: French Anti-Slavery Discourses on Haiti Under the Restoration, 1814–30," *Atlantic Studies* 8, no. 3 (2011): 318; Vanessa Mongey, "Going Home: The Back-to-Haiti Movement in the Early Nineteenth Century," *Atlantic Studies: Global Currents* 16, no. 2 (2019): 184–202.

91. *Courrier français*, March 26, 1823.

92. Scholten to de la Torre and Gonzalez de Linares, November 25, 1822, Archivo General de Puerto Rico, Records of the Spanish Governors of Puerto Rico. Political and Civil Affairs. Consuls Panama—Saint Thomas, RG 186, box 32, entry 16.

93. Miguel de la Torre to Governor of Barbados, October 14, 1822, TNA, CO 28/91, fol. 122.

94. Ibid.

95. Grotius, *On the Law of War and Peace*, book II, chap. 20; Vattel, *Droit des gens*, book I, chap. 19.

96. Governor of Curacao to Governor and Captain-General of Puerto Rico, October 25, 1822, in "Rapport sur l'expedition," attachment 4.

97. Pedro Tomás Códova, *Memorias geográficas, históricas, económicas, estadísticas de la isla de Puerto Rico* (San Juan: Ofician del Gobierno, 1831), 3: 473–479, 4: 12–22.

98. Lidio Cruz Monclova, *Historia de Puerto Rico* (Rio Piedras: Editorial Universitaria, 1970), 1: 162–164, 187–189.

99. Scholten to de la Torre, November 25, 1822, AGPR/RSGPR, Cónsules Panamá-Saint Thomas, RG 186, box 32, entry 16; Scholten to King, October 13, 1823, DNA, Government-General: copybooks of letters sent to the king, 1816–1826, fol. 59.

100. Monclova, *Historia de Puerto Rico*, 1: 175–176.

101. Ekman, "Slave Trade," 226.

102. Joseph Dorsey, *Slave Traffic in the Age of Abolition: Puerto Rico, West Africa, and the Non-Hispanic Caribbean, 1815–1859* (Gainesville: University Press of Florida, 2003).

103. Correspondence of Nordeling, March 1824, ANOM, FSSB, série C, vol. 258.

104. See, for example, the correspondence between Nordeling and Philippe (alias Titus) Bigard, March 1825, ANOM, FSSB, série C, vol. 258. The Case of the *Nirzee (a) Neirsée (a) Estafette* with 300 Africans from Calabar and Gulf of Guinea in 1829, destined for Havana and captured in Guadeloupe, Transatlantic Slave Trade Database, voyage identification number 931.

105. Traité pour la répression de la Traite des Noirs, November 6, 1824, and proclamation concerning the owners of Swedish vessels carrying the slave trade, January 12, 1825, in James Haasum, *Très Humble Rapport sur le nombre de la population et sur des questions relatives aux Esclaves*, no. 191, Mémoire St Barth, http://www.memoirestbarth.com.

106. *St Christopher Advertiser*, July 5, 1825.

107. *Niles' Weekly Register*, July 15, 1823.

108. Ducoudray-Holstein, *Histoire de Bolivar*, 2: 300.

109. Irvine to Clay, January 18, 1824, in *The Papers of Henry Clay: Presidential Candidate* (Lexington: University Press of Kentucky, 1963), 3: 595.

110. Parker to Secretary of State, October 18, 1822, "Expedition Against the Island of Porto Rico," 1038.

111. Parker to Secretary of State, September 2, 1824, NARA, Consular Despatches: Curacao, T 197, vol. 1.

112. *Niles' Weekly Register*, December 7, 1822.

113. *Niles' Weekly Register,* March 22, 1823. Irvine quoted Vattel, *Droit des gens,* book III, chap. 18.

114. Irvine to Clay, January 1824, in *Papers of Henry Clay,* 3: 595.

115. *Niles' Weekly Register,* April 22, 1823.

116. Ducoudray-Holstein, *Histoire de Bolivar,* 2: 300–302.

117. Ibid.

118. Irvine to Clay, in *Papers of Henry Clay,* 3: 18–19; *Niles' Weekly Register,* April 10, 1824; Adams, *Memoirs,* 6: 104, 430–431.

119. Dudley W. Knox, ed., *Naval Documents Related to the Quasi-War Between the United States and France* (Washington, DC: U.S. Government Printing Office, 1935–1938), 7: 364–371.

120. Annals of Congress, 14th Cong., 2nd sess., Jan. 24, 1817, 719–720.

121. Act of March 3, 1817, chap. 58, *United States Statutes at Large* (Washington, DC: Library of Congress, 1817), 370–371.

122. "An Act to Protect the Commerce of the United States, and Punish the Crime of Piracy and to Make Further Provisions for Punishing the Crime of Piracy, May 8, 1820," Annals of Congress, 16th Cong., 1st sess., 2207–2211; Jenny S. Martinez, *The Slave Trade and the Origins of International Human Rights Law* (New York: Oxford University Press, 2012), 48–50; Alfred Rubin, "The United States of America and the Law of Piracy," *International Law Studies* 63 (1988): 122–199. On the heightened prosecution rates after the passing of the laws, see David Head, "A Different Kind of Maritime Predation: South American Privateering from Baltimore, 1816–1820," *International Journal of Naval History* 7, no. 2 (2008): 14–16; Arlyck, "Plaintiffs v. Privateers," 245–276; Reeder, "'Sovereign Lords,'" 323–346.

123. Matthew Mason, "Keeping Up Appearances: The International Politics of Slave Trade Abolition in the Nineteenth-Century World," *William and Mary Quarterly* 66, no. 4 (2009): 809–832.

124. South American privateering had almost disappeared in the United States after the panic of 1819 ruined many investors. Head, *Privateers,* 90–91.

125. Declaration of Jean Martin, October 17, 1822, in "Rapport sur l'expedition."

126. Joel R. Poinsett, *Notes on Mexico, Made in the Autumn of 1822* (London: J. Miller, 1825), 6.

127. *Niles' Weekly Register,* December 14, 1822.

128. *Niles' Weekly Register,* December 7, 1822.

129. Crawford to Treasury Department, December 30, 1822, "Expedition Against the Island of Puerto Rico," 1039.

130. Ingersoll to Secretary of State, January 8, 1823, "Expedition Against the Island of Puerto Rico," 1028.

131. *Niles' Weekly Register,* April 19, 1823.

132. *East Florida Herald,* February 8, 1823.

133. *National Advocate,* December 17, 1822.

134. "Monroe to 17th Congress of the United States, December 3, 1822," in Manning, *Diplomatic Correspondence,* 2: 162–163.

135. "Correspondence on the Course Pursued by Commodore David Porter, in Command of the Squadron for the Suppression of Piracy in the West Indies, March 21, 1826," House of Representatives, 19th Cong., 1st sess., ASP: NA 2: 648–649.

136. "Affidavit of George Brown, on Murders and Atrocities by Pirates Near Island of Cuba," January 31, 1825, 18th Cong., 2nd sess., ASP: Foreign Relations 5: 398.

137. "Expenditures of the Navy, 1794 Through 30 June 1960," *Financial Report Fiscal Year 1960 by the Department of the Navy, Office of the Comptroller* (Washington, DC: U.S. Government Printing Office, 1960), 43–44; "Conditions of the Navy and Its Expenses Communicated to House of Representatives," January 25, 1821, 16th Cong., 2nd sess., ASP: House of Representatives, Naval Affairs 1: 712.

138. Regulations for the suppression of piracy, Title 33, U.S. Code, chap. 7, § 381, 1823.

139. "Additional Force for the Suppression of Piracy Communicated to the Senate by the Chairman of the Committee on Naval Affairs," December 10, 1822, 17th Cong., 2nd sess., no. 213.

140. *American Mercury*, April 29, 1823; Porter to Vives, July 13, 1823, ASP: NA 1: 1114.

141. De la Torre to Porter, March 6, 1823, ASP: NA, 1: 1104.

142. Porter to de la Torre, March 11, 1823, ASP: NA, 1: 1105.

143. Case of Commodore Porter, January 23, 1826, *Register of Debates in Congress* (Washington, DC: Gales & Seaton, 1826), 55–66.

144. Porter to de la Torre, March 11, 1823, ASP: NA, 1: 1105.

145. Consul to Ministry of Navy, January 15, 1823, CAD, Correspondence Consulaire: Philadelphia, fol. 244; Fernando Geigel, *Corsarios y piratas de Puerto Rico; estudio en Puerto Rico durante la guerra de los Estados Unidos con las piratas de las indias occidentales, 1819–1835* (San Juan, PR: Cantero Fernández & cía., 1946), 40–42.

146. *Dansk Vestindik Regiering Avis*, May 29, 1823.

147. Harold Temperley, "The Instructions to Donzelot, Governor of Martinique, 17 December 1823," *English Historical Review* 41, no. 164 (1926): 587.

148. "Suppression of Piracy, January 31, 1825," in *Debates in Congress* (Washington, DC: Gales and Seaton, 1825), 2469.

149. *Memoirs of John Quincy Adams* (Philadelphia: J. B. Lippincott, 1875), 6: 71.

150. "Lawless Expedition Against Puerto Rico, December 12, 1822," in *Abridgment of the Debates of Congress, from 1789 to 1856*, ed. Thomas Hart Benton (New York: D. Appleton, 1858), 7: 383.

151. Simón Bolívar, *Obras completas* (La Habana: Editorial Lex, 1947), 1: 1097; Hernán Venegas Delgado, "Los Planes Colombo-mexicanos de expedición conjunta para la liberación de Cuba (1820–1827)," *Caribbean Studies* 36, no. 1 (2008): 3–23.

152. Clay to Brown, October 25, 1825, "Commission of American Ministers to the Congress at Panama," Senate, 19th Cong., 2nd sess., ASP: FR, 6: 383.

153. Foreign Office, Instructions to the Agents to the Panama Congress, March 18, 1826, TNA, FO 97/115, fol. 45–50.

154. Bassi, *Aqueous Territory*, 168–169.

155. Bolívar to Santander, May 30, 1825, *Cartas Santander-Bolívar*, IV: 50.

156. Jean-François Brière, *Haïti et la France 1804–1848. Le rêve brisé* (Paris: Karthala, 2008).

157. Blaufarb, "Western Question," 762.

158. Ducoudray-Holstein, *Histoire de Bolivar*, 1: 300.

159. Proclamation of captain general of Puerto Rico, October 18, 1822, ADMAE, Correspondance Consulaire: Philadelphia, vol. 12.

160. H.L.V. Ducoudray-Holstein, *Memoirs of Gilbert Motier La Fayette* (New York: Charles Wiley, 1824), 305.

161. Edward Everett, "Lafayette," *North American Review* XLVI (1825); Louis Gottschalk, *Lafayette Comes to America* (Chicago: University of Chicago Press, 1935), 47.

162. *Le glaneur francais* (Geneva: Russell Robbins, 1833); *Zodiac*, January 1837, 101.

163. Robert R. Beale, *A Report of the Trial of Commodore David Porter: of the Navy of the United States, Before a General Court Martial, Held at Washington, in July 1825* (Washington, DC, 1825), 19.

164. Matthew Brown and Gabriel Paquette, "The Persistence of Mutual Influence: Europe and Latin America in the 1820s," *European History Quarterly* 41, no. 3 (2011): 387–396; Centeno, *Blood and Debt*, 25–29. Haiti borrowed money from French banks to help repay the indemnity imposed by the French government in the 1825 treaty of recognition. Brière, *Haïti et la France*, 160–186; François Blancpain, *Un siècle de relations financières entre Haïti et la France, 1825–1922* (Paris: L'Harmattan, 2001), 43–78.

Chapter 5

1. Ferrari, *Memorie*, 184–185.

2. Homi K. Bhabha, ed., *Nation and Narration* (London: Routledge, 1990); Eric Hobsbaw and Terence Ranger, eds., *The Invention of Tradition* (Cambridge: Cambridge University Press, 1983); Miguel Angel Centeno, "War and Memories: Symbols of State Nationalism in Latin America," *Revista Europea De Estudios Latinoamericanos y Del Caribe/European Review of Latin American and Caribbean Studies* 66 (1999): 75–105; Matthew Brown, "Soldier Heroes and the Colombian Wars of Independence," *Hispanic Research Journal* 7, no. 1 (2006): 41–56; Christopher Schmidt-Nowara, *The Conquest of History: Spanish Colonialism and National Histories in the Nineteenth Century* (Pittsburgh: University of Pittsburgh Press, 2006); Erin Zavitz, "Revolutionary Narrations: Early Haitian Historiography and the Challenge of Writing Counter-History," *Atlantic Studies: Global Currents* 14, no. 3 (2017): 336–353.

3. Ann Fabian, *The Unvarnished Truth: Personal Narratives in Nineteenth Century America* (Berkeley: University of California Press, 2000); William L. Andrews, *To Tell a Free Story: The First Century of Afro-American Autobiography, 1760–1865* (Urbana: University of Illinois Press, 1986); Sylvia Molloy, *At Face Value: Autobiographical Writing in Spanish America* (Cambridge: Cambridge University Press, 1991); Frederika J. Teute, ed., *Through a Glass Darkly: Reflections on Personal Identity in Early America* (Chapel Hill: University of North Carolina Press, 1997); Steven V. Hunsaker, *Autobiography and National Identity in the Americas* (Charlottesville: University of Virginia Press, 1999).

4. Philip G. Dwyer, "Public Remembering, Private Reminiscing: French Military Memoirs and the Revolutionary and Napoleonic Wars," *French Historical Studies* 33, no. 2 (2010): 231–258; Damien Zanone, *Ecrire son temps, les Mémoires en France de 1815 à 1848* (Lyon: Presses Universitaires de Lyon, 2006).

5. "The geographic enterprise of 'becoming identities in places' is a performative construction/practice in which ongoing memories play a pivotal role." Owain Jones and Joanne Garde-Hansen, *Geography and Memory: Explorations in Identity, Place and Becoming* (Basingstoke: Palgrave Macmillan, 2012), 2; Danielle Drozdzewski, Sarah De Nardi, and Emma Waterton, "Geographies of Memory, Place and Identity: Intersections in Remembering War and Conflict," *Geography Compass* 10 (2016): 447–456; Pamela Ballinger, *History in Exile: Memory and Identity at the Borders of the Balkans* (Princeton, NJ: Princeton University Press, 2003).

6. On state membership in the early modern period, see Tamar Herzog, *Defining Nations: Immigrants and Citizens in Early Modern Spain and Spanish America* (New Haven, CT: Yale University Press, 2003); Peter Sahlins, *Boundaries: The Making of Modern France and Spain in the Pyrenees* (Berkeley: University of California Press, 1898). On national identities during the

revolutionary period, see Linda Colley, *Britons: Forging the Nation, 1707–1837* (New Haven, CT: Yale University Press, 1992); David Waldstreicher, *In the Midst of Perpetual Fetes: The Making of American Nationalism, 1776–1820* (Chapel Hill: University of North Carolina Press, 1997); David A. Bell, *The Cult of the Nation in France: Inventing Nationalism, 1680–1800* (Cambridge, MA: Harvard University Press, 2001); Rogers Brubaker, *Citizenship and Nationhood in France and Germany* (Cambridge, MA: Harvard University Press, 1992). For a summary of Borderlands scholarship, see Jared Orsi, "Construction and Contestation: Toward a Unifying Methodology for Borderlands History," *History Compass* 12, no. 5 (2014): 433–443. Many people resisted or ignored these centralizing forces, especially residents living great distances from centers of power or sailors at sea.

7. Codazzi's memoirs belonged to Conde Giacomo Manzoni and Doctor Carlo Piancastelli before ending in a library in Folrí, not far from where he grew up. The social-democratic leader, Mario Longhena, edited and published the memoirs in 1930; his edition was translated into Spanish in 1973. Some of Codazzi's letters are in Lugo, others are in the National Archives in Caracas, and his service records are in the National Archives in Bogotá. A small local press posthumously published Ferrari's memoirs in 1855. See Nicolàs Perazzo, *Constante Ferrari, companero de aventuras de Codazzi* (Caracas: Editorial Cromotip, 1954).

8. Walter Benjamin, *Illuminations* (New York: Houghton Mifflin Harcourt, 1968), 83.

9. On memoirs, see Paul Lovejoy, "Biography as Source Material: Towards a Biographical Archive of Enslaved Africans," in *Source Material for Studying the Slave Trade and the African Diaspora*, ed. Robin Law (Sterling: Center of Commonwealth Studies, University of Sterling, 1997): 119–140; Mark Freeman, *Rewriting the Self: History, Memory, Narrative* (London: Routledge, 1993); Paul Ricoeur, *La mémoire, l'histoire, l'oubli* (Paris: Seuil, 2000); Arthur F. Saint-Aubin, *The Memoirs of Toussaint and Isaac Louverture: Representing the Black Masculine Subject in Narratives of Mourning and Loss* (Bethlehem, PA: Lehigh University Press, 2015): 41–69.

10. Wendy Anne Warren, "'The Cause of Her Grief': The Rape of a Slave in Early New England," *Journal of American History* 93, no. 4 (2007): 1031–1049; Patricia Saunders, "Defending the Dead, Confronting the Archive: A Conversation with M. NourbeSe Philip," *Small Axe* 26 (2008): 63–79.

11. Cited in Giorgio Antei, *Mal de América. Las obras y los días de Agustín Codazzi, 1793–1859* (Caracas: Biblioteca Nacional de Venezuela, 1993), 18.

12. Ferrari, *Memorie*, 468.

13. Alexander Grab, "Army, State and Society: Conscription and Desertion in Napoleonic Italy (1802–1814)," *Journal of Modern History* 67, no. 1 (1995): 25–54; Daniel Ziblatt, *Structuring the State: The Formation of Italy and Germany and the Puzzle of Federalism* (Princeton, NJ: Princeton University Press, 2006), 1–17.

14. Baron Gaspar Gourgaud, *Memoirs of the History of France During the Reign of Napoleon* (London: Colburn and Bossange, 1824), 4: 182; Preamble to the Constitution of the Cisalpine Republic, 20 messidor an V (July 7, 1797).

15. On Italy at the end of the eighteenth century and the concept of "passive revolution," see Francesca Morelli, "El trieno republican italiano y las revoluciones hispanoàmericas" in *Revoluciones del mundo atlàntico*, ed. Clément Thibaud and Maria Teresa Calderón (Bogotà: Taurus, 2006), 81–99.

16. Ferrari, *Memorie*, 9.

17. Ibid., 11.

18. Ibid., 64.

19. Cited in Antei, *Mal de América*, 18.

20. The term "Grande Armée" refers to all the multinational forces gathered by Napoléon in his campaigns. Guy C. Dempsey, *Napoleon's Mercenaries: Foreign Units in the French Army Under Consulate and Empire, 1799 to 1814* (London: Greenhill, 2002); Alan Forrest, *Napoleon's Men: The Soldiers of the Revolution and Empire* (London: Hambledon and London, 2002); Jean-François Brun, "Les unités étrangères dans les armées napoléoniennes: Un élément de la stratégie globale du Grand Empire," *Revue historique des armées* 255 (2009): 22–49.

21. Antei, *Mal de América*, 41–44.

22. Ferrari, *Memorie*, 319.

23. Ibid., 395.

24. Ibid., 396–397.

25. Ibid., 414–418.

26. Brian Joseph Martin, *Napoleonic Friendship: Military Fraternity, Intimacy, and Sexuality in Nineteenth-Century France* (Hanover: University of New Hampshire Press, 2011); Talissa Ford, *Radical Romantics: Prophets, Pirates, and the Space Beyond Nation* (Edinburgh: Edinburgh University Press, 2016).

27. Ferrari, *Memorie*, 318.

28. Ibid., 420.

29. Harold A. Bierk Jr., *Vida pública de don Pedro Gual* (Caracas: Ministerio de Relaciones Exteriores, 1983), 144.

30. Ferrari, *Memorie*, 420–421.

31. Ibid., 399.

32. Codazzi, *Memorias*, 254.

33. Persat, *Mémoires*, 21–25.

34. Codazzi, *Memorias*, 436.

35. *La voce della verità: gazzetta dell'Italia Centrale*, July 13, 1833.

36. Ferrari, *Memorie*, 466.

37. Ibid., 467–468.

38. William St. Clair, *That Greece Might Still Be Free: The Philhellenes in the War of Independence* (Oxford: Oxford University Press, 1972).

39. Ferrari, *Memorie*, 475.

40. Michael J. Hughes, *Forging Napoleon's Grande Armée: Motivation, Military Culture, and Masculinity in the French Army, 1800–1808* (New York: New York University Press, 2012).

41. Ferrari wrote about hearing about the capture and execution of Mina and his "liberal or republican" troops from a boat that moored in Amelia in December 1817. Ferrari, *Memorie*, 429.

42. Codazzi, *Memorias*, 262.

43. Ferrari, *Memorie*, 425. Codazzi's own memoirs, written in 1825, clash with the service records his widow sent the Colombian government in 1859. She dated the beginning of Codazzi's career for the Spanish American independence movements to February 1818 and recorded his service with Aury in Amelia, AGNC, República, Hoja de Servicio, t. 12, fol. 525–528.

44. Codazzi, *Memorias*, 420.

45. Ibid., 432–436.

46. Ibid., 476.

47. Ferrari, *Memorie*, 463.

48. Marina Foschi, *Architectes et ingénieurs de l'Emilie-Romagne dans le monde* (Bologna: Tipolitografia FR, 2009), 58.

49. Jean Savant, *Les Mamelouks de Napoléon* (Paris: Calmann-Levy, 1949); Edmund Burke, "The Mediterranean Before Colonialism: Fragments from the Life of 'Ali bin' Uthman al-Hammi in the Late Eighteenth and Nineteenth Centuries," *Journal of North African Studies* 6, no. 1 (2001): 129–142.

50. Human and material merchandise as well as the *Catalina* itself were sold for over $35,000; Aury's government received $5,791. As an outfitter, Aury received a share of almost $7,000, LOC/MD/LA, folder 6.

51. "List of Spanish Vessels Which Have Cleared Out for the Coast of Africa, from the Port of the Havannah, Between the 1st of January, 1819, and the 30th of May, 1823," *British and Foreign State Papers* (London: James Ridgway and Sons, 1848), 13: 85–86.

52. These figures come from the transatlantic slave trade database: www.slavevoyages.org.

53. Christopher Schmidt-Nowara, *Slavery and Antislavery in Spain's Atlantic Empire* (New York: Berghahn, 2013); David R. Murray, *Odious Commerce: Britain, Spain and the Abolition of the Cuban Slave Trade* (Cambridge: Cambridge University Press, 1980); Leslie Bethell, "The Mixed Commissions for the Suppression of the Transatlantic Slave Trade in the Nineteenth Century," *Journal of African History* 7, no. 1 (1966): 79–93.

54. The records of the mixed commission courts are in the Foreign Office series (TNA, FO 313, FO 314, FO 315, FO 129, and FO 131); Rosanne M. Adderley, *"New Negroes from Africa": Slave Trade Abolition and the Free African Settlement in the Nineteenth-Century Caribbean* (Bloomington: Indiana University Press, 2006); Natasha Ligthfoot, *Troubling Freedom: Antigua and the Aftermath of British Emancipation* (Durham, NC: Duke University Press, 2015).

55. Ferrari, *Memorie*, 103, 438.

56. Ferrer, "Haiti," 43–47.

57. "Numeración de los esclavos de la Isla de Vieja Providencia," October 9, 1822, AGNC, SGM, t. 343, fol. 964.

58. AGNC, República, Manumisión, t. 1.

59. Ferrari, *Memorie*, 434.

60. Trouillot, *Silencing the Past*, 45.

61. Ferrari, *Memorie*, 432.

62. Ibid., 477.

63. Ira Berlin, "From Creole to African: Atlantic Creoles and the Origins of African-American Society in Mainland North America," *William and Mary Quarterly* 53, no. 2 (1996): 251–288; Michael A. Gomez, *Exchanging Our Country Marks: The Transformation of African Identities in the Colonial and Antebellum South* (Chapel Hill: University of North Carolina Press, 1998).

64. James H. Sweet, "Mistaken Identities? Olaudah Equiano, Domingo Alvarez, and the Methodological Challenge of Studying the African Diaspora," *American Historical Review* 114, no. 2 (2008): 283; David Eltis, Phil Morgan, and David Richardson, "Agency and Diaspora in Atlantic History: Reassessing the African Contribution to Rice Cultivation in the America," *American Historical Review* 112, no. 5 (2007): 1329–1358; Herman L. Bennet, "The Subject in the Plot: National Boundaries and the 'History' of the Black Atlantic," *African Studies Review* 43 (2000): 101–124; Roquinaldo Ferreira, *Cross-Cultural Exchange in the Atlantic World: Angola and Brazil During the Era of the Slave Trade* (New York: Cambridge University Press, 2012); Randy Sparks, *Africans in the Old South: Mapping Exceptional Lives Across the Atlantic World* (Cambridge, MA: Harvard University Press, 2016).

65. On the decolonial work challenging the authority of archival records produced within colonial conditions, see Anjali Arondekar, *For the Record: On Sexuality and the Colonial Archive*

in India (Durham, NC: Duke University Press, 2009) and Marisa Fuentes, *Dispossessed Lives: Enslaved Women, Violence, and the Archive* (Philadelphia: University of Pennsylvania Press, 2016).

66. Codazzi, *Memorias*, 325, 397.

67. Felicity Nussbaum, *Torrid Zones: Maternity, Sexuality, and Empire in Eighteenth-Century English Narratives* (Baltimore: Johns Hopkins University Press, 1995); Lisa Ze Winters, *The Mulatta Concubine: Terror, Intimacy, Freedom, and Desire in the Black Transatlantic* (Athens: University of Georgia Press, 2016).

68. Codazzi, *Memorias*, 580.

69. Natalie A. Zaceck, "Searching for the Invisible Woman: The Evolution of White Women's Experience in Britain's West Indian Colonies," *History Compass* 7, no. 1 (2009): 329–341; Loraine Vollmer, *La Historia del poblamiento del Archipiélago de San Andrés, Vieja Providencia y Santa Catalina* (San Andrés: Ediciones Archipiélago, 1997).

70. Margaret B. Crosby-Arnold, "A Case of Hidden Genocide? Disintegration and Destruction of People of Color in Napoleonic Europe, 1799–1815," *Atlantic Studies: Global Currents* 14, no. 3 (2017): 354–381.

71. John Quincy Adams to John Forbes, June 5, 1820, in Manning, *Diplomatic Correspondence*, 1: 131.

72. Janice E. Thomson, *Mercenaries, Pirates, and Sovereigns* (Princeton, NJ: Princeton University Press, 1994).

73. See Nancy Green, "Expatriation, Expatriates, and Expats," *American Historical Review* 114, no. 2 (2009), 131–132; Rogers Smith, *Civic Ideals: Conflicting Visions of Citizenship in U.S. History* (New Haven, CT: Yale University Press, 1997), 155–160.

74. Adams to Shaler, January 13, 1818, in *A Digest of International Law*, ed. John Bassett Moore (Washington, DC: Government Printing Office, 1906), 3: 735–736; Gideon M. Hart, "'The Original' Thirteenth Amendment: The Misunderstood Titles of Nobility Amendment," *Marquette Law Review* 94 (2010): 311.

75. French Civil Code (1804), book I, title I, chapter II, section I, articles 17 and 21.

76. To Special Commissioners of the United States to South America from Secretary of State John Quincy Adams, November 21, 1817, in Manning, *Diplomatic Correspondence*, 1: 49.

77. *Archives parlementaires de 1787 à 1860* (Paris: P. Dupont, 1866), 7: 471.

78. James H. Kettner, *The Development of American Citizenship, 1608–1870* (Chapel Hill: University of North Carolina Press, 1978); Douglas Bradburn, *The Citizenship Revolution: Politics and the Creation of the American Union, 1774–1804* (Charlottesville: University of Virginia Press, 2009); Jordana Dym, "Citizens of Which Republic? Foreigners and the Construction of National Citizenship in Central America, 1823–1845," *Americas* 64, no. 4 (2008): 497–500; Nathan Perl-Rosenthal, *Citizen Sailors: Becoming American in the Age of Revolution* (Cambridge, MA: Harvard University Press, 2015).

79. Perl-Rosenthal, *Citizen Sailors*, 270–279.

80. Ferrari, *Memorie*, 420.

81. Manuel Ancizar, "Biografía de Codazzi," *Mosaico de Bogotá* 11 (1859); Antei, *Mal de America*, 43.

82. Brown, *Adventuring*, 156–170; Reuben Zahler, *Ambitious Rebels: Remaking Honor, Law, and Liberalism in Venezuela, 1780–1850* (Tucson: University of Arizona Press, 2013), 213; Véronique Hébrard, "¿Patricio o soldado: Qué uniforme para el ciudadano? El hombre en armas en la construcción de la nación," *Revista de Indias* 62, no. 225 (2002): 429–462; Arlene Diaz, *Female*

Citizens, Patriarchs, and the Law in Venezuela, 1786–1904 (Lincoln: University of Nebraska Press, 2004), 150–159.

83. Constitution of 1819, título 3, sección primera, articulo 7, in *Primeras constituciones de Colombia y Venezuela, 1811–1830*, ed. Carlos Restrepo (Bogotá: Universidad Externado de Colombia, 1993), 249.

84. Matthew Brown, "Soldier Heroes," 41–56; Francois-Xavier Guerra and Annick Lemperiere, eds., *Los espacios públicos en Iberoamérica: Ambigüedades y problemas, siglos XVIII–XIX* (México D.F: Centro Francés de Estudios Mexicanos y Centroamericanos: Fondo de Cultura Económica, 1998).

85. "Ley sobre la naturalización de extranjeros," *Gaceta de Colombia*, May 30, 1824.

86. Naturalization Law, July 4, 1823. Many foreign veterans who had remained after the war had trouble earning a living and remained in the military. Matthew Brown found that out of nearly 400 British veterans, 83 percent remained in the military. Brown, *Adventuring*, 174–183.

87. Rebecca Earle, "Padres de la Patria and the Ancestral Past: Commemorations of Independence in Nineteenth-Century Spanish America," *Journal of Latin American Studies* 34, no. 4 (2002): 775–805.

88. Claudio Lomniz, "Nationalism as a Practical System: A Critique of Benedict Anderson's Theory of Nationalism from a Spanish American Perspective," in *The Other Mirror: Grand Theory Through the Lens of Latin America*, ed. Miguel Angel Centeno and Fernando López-Alves (Princeton, NJ: Princeton University Press, 2001), 348–351.

89. Pedro Cunill Grau, *Historia de la Geografía de Venezuela* (Caracas: Consejo Nacional de Universidades, 2009), 124–125.

90. Rodrigo de J. Garcia Estrada, "La condición de extranjero en el tránsito de la Colonia a la Republica en la Nueva Granada, 1750–1830" (PhD diss., Universidad Andina Simón Bolívar, 2012).

91. Reproduced in Codazzi, *Atlas físico y político de la República de Venezuela* (Paris: Lithographie de Thierry Frères, 1840), 2; Nancy P. Applebaum, "Envisioning the Nation: The Mid-Nineteenth Century Colombian Chorographic Commission," in *State and Nation Making in Latin America and Spain*, ed. Miguel A. Ceneno and Agustin E. Ferraro (Cambridge: Cambridge University Press: 2013), 375–395; Jose Lopez Rojas, "Agustin Codazzi y los paisajes de une geografía imaginaria en Venezuela," *Revista Geográfica Venezolana* 48, no. 2 (2007): 299–308; Efraín Sánchez, *Gobierno y geografía: Agustín Codazzi y la Comisión Corográfica de la Nueva Granada* (Bogotá: El Ancora Editores, 1999); Arturo Uslar Pietri, *Del hacer y deshacer de Venezuela* (Caracas: Italgrafica, 1962); Lina del Castillo, *Crafting a Republic for the World: Scientific, Geographic and Historiographic Inventions of Colombia* (Lincoln: University of Nebraska Press, 2018).

92. Nancy P. Applebaum, *Mapping the Country of Regions: The Chorographic Commission of Nineteenth-Century Colombia* (Chapel Hill: University of North Carolina Press, 2016), 38.

93. Bassi, *Aqueous Territory*, 172–203; John K. Wright, "Map Makers Are Human: Comments on the Subjective in Maps," *Geographical Review* 32, no. 4 (1942): 527–544; Raymond B. Craib, *Cartographic Mexico: A History of State Fixations and Fugitive Landscapes* (Durham, NC: Duke University Press, 2004); Jordan Branch, "Mapping the Sovereign State: Technology, Authority, and Systemic Change," *International Organization* 65, no. 1 (2011): 1–36.

94. Codazzi, *Atlas*, 4.

95. William Richard Hamilton, "Address to the Royal Geographical Society of London," *Journal of the Royal Geographical Society of London* 12 (1842): 76.

96. José Lovera, *Codazzi y la comisión corográfica 1830–1841* (Caracas: Biblioteca Nacional de Venezuela, 1993), 36; Frédérique Langue, "La independencia de Venezuela, une historia

mitificada y un paradigma heroico," *Anuario de Estudios Americanos* 66, no. 2 (2009): 245–276; Elena Plaza, "Historiografía y nacionalidad: El *Resumen de la historia de Venezuela* de Rafael María Baralt," *Tiempo y Espacio* 7, no. 13 (1990): 63–96.

97. Rafael María Baralt, *Resumen de la Historia de Venezuela* (Paris: Imprenta de H. Fournier y Comp., 1841), 92–93.

98. Codazzi, *Atlas*, 8.

99. Ferrari, *Memorie*, 472.

100. Cited in Gioacchino Vicini, *La rivoluzione dell' anno 1831 nell Stato romano* (Imola: Galeati e figlio, 1889), 39.

101. Rumor of Ferrari's death in the hands of "a banda de Centurioni e di Carabinieri Pontifici" appeared in *La voce della verità: Gazzetta dell'Italia Centrale*, no. 303, July 13, 1833, 22.

102. Carlo Ginzburg, introduction to M. Baxandall, *Episodes: A Memorybook* (London: Frances Lincoln Limited, 2010), 10.

103. Ferrari, *Memorie*, 487–500.

104. Perazzo, *Agustín Codazzi*, 66.

105. Ibid., 62–63.

106. Cited in Zahler, *Ambitious Rebels*, 52.

107. *Recopilación de leyes y decretos de Venezuela* (Caracas: Impr. de La Opinión Nacional, 1874), 1: 116–117.

108. *Boletín de la Colonia Tovar*, nos. 1–5, August 8, 1843, British Library.

109. Codazzi to Secretary of State, November 11, 1841, in *El Liceo Venezolano*, numero estraordinario (Caracas: George Corser, 1842), 99.

110. *Boletín*, 3.

111. Oscar Olinto Camacho, "Venezuela's National Colonization Programme: The Tovar Colony, a German Agricultural Settlement," *Journal of Historical Geography* 10, no. 3 (1984): 279–289. The scheme benefited mostly the Tovar family but was presented publicly as essential to the "national interest."

112. Antei, *Mal de America*, 42.

113. Susan Berglund, "Italian Immigration in Venezuela: A Story Still Untold," *Center for Migration Studies* 11, no. 3 (1994): 175–177. Colonel Carlos Castelli, for example, contracted to bring 300 to 500 Italian and German immigrants. Codazzi, *Liceo Venezolano*, 109. On Codazzi's activities, see Giorgio Antei, ed., *Immagini della Nueva Granada. L'opera cartografica di Agostino Codazzi nel fondo manoscritto della Biblioteca Nazionale Universitaria* (Turin: Ministero per i Beni Culturali e Ambientali / Biblioteca Universitaria di Torino, 1995); Nicolás Perazzo and Manuel Pinto, *La inmigración en Venezuela, 1830–1850* (Caracas: Archivo General de la Nación, 1973), 21–22.

114. Diaz, *Female Citizens*, 157.

115. Cited in Antei, *Mal de America*, 46.

116. Applebaum, *Mapping the Country of Regions*, 2.

117. Eduardo Posada Carbó, *La nacion soñada: Violencia, liberalismo y democracia en Colombia* (Bogotá: Norma, 2006).

118. Sanchez, *Gobierno y geografía*, 910–911; Applebaum, "Envisioning the Nation," 377–378.

119. Jordana Dym and Karl Offen, eds., *Mapping Latin America: A Cartographic Reader* (Chicago: University of Chicago Press, 2011), 8.

120. Cited in Applebaum, *Mapping the Country of Regions*, 37.

121. Eduardo Restrepo, "'Negros indolentes' en las plumas de corógrafos: Raza y progreso en el occidente de la Nueva Granada de mediados del siglo XIX," *Nómadas* 26 (2007): 28–43.

122. Codazzi, *Memorias*, 325.

123. Cited in an 1853 letter in Beatriz Rodríguez, "El Ensamblaje visual del cuerpo negro: El caso de la Comisión Corográfica de la Nueva Granada," *Tabula Rasa* 17 (2012): 55.

124. Benigno Trigo, *Subjects of Crisis: Race and Gender as Disease in Latin America* (Middletown, CT: Wesleyan University Press, 2000), 43, n. 80.

125. George Reid Andrews, *Afro-Latin America: Black Lives, 1600–2000* (Cambridge, MA: Harvard University Press, 2016), 117–150.

126. Eugenio Bonvicini, *Commemorazione del cav. colonnello Costante Ferrari fatta a Villa Serraglio* (Tip. d'I. Galeati e figlio, 1895), 3. For a broader historical context, see Claudia Baldoli, *History of Italy* (Basingstoke: Palgrave Macmillan, 2009), 204–210.

127. Juan José Perez Rancel, ed., *Augustin Codazzi Arquitecto del territorio* (Caracas: Facultas de Arquitectura y Urbanismo, 2000).

128. Graham Dawson, *Soldier Heroes: British Adventure, Empire, and the Imagining of Masculinities* (New York: Routledge, 1994), 53–77; Mrinalani Sinha, *Colonial Masculinity: The 'Manly Englishman' and the 'Effeminate Bengali' in the Late Nineteenth Century* (Manchester: Manchester University Press, 1995); James M. McPherson, *For Cause and Comrades: Why Men Fought in the Civil War* (Oxford: Oxford University Press, 1997), 77–88.

Conclusion

1. Brian Hamnett, "Process and Pattern: A Re-Examination of the Ibero-American Independence Movements, 1808–1826," *Journal of Latin American Studies* 29 (1997): 279–328; Timothy E. Anna, *Forging Mexico: 1821–1835* (Lincoln: University of Nebraska Press, 1998); Elías Palti, *La nación como problema. Los historiadores y la "cuestión nacional"* (Buenos Aires: Fondo de Cultura Económica, 2002).

2. José Manuel Restrepo, *Historia de la revolución de Colombia en la América Meridional* (Paris: Librería Americana, 1827), 6: 149 and 7: 164; Daniel Gutiérrez Ávila, "La campana de propaganda de los estados hispanoamericanos en Europa (1810–1830)," *Anuario de Historia Regional y de las Fronteras* 13, no. 1 (2009): 9–38; Sergio Mejía, *La revolución en letras. La Historia de la revolución de Colombia de José Manuel Restrepo, 1781–1863* (Bogotá: Universidad de los Andes, 2007). Restrepo published a revised version of the *Historia* in 1858. On postindependence Colombia's efforts to delink the new nation from the Caribbean world and link it to the Andes and the North Atlantic (Europe and the United States), see Bassi, *Aqueous Territory*, 172–203.

3. Restrepo, *Historia de la revolución*, 1: 225.

4. Restrepo used Spanish maps from the hydrographic deposit of Madrid to draw the Atlantic coast of Gran Colombia. Restrepo, *Carta de la República de Colombia* (Paris: Librería Americana, 1827), 5–6.

5. Ineke Phaf and Matthias Röhrig Assunção, "History of Bunk! Recovering the Meaning of Independence in Venezuela, Colombia, and Curacao: A Cross-Cultural Image of Manuel Piar," in *History of Literature in the Caribbean*, ed. A. James Arnold (Amsterdam: John Benjamin, 1997), 2: 161–174.

6. Vicente Perez Rosales, *Times Gone By: Memoirs of a Man of Action: Memoirs of a Man of Action*, trans. Brian Loveman and John H. R. Polt (New York: Oxford University Press, 2003), 63–64.

7. Friedrich Saalfedl, *Handbuch das positive Volkerrechts* (1833), cited in Crawford, *Creation of States*, 97.

8. Fabry, *Recognizing States*, 7.

9. Barry Buzan and Richard Little, *International Systems in World History* (Oxford: Oxford University Press, 2000), 17–34; Andrew Phillips, "Global IR Meets Global History: Sovereignty, Modernity and the International System's Expansion in the Indian Ocean region," *International Studies Review* 18, no. 1 (2016): 62–77; Charles Butcher and Ryan Griffiths, "Between Eurocentrism and Babel: A Framework for the Analysis of States, State Systems, and International Orders," *International Studies Quarterly* 61 (2017): 328–336.

10. Vattel, *Droit des gens*, book I, chap. I, 4.

11. Arthur Nussbaum, *A Concise History of the Law of Nations* (New York: Macmillan, 1947); C. H. Alexandrowicz, "Doctrinal Aspects of the Universality of the Law of Nations," *British Yearbook of International Law* 37 (1961): 506–515; Jennifer Pitts, "Empire and Legal Universalism in the Eighteenth Century," *American Historical Review* 117, no. 1 (2012): 92–121.

12. Greg Grandin, "The Liberal Traditions in the Americas: Rights, Sovereignty, and the Origins of Liberal Multilateralism," *American Historical Review* 117, no. 1 (2012): 69.

13. Thomson, *Mercenaries*, 69–105.

14. Edward Dumbauld, "Neutrality Laws of the United States," *American Journal of International Law* 31, no. 2 (1937): 258–270.

15. "Piracy and Outrage on Commerce of the United States by Spanish Privateers, January 24, 1825," House of Representatives, 18th Cong., 2nd sess., ASP: FR, 5: 585–587.

16. Francis R. Stark, *The Abolition of Privateering and the declaration of Paris* (New York: Columbia University Press, 1897), 40–42.

17. Nicholas Parillo, "The De-Privatization of American Warfare: How the U.S. Government Used, Regulated, and Ultimately Abandoned Privateering in the Nineteenth Century," *Yale Journal of Law of the Humanities* 19, no. 1 (2007): 55–57.

18. The United States was more successful in pushing for the rule "free ships, free goods" and concluded treaties with Latin American states, Algiers, Morocco, Spain, Tripoli, Russia, and France. H. W. Malkin, "The Inner History of the Declaration of Paris," *British Year Book of International Law* 8 (1927): 1–44. During the Civil War (1861–1865), the Confederate States of America commissioned privateers to attack the shipping of the Union navy. Jan Martin Lemnitzer, *Power, Law and the End of Privateering* (London: Palgrave Macmillan, 2014), 115–153.

19. William Duane to Secretario de Guerra y Marina de Colombia, April 8, 1820, in Charles H. Bowman, "Correspondence of William Duane in Two Archives in Bogotá," *Revista de Historia de America* 82 (1976): 119.

20. Consejo ordinario de gobernio del 12 de julio de 1824, in *Acuerdos*.

21. "Provisional Ordinance of the Republic of Colombia Relative to the Equipment and Service of Vessels Bearing Letters of Marque," March 30, 1822, in *British and Foreign State Papers* (London: H. M. Stationery Office, 1846), 12: 647–661. On the defense of privateering as a privilege of sovereign states, see *El Venezolano*, December 27, 1823.

22. The executive branch had the right to issue privateering commissions during wartime, often in agreement with the Congress: constitutions of Colombia 1832, 1853, and 1843 (it is absent from the 1853 Constitution); constitution of Venezuela (1830); and constitution of Mexico (1824).

23. Miguel C. Carranza y Castillo, *Y la Independencia se consolido en el mar. Ensayo histórico sobre la guerra entre México y España* (México D.F.: Instituto Nacional de Estudios Históricos de la Revoluciones, 2009), 89–99.

24. Charles Tilly, *Coercion, Capital, and European States, AD 990–1992* (Cambridge: Blackwell, 1992), 58, 69; Thomson, *Mercenaries*, 10–11.

25. Lauren Benton, "Towards a New Legal History of Piracy: Maritime Legalities and the Myth of Universal Jurisdiction," *International Journal of Maritime History* 23, no. 1 (2011): 225–240.

26. William H. Gray, "American Diplomacy in Venezuela 1835–1865," *Hispanic American Historical Review* 20, no. 4 (1940): 569–570.

27. Thomas R. Dew, *Review of the Debate in the Virginia Legislature of 1831 and 1832* (Richmond, VA: TW Whites, 1832), 104.

28. A summary of the debate is in Ginsburg, Lansberg-Rodriguez, Versteeg, "When to Overthrow Your Government," 1203–1206; Fritz, *American Sovereigns*, 24–27, 283–290.

29. Juan Pablo Scarfi, "In the Name of the Americas: The Pan-American Redefinition of the Monroe Doctrine and the Emerging Language of American International Law in the Western Hemisphere, 1898–1933," *Diplomatic History* 40, no. 2 (2016): 189–218.

30. Fabry, *Recognizing States*, 66–77.

31. Anthony Anghie, *Imperialism, Sovereignty, and the Making of International Law* (New York: Cambridge University Press, 2017).

32. Benjamin Allen Coates, *Legalist Empire: International Law and American Foreign Relations in the Early Twentieth Century* (New York: Oxford University Press, 2016).

33. Walter Johnson, *River of Dark Dreams: Slavery and Empire in the Cotton Kingdom* (Cambridge, MA: Harvard University Press, 2013), 303–329; Robert E. May, *Manifest Destiny's Underworld: Filibustering in Antebellum America* (Chapel Hill: University of North Carolina Press, 2002); Amy S. Greenberg, *Manifest Manhood and the Antebellum American Empire* (New York: Cambridge University Press, 2005), 170–196; Víctor Hugo Acuña Ortega, ed., *Filibusterismo y Destino Manifesto en Las Américas* (San José: Museo Histórico Cultural Juan Santamaría, 2010); Michel Gobat, *Empire by Invitation: William Walker and Manifest Destiny in Central America* (Cambridge, MA: Harvard University Press, 2018).

34. Bertrand Taithe, *The Killer Trail: A Colonial Scandal in the Heart of Africa* (New York: Oxford University Press, 2009); Steven Press, *Rogue Empires: Contracts and Conmen in Europe's Scramble for Africa* (Cambridge, MA: Harvard University Press, 2017).

INDEX

ACKNOWLEDGMENTS

This manuscript traveled with me through at least three countries and six cities—such is the life of a precariously employed academic. I have been fortunate to meet many wonderful people along the way. This book would not exist without them.

Many thanks go to Kathleen Brown, who helped me to develop key aspects of the argument. Her own groundbreaking work is a source of inspiration. Bob Lockhart gave me helpful editorial suggestions and unflagging encouragement. Kathleen Kearns assisted me in making it a more readable book. The readers of the University of Pennsylvania Press gave me very thoughtful and thought-provoking comments. I am indebted to the people who generously shared their expertise: Amy Kaplan, Daniel Richter, Marcus Rediker, Seymour Dresher, Chelsea Stieber, Michele Reid-Vasquez, Lara Putnam, Rogers Smith, John Stoner, Pernille Røge, and Molly Warsh. I have been lucky to meet wonderful scholars as I was just finishing the manuscript. My deepest gratitude to Sarah Liu, Annie Tindley, Sarah Winkler-Reid, and Joseph Lawson for their comments and their friendship. Loes Veldpaus and Moozhan Shakeri shared their mapmaking skills with a vigorous sense of humor and a steady supply of doughnuts. I try to follow Loes's advice to bring kindness into the world: "Listen, acknowledge, and do not dismiss power inequalities. Bring others up with you."

I am grateful to the institutions and individuals that helped me at different and equally crucial stages of my research. L'argent est le nerf de la guerre, and I received financial support from the University of Pennsylvania (including a fellowship from the Penn Democracy, Citizenship, and Constitutionalism Program), the Mellon Foundation, the Society for Historians of American Foreign Relations, the New-York Historical Society, and the University of Pittsburgh. In addition, the Historic New Orleans Collection, the Newberry Library, and the John Carter Brown Library offered much-needed short-term fellowships. The staff at the New Orleans Public Library, the Center for American History at the University of Texas, the Library of Congress, and the Smathers Libraries at the University of Florida kindly shared their knowledge with me. I also extend my gratitude to the Archivo General de la Nación in Mexico D.F., the Archivo General de la Nación, and the Biblioteca Luis Ángel Arango in Bogotá. On the other side of the Atlantic, I have been lucky to do research in such wonderful places as the Archivo General de las Indias, the Centre des Archives d'Outremer, the Archives du Ministère des Affaires Etrangères, the Archives Nationales, the Centre des Archives Diplomatiques, and the Bibliothèque Nationale, as well as the British Library and the National Archives.

I owe the biggest thank you to my family and friends. They are scattered around the world: Yvie Fabella, Caroline Cunill, Esen Kirdis, Cristina Pangilinan, Kathleen Paugh, Juan José Ponce-Vasquez, Adelina Stefan, and Madalina Veres: I hope you know that I miss you all very much. I am especially grateful to Connie Aust and Yael Rice for their support through graduate school and beyond. I can only hope that Laurence will remain my biggest supporter for the rest of our adventures together. There are no words to describe my gratitude for my grandmother, Jacqueline, and my parents, Richard and Mauricette. They have always provided me with unconditional support and acceptance. I am very lucky to have them in my life. My grandfathers, César and André, passed away as research and writing were in progress. They taught me about crossing borders and carrying on when life gets tough. Affected by Alzheimer disease, their final lesson was to teach me that memory is fleeting and fragile and that only love endures.

Portions of Chapter 1 appeared in "A Tale of Two Brothers: Haiti's Other Revolutions," *Americas* 69, no. 1 (2012): 37–60. Copyright © 2012 Academy of American Franciscan History.